101 INTER
IN FAMILY THERAPY

Thorana S. Nelson, PhD
Terry S. Trepper, PhD

SOME ADVANCE REVIEWS

"An outstanding resource which provides practical guidelines for clinical interventions. . . . I quickly discovered this volume to be an exciting and energizing grab bag of straightforward advice for both the beginning student and the experienced family therapy practitioner. The editors and contributors are to be commended for bringing together a wide range of clinical situations with practicality and applicability! This is an enjoyable, highly readable, and useful book. It should become part of our library for years to come."

John S. Shalett, MSW, ACSW, BCD
Director of Counseling
Family Service of Greater New Orleans

"Creativity just oozes from the pages of this book as clinicians of all levels and ilk tell their most rewarding interventions. Most importantly, authors in the last section reflect on how to approach intervening and prevent the selecting of a juicy interpretation that is used indiscriminantly, out of context, without proper preparation or knowledge."

Cheryl L. Storm, PhD
Associate Professor
Marriage and Family Therapy Program
Pacific Lutheran University

"Trepper and Nelson wanted to provide the reader with a smorgasbord of interventions – ideas that worked for therapists. They have succeeded in providing clinicians with practical, sometimes unusual and often imaginative interventions. It is both highly entertaining and enlightening."

William J. Hiebert, STM
Executive Director
Marriage & Family Counseling Service
Rock Island, Illinois

101 Interventions
in Family Therapy

HAWORTH Marriage and the Family
Terry S. Trepper, PhD
Senior Editor

New, Recent, and Forthcoming Titles:

Christiantown, USA by Richard Stellway

Marriage and Family Therapy: A Sociocognitive Approach by Nathan Hurvitz and Roger A. Straus

Culture and Family: Problems and Therapy by Wen-Shing Tseng and Jing Hsu

Adolescents and Their Families: An Introduction to Assessment and Intervention by Mark Worden

Parents Whose Parents Were Divorced by R. Thomas Berner

The Effect of Children on Parents by Anne-Marie Ambert

Multigenerational Family Therapy by David S. Freeman

101 Interventions in Family Therapy edited by Thorana S. Nelson and Terry S. Trepper

Therapy with Treatment Resistant Families: A Consultation-Crisis Intervention Model by William McCown and Judith Johnson

101 Interventions in Family Therapy

Thorana S. Nelson, PhD
Terry S. Trepper, PhD
Editors

The Haworth Press, Inc.
New York • London • Norwood (Australia)

The Haworth Press, Inc., 10 Alice Street, Binghamton, NY 13904-1580

Library of Congress Cataloging-in-Publication Data

101 interventions in family therapy / Thorana S. Nelson, Terry S. Trepper, editors.
    p. cm.
   Includes bibliographical references.
   ISBN 0-86656-902-2 (alk. paper) – 1-56024-193-4 (pbk.: alk. paper).
   1. Family psychotherapy. 2. Family psychotherapy – Case studies. I. Nelson, Thorana
Strever. II. Trepper, Terry S. III. Title: One hundred one interventions in family therapy.
RC488.5.A17   1992
616.89'156 – dc20   91-22252
                                                              CIP

Thorana S. Nelson, PhD

To my mom

Terry S. Trepper, PhD

To Scotty, King of Tots

ABOUT THE EDITORS

Thorana S. Nelson, PhD, is Director of the Marriage and Family Therapy Program and Associate Professor, Department of Family and Human Development at Utah State University. She has published in the areas of gender, transgenerational family therapy, and basic skills in family therapy.

Terry S. Trepper, PhD, is Director of the Family Studies Center at Purdue University Calumet where he is also Professor of Psychology. An expert in sex therapy, family therapy of sexual abuse, and family therapy treatments for substance abuse, he is editor of the *Journal of Family Psychotherapy*.

CONTENTS

REFLECTIONS ON INTERVENTION

Foreword

One of the major "mystiques" of family therapy, and probably therapy in general, has to do with what really goes on behind closed doors. Next to the nebulous middle phase of treatment, actual interventions used by therapists remain the least documented area within the field. Therapeutic exhibitionism (the willingness to and comfort in having your work observed) and voyeurism (watching videotapes and observing treatment) are commonplace throughout family therapy training programs and clinical practice. Yet opportunities to gain broad exposure to the myriad of creative techniques that "therapists in the trenches" employ have been scattered and limited.

This book fills a major void that exists in the family therapy literature. Rather than inundate the reader with theoretical constructs, or descriptions of the uniqueness of certain specialized clinical populations, it provides a smorgasbord of therapeutic techniques and interventions. In much the same way that live supervision does, this book allows the reader to enter the private worlds of therapists behind closed doors. The editors have done an excellent job of selecting for the book a wide range of interventions that draw from every existing family therapy theory. Since the compilation of interventions is applied to a variety of presenting problems and client types, therapists from divergent world views and clinical specializations will find the book stimulating, provocative, and useful.

This book is destined to become a major sourcebook in the field. Students, teachers, and practitioners of family therapy will find it a refreshing departure from most of the existing family therapy literature.

One of the chief complaints often cited about therapy books is that the author did not spend enough time discussing the "how to" part of the process. This book is unique in that this part of the process receives sole attention by the editors. While there are not detailed rationales given for why certain interventions are used, this omission does not detract from the plethora of useable clinical material contained in this book.

I know of no other family therapy collection that draws from the wealth of clinical knowledge and experience of therapists, male and female, ethnic minority and non-minority, as does this book. After reading the book, I am convinced that there are actually 102 interventions . . . the one not included in the book is the one represented by the impact this book will have on the field for years to come.

Kenneth V. Hardy, PhD
Marriage and Family Therapy Program
Syracuse University

Preface

This book had its origins at a family therapy conference. The two of us (Nelson and Trepper) were sitting with a group of therapists talking about interesting cases when someone in the group asked what must be the universal "when-therapists-meet" question: "What would you do in this case?" What followed was a fascinating hour or so of wonderful strategies, interventions, and ways of thinking about cases. Each person's favorite led to examples of how some of us had used similar interventions or how we might try these ideas with our current clients. We all agreed that this is one of the reasons we come to meetings and that these ad hoc colloquy are often more useful than the "how-to" workshops offered by "experts."

After we had exchanged our "tips," someone in the group said the magic words: "What do you suppose is Jay Haley's favorite intervention?" Someone replied, "We know *his* favorite interventions; he wrote about them. I'd like to see a book of *our* favorite interventions; you know, the ones that work for folks like us." Terry Trepper, editor of the *Journal of Family Psychotherapy*, and Senior Editor for Haworth Marriage and the Family, took note of this excellent book idea that emerged from the group. Later that evening, he and Thorana Nelson, Associate Professor of Family and Human Development at Utah State University, discussed the nefarious notion.

"Let's steal the idea!" Terry subtly suggested.

Thorana was convinced by this compelling argument. "Yeah!" she not-so-subtly assented.

We agreed that we wanted, as much as possible, a replication of our recent "colloquium" in book form. We wanted to have a large number of practicing clinicians share their favorite, most successful interventions, so that others could learn from and possibly use them in their work. We agreed that we wanted "therapists-on-the-street," not just famous, prolific family therapy writers. We also knew that we wanted ideas that worked for therapists, not necessarily the intriguing, exotic, "glitzy" interventions found in other publications. Finally, we wanted to include interventions that could be used by different levels of therapists, that represented a variety of theoretical models, and that reflected many personal therapeutic styles.

Our first problem was: who would be first editor. Terry, who already possessed the big T (tenure), generously and graciously offered the first editorship to Thorana, who didn't. Thorana, scared out of her mind with the thought of such a formidable task, paled. Terry, however, prevailed, suggesting that it would be a perfect book for Haworth to publish and it would therefore be inappropriate for him to be first editor. (Besides, he told her later, it was time for her to learn the joys of editing a book, and what better way to start than this?)

Our second problem was finding contributors. Knowing that we wanted submissions from practicing clinicians, we randomly selected a large number of Clinical Members of the American Association for Marriage and Family Therapy. We also contacted everyone who had undertaken clinical presentations at an AAMFT Annual Conference. Finally, we wrote to the faculty of training programs in family therapy to encourage them and their students to contribute to the book, since these people were dealing extensively with basic issues in clinical practice.

We sent letters to all of these people, asking them to submit their favorite or most successful or most interesting interventions. We suggested a format which included theoretical credit (i.e., from whom did you plagiarize this); a description of the interventions (not just case studies and crayon drawings); indications and contra-indications (those words were explained to us); and a brief case example (as you might expect, we did get a few *briefcase-size* examples, but we sent them back). We were delighted, however, that not everyone followed our format, since the responses were rich and varied in writing style and content. We were quite pleased with what we received. We had been afraid that the submissions would be prosaic, pedantic, or out-and-out weird. Instead, they were creative, useful, and fun to read.

Not everyone responded to our requests for interventions. A few wrote letters, reflecting upon the notion of *intervention*. We included these letters under a special section, "Reflections on Intervention," to stimulate the readers' thinking about larger concepts involved in therapy.

We ("Who's this *we* business?" asks the first editor) did only minor editing, since most of the interventions were written quite well to begin with. More importantly, however, we decided that we needed to allow the therapists' own words to tell the stories, giving special flavor to the interventions. This turned out to give the book a true "case-conference" feeling.

ORGANIZATION OF THE BOOK

We struggled a great deal with the decision of how to present the interventions. At first, we thought we would organize it by theoretical models, such as *behavioral interventions, strategic interventions*, and *interventions involving the "self" of the therapist*. This became clearly impossible to do, since many, if not most, of the interventions crossed over theoretical boundaries, were based on multiple theories, or were atheoretical. Next, we thought we might organize it by client populations, such as *interventions for couples* or *interventions for families with anorectic, drug-abusing adolescents whose parents are divorced and who have handicapped siblings*. That turned out to be an even worse idea than the first, since part of a reader's creativity is the ability to modify interventions from one context to another. We then thought we would alphabetize the interventions by first author. This wouldn't work since we each had forgotten how to alphabetize. Besides, the A's always get to go first when alphabetizing and both N and T come later in the alphabet (and N had been an S growing up), so we hated alphabetizing.

We finally decided to do the unthinkable: we would present the interventions in random order, trying not to put similar interventions or two long ones together. We also decided not to provide a detailed index, since we didn't want this to be a "cookbook" organized by theory, topic, or client population. We wanted to encourage our readers to really *read* the book, not simply skim it for specific concepts or ideas.

We think of this book as a smorgasbord: Not everything is on the menu; instead, we invite readers to "view and taste" everything, and to remain open to surprises and enjoyment.

WHO IS THIS BOOK FOR?

We believe that both intermediate and advanced clinicians will enjoy this book because of its similarity to case conference experiences. Many therapists, particularly those in private practice, do not have the opportunity to staff cases on a regular basis and look forward to hearing what other clinicians are doing.

Teachers of courses on psychotherapy and family therapy will find this book useful to stimulate discussion on various models and strategies for intervention and for making decisions about when and how to intervene. We have used many of the interventions presented here with our own students as points of departure: "So this is how this clinician intervened; what else could a therapist do?"

Finally, students of therapy will find this book particularly useful. Most therapy texts are long on theory and short on examples, or simply long on examples without explaining the interventions. This is a compendium of interventions with short case examples that can be of immediate use. Students, who often have not yet established their therapeutic "voices," will find the book useful because it presents 101 interventions offered in a number of real-life therapeutic styles, not just those of the "masters."

HOW SHOULD THIS BOOK BE USED?

After spending a great deal of time with this book, we believe the best way to read it is for fun and leisure. The book can be read, for example, like a book of short stories. It lends itself to that, since the interventions are unique and engaging.

Of course, no one will like every intervention, nor will each fit the style or theoretical orientation of every therapist. Some may even be concerned about some of the interventions. However, we expect therapists to take the interventions, think about them, perhaps modify one to fit his/her style, try it out, and then evaluate its usefulness in his or her own work.

ACKNOWLEDGEMENTS

We must first thank, of course, the over 100 authors who were willing to put their work on the line and share with their fellow clinicians their favorite interventions. It takes courage to expose oneself professionally. For taking that risk, we gratefully thank our authors.

We would also like to thank graduate assistants Gabriella Heilbrun and Sherry Rediger, who put many hours into this book: mailing, collecting, editing, checking references, etc.

Finally, we would like to thank the Purdue colleagues who put up with us and our antics during the process of Codename: Dalmatians.

Thorana S. Nelson, PhD
Terry S. Trepper, PhD

The Other Side

D. Ray Bardill

Several years ago I agreed to see a highly successful young professional man for the stated purpose of "improving my marriage relationship." From the beginning of the initial interview I sensed an incongruence between his stated reasons for seeking help (improve my marriage relationship) and the words he used to describe his marital situation (reasons to get out of the marriage). In order to more clearly determine what he wanted out of the therapeutic experience I asked him to try something for me. I gave him three pieces of paper and a pencil. First, I asked him to complete in writing the following statement:

"I am coming to see you in-order-to . . . ." (*your statement*).

When he had written his response, I asked him to take the second piece of paper and complete the sentence again. However, this time I asked him to fill in the blank with a statement that seemed to him to be totally opposite to the first statement he had written.

"I am coming to see you in-order-to . . . ." (*reason is to be totally opposite to the first statement*).

He looked a bit confused, hesitated a moment and wrote his second statement. When he finished I asked him to take the third piece of paper and complete the sentence again. This time he was instructed to "give another reason" for coming to see me.

"I am coming to see you in-order-to . . . ." (*another reason*).

This time he hesitated even longer before writing his statement.

The ideas for this intervention are similar to those suggested in Miller, B., & Maloney, D. (1972). Turn over. *Transactional Analysis Journal, 2*, 117-121.

When he had written his third statement, he put the pencil down, stared at me momentarily and said, "Now, I know why I am here today." He went on to say that he realized that he had sought help with his marriage, not to improve it; he wanted to be able to tell himself, and others, that he had tried to save the marriage. He did not intend to remain in the marriage. He reported having an extramarital relationship with a woman he intended to marry.

After talking about his affair for awhile he looked directly at me, gave me a sad but knowing facial expression and said, "I know something else." The patient went into a rather lengthy discussion about his awareness that he would not marry this other woman. He was using her to get out of his current marriage. He now knew he did not want to marry his girlfriend.

For the rest of the therapy session the patient went into detail about the marriage, his own tendency to go to great lengths to use other people to do what he wished, and his intention to seek psychotherapy "to resolve my guilt about my need to use other people."

I have used the intervention I call "the other side" many times since that first experience. While the results have been different each time, "the other side" has always provided useful information. As Virginia Satir often said, "We know more than we know we know."

There are at least two important dynamics at play in the "other side" intervention. First, purpose (in-order-to) creates a perceptual medium through which all ideas, actions, and thoughts must go. Purpose establishes a cognitive map, or context, which serves as a guide for whatever follows. When what is said or done does not match the purpose, there is a sense of incongruence, which is experienced at some level by the patient. The nature of the incongruence may or may not be apparent to the therapist. A frequent therapist reaction in such a situation is an inability to make any sense out of the patient's presentation of his/her problem. In the ordinary course of events the therapist will probe into a series of different areas of the patient's situation. The probes will be an effort to clarify just why the patient is seeking help. The emotion felt when the basis for the incongruence is resolved is much like the feelings experienced when committee members discover a "hidden agenda." The discovery of that which has interfered with the work of the committee clears the air for the moment. While sometimes painful, the emergence of the hidden agenda ordinarily is accompanied by a sense of relief by the committee members. Such is the sense of relief felt by a patient and the therapist when the underlying purpose for seeking help is revealed.

Second, the "other side" intervention helps differentiate between the "why" (reasons) for seeking help and the purpose (in-order-to) dynamics in the therapy process. In this frame, the question is not "why" are you doing what you are doing. *Why* ordinarily taps into some well thought out, or not so well thought out, justifications for actions. Purpose gets to the background or context within which the patient is behaving. In the case example given above, the patient's actions relating to his request for therapy made sense to him only after he became aware that his intention to get rid of his intense feelings of guilt was his purpose for seeking help. To put it another way, if I tell my therapist I want a more positive relationship with my wife and I then proceed to attack her with every word I utter, my behavior and my stated purpose are incongruent. Exploring this incongruency gets to the purpose that is driving my behavior. When I know the context (purpose) out of which my statements come, I can better understand the meaning of my behavior.

Additionally, the "other side" intervention is firmly rooted in the communications dimension of systemic thinking. Communications theory tells us that disagreement between a stated intention and a strongly held underlying intention(s) has a high probability of showing up in incongruent communication. As in the case above, exploring the basis for the incongruency often clarifies some of the factors behind other troublesome behavior patterns.

The "other side" intervention is most powerful when the therapist does not give any hints about what the patient should, or might, say to complete the in-order-to sentence. The ideas need to be those of the patient. Initially, some patients will resist dealing with alternative ideas. A simple statement such as "just try it, let's see what comes up" is ordinarily enough to move the process forward. When the therapist responds to the second and third "other-side" ideas provided by the patient, alternative interview subjects naturally emerge. The fact of hidden frames for dealing with the issues at hand has been demonstrated through the process.

Now, give me your *response* to the usefulness of this intervention. Next, give me a response that is totally *opposite* to your first response. Finally, give me *another* response. GOOD!

2

The Case of the Missing Client: Using Non-Pejorative Language with Strong Denial Systems

Yolanda Reyna
Vincent Taylor

There are occasions when clients come to therapy of their own volition with a growth plan in mind, seeking a psychological guide through the maze of life. This article is not about those clients. Nor is this article about those clients who come to therapy to change anything about themselves. This article should be read only by therapists who have clients who are mandated and often resent having to "waste their time coming to therapy." After all, they aren't the problem, don't have a problem, and are not interested in changing anything about themselves — only the circumstances that coerced them into therapy. While they believe the problem to be imaginary, their covertly and overtly expressed sentiments of anger and denial are very evident. Confrontation, while making the therapist feel better, only makes the denial and anger worse. This article uses a case illustration of an incest offender to demonstrate the advantage of non-pejorative language in therapy to circumvent denial and better monitor the safety of the child.

Anderson and Goolishian (1988) offer a framework for understanding human systems as linguistic systems. They outlined eight tenets to guide the therapeutic interview. This article will apply those eight tenets to the problem of extreme denial in a sexual offender.

TENET #1

The therapist keeps the inquiry within the parameters of the problem as described by the client.

The client, Mr. C, read a prepared statement in which he described the sexual involvement with his daughter as "massage therapy and desensitization of the lower part of her body for a bedwetting problem." He also described the sexual incidents as education sessions and advice on how to deal with boyfriends. While Mr. C's language was part of the denial process, it was possible to expand his descriptions of his behaviors without challenging his unusual use of language. For example, without getting into any disagreements, Mrs. C was brought into the dialogue and it was clear that she did not describe the abuse in the same language Mr. C used.

Therapist: Did Mr. C share his educational strategies with you and which strategies did you like and which ones did you not like?

Mrs. C: I am a pretty sound sleeper myself and he used to get up to take her to the bathroom about midnight. But I didn't know about the rest.

Therapist: So you agreed that taking your daughter to the bathroom during the night might help the bed-wetting? Did you decide who would take her and when to take her together or did Mr. C just take the responsibility upon himself?

TENET #2

The therapist entertains multiple and contradictory ideas simultaneously.

From Mr. C's point of view, he loved his daughter and wanted to protect her, as he said, "from the wolves." This protection included monitoring any phone calls to her from boys, reading letters or diaries for explicit discussion of boys, restricting her use of any make-up and ending friendships that were not approved by him. From the judicial system's perspective, including the District Attorney, caseworker, and probation officer, Mr. C's actions demonstrated poor parenting skills, pathological boundaries between family members, and no apparent motivation to remediate his problem or for the family to provide protection for their daughter. As can be seen, Mr. C's and the other system members' perspectives were worlds apart yet the therapist's job was to establish multipartiality (Anderson & Goolishian, 1988) and to simultaneously agree with both perspectives. Agreement would be impossible without viewing both perspectives as double description (Bateson, 1980) of a unified concept. We described both sides as trying their best to protect the girl — a concept that described the legal perspective and Mr. C. However, we acknowledged that they were far apart concerning how to protect her, who best knew how to protect her, and about what she was being protected from. That is when therapy began.

TENET #3

The therapist chooses cooperative rather than uncooperative language.

At the initial interview, Mr. C came in with a five-page written confession of his sexual involvement with his daughter. His demeanor was nervous but stoic. Often in therapy, choosing a cooperative stance involves what you don't do or say as much as what you do or say. Mr. C's demeanor communicated an expectation that therapy would be an hour of interrogation followed by possible torture. A cooperative stance involved not allowing him to confess in the same manner he had at the Department of Child Protective Services, which made him feel like he paid for his offense and that it was behind him, since he had been forgiven by God and would never do it again.

Therapist: (Interrupting after about one minute of Mr. C's prepared statement) I know you wrote this about two weeks ago. I want you to feel free to bring up any additional thoughts or explanations that might help us understand what you are telling us.

TENET #4

The therapist learns, understands, and converses in the client's language because that language is a metaphor for the client's experiences.

Mr. C viewed his role in the family as the provider, protector and teacher. The metaphor *teacher* provided an avenue of entrance into his world. Teachers have gone to school to learn what they know. Mr. C revealed that his school began with a very harsh father who sexually abused him once. His further schooling came when he "went with girls just to get what I could get." From this understanding, we were able to dialogue with Mr. C about his "teaching techniques." For example, "There are a lot of guys who would take advantage of your daughter and it is important to help protect her. However, I am concerned that when she becomes eighteen and leaves home she won't have you to shelter her. Is she learning to recognize danger signs herself and learning how to handle herself without your supervision?"

TENET #5

The therapist is a respectful listener who does not understand too quickly (if ever).

Therapist: I am sure you've talked to other parents. How do the letters your daughter writes differ from those that other girls her age are writing?

Mr. C: I am just concerned that her love letters will give people the wrong impression.

Therapist: If you could have written the letters for your daughter, what could you have said that would convey the right impression?

TENET #6

The therapist asks questions, the answers to which require new questions. This idea is similar to Penn's (1982) circular questioning.

Therapist: When your daughter shows an interest in a boy, how do you know when you've taught her enough so that she's ready?

Mr. C: Well, she's not ready to date like guys who are eighteen or older. And I make sure I've met them before she goes out.

Therapist: And are there some places where she can go with boys that you feel safer than others?

TENET #7

The therapist takes the responsibility for the creation of a conversational context that allows for mutual collaboration in the problem-defining process.

Therapist: Since it is mandatory that you attend these sessions, how can you convince the judge and your probation officer that you have changed and that it would not happen again?

Mr. C: I was hoping you would write him a letter telling him that I am, you know, okay.

Therapist: If at some point we were to write to the probation officer, what kind of things would he take our word about and what would you have to prove to him by demonstrating that you've changed since you were charged?

TENET #8

The therapist maintains a dialogical conversation with himself or herself.

Throughout this case, the therapy team was torn between our desire to protect the daughter, who lived in the home where the father returned to live after only a few weeks of banishment at the insistence of the caseworker, and our desire to break through Mr. C's denial so a change in the quality of his relationships could be accomplished. In early sessions, these two goals seemed diametrically opposed. As we saw how Mr. C responded to direct confrontation/lectures and one cussing from a judicial system worker, we developed the view that the non-pejorative languaging approach best allowed us to monitor the family dynamics, thereby protecting the daughter somewhat, while helping to co-evolve new meaning into an epistemology that held Mr. C in prison even before his day in court. This dynamic team dialogue kept us from losing sight of either our duty to protect or our desire to facilitate an environment for change.

EPILOGUE

While Mr. C was seen as a high risk client capable of re-offending and being overbearing, neither the caseworker nor the probation officer were in a position of effectively monitoring this family. Through the non-pejorative language approach, he softened some of his parenting positions, involved the wife more in decisions, and admitted that he was wrong in what he did. He did, however, maintain that the daughter was at fault, the courts were being too unfair, and that he did not care if men forgave him as long as God forgave him. Our approach seemed to allow for dialogue concerning his feelings, thoughts, and behaviors that were closed off to the caseworker and probation officer. Therefore, the therapists positioned themselves to be an effective monitor of the family, affording more protection to the teenage girl.

REFERENCES

Anderson, H., & Goolishian, H. (1988). Human systems as linguistic systems: Preliminary and evolving ideas about clinical theory. *Family Process, 27*, 371-391.

Bateson, G. (1980). *Mind and nature: A necessary unity.* New York: Bantam Books.

Penn, P. (1982). Circular questioning. *Family Process, 21*, 267-280.

3

Read Aloud

Diane B. Brashear

Most of my work is as a marital and sex therapist. The majority of couples present with serious deficits in their ability to verbally and sexually communicate. The therapist's role is commonly a combination of educator and permission-giver. Interventions may be used not only to aid problem solving, but may be quite positive in enhancing the couples' awareness of the deficits they have either in communication skills or faulty assumptions about sexual performance. Although I may not be surprised about the result of a couple's use of an intervention technique, I cannot predict how they experience the intervention. What I do is use their response to the experience as an entrée into furthering awareness and skill development.

My favorite intervention is to ask the couple to share in reading out loud to each other. I qualify this by asking the less verbal partner (usually the male) to do most of the reading. I give him a book which I select based on what I know of his interests. One favorite selection is *Golf in the Kingdom*, by Michael Murphy. In this, golf is a metaphor for problem solving. Most males find this book fascinating and they become enthusiastic about it. If they are poor readers, I use popular comic strip books such as "Peanuts" or "Garfield." The couple is usually puzzled about this assignment, but are intrigued enough to follow through. Results are reported in the following session. For example, she (or the more expressive partner) was bored, had difficulty listening, did not keep quiet. This of course usually replicates other verbal interactions, yet is less threatening and can therefore be the basis for self-awareness and altered communication patterns.

This intervention is usually used after an assessment in which the couple is determined to be committed to their relationship and to therapy. It is used early in the treatment process, and is often helpful prior to the assignment of sensuality and sexuality orientated behavior prescriptions. Some couples continue to use reading out loud as they proceed through sensate focus type exercises.

$$-4-$$

Stepfamily Enrichment: Assets Feedback

Lorna Hecker

TARGETED POPULATION

This intervention is for families who have fairly good stepfamily relationships already. It is not designed for families with depression, intense conflict, or severe pathology. It not suited for children who are not school age. It is designed to enhance relationships that have a fairly good foundation.

THEORETICAL FOUNDATION

This intervention is based in enrichment theory and success training interventions introduced by Barb Sher (1979) in the popular press book *Wishcraft: How to Get What You Really Want*. The intervention is an adaptation of Ms. Sher's work with success group training.

PREPARATORY ACTIVITY

In preparation for an assets feedback exercise, a session is spent discussing the changes family members have experienced since the birth of the stepfamily. Possible losses included when a stepfamily is born include (Visher & Visher, 1988):

1. Relationship losses
2. Loss of marriage dreams
3. Major changes for children
   a. Change in ordinal position
   b. Remarriage explodes the fantasy that biological parents will get back together
   c. More need to share
   d. Sharing parental time
   e. Loss of former role in household
4. Loss of former traditions
5. Lack of affirmation from former spouse
6. Continuing transitions: Shifts and ambiguities of stepfamily life can be difficult
7. Custodial changes
8. Fear of further losses

RATIONALE

"A major task of therapy can be to help individuals identify their losses, be able to express their sadness and anger, and then move on to recognizing present gains and potential satisfactions" (Visher & Visher, 1988, p. 119). The preparatory activity aids the family in identifying losses and mourning the losses brought about by the formation of the stepfamily.

THE INTERVENTION: ASSETS FEEDBACK

Therapist's introduction: "Last week we talked about the losses brought about by the birth of this stepfamily. There was sadness and anger brought about by some of the changes."

(The therapist lists some of the losses.)

"Everyone, in spite of how much you may have wanted to form this new family, has had goodbyes to say and losses to feel.

"Today, since we talked about these losses last week, with your permission, I would like to explore your gains with you. Can I have your permission to do a little experiment?

"Praise in our busy lives is sometimes hard to come by. In order to realize the new strengths that members bring to this family, I would like you to think about each other's strengths and the good things each person here has brought to this new family.

"I am going to ask you to give each other Positive Precise Feedback. This means, I'm going to ask you, one at a time, to turn your chair away from the others. When your chair is turned away, you are not allowed to talk — not even to say thank you. You must just sit and listen to the positive feedback the others give you and write it down. The rest of you will have three minutes to talk about this person and say what you like about him/her and what you think that person's assets and strengths are. This can be as simple as he/she has nice eyes to he/she balances the checkbook wonderfully! or I appreciate his/her patience. Who wants to start?"

At this time, each member takes his/her turn receiving positive feedback from the other members and writing down each thing he/she hears for future reference. (Note: If you have young members, an older sibling or the therapist can be the scribe for the family.)

Afterwards, process the activity with questions such as: "What was it like to hear the comments?" and so on. Finish with, "I'd like you to take these papers home and place them where you can see them daily."

Rationale: Assets feedback aids the step family in recognizing "present gains and potential satisfactions." This exercise brings out the strengths of the newly formed family, aids in the formation of a family bond, and puts the family in a position where they may be more willing to work on new therapeutic activities.

OUTCOMES

With the stepfamily members having affirmed each other, members will feel good about themselves, as well as feel good about the compliments they gave to others. Some statements I've encountered with this intervention include: "I like it when my Daddy plays games with me"; "I appreciate Wayne's patience with the kids"; "She is really a kind person," etc.

This type of outcome provides a good framework for therapy to continue with a solution-focus. It also makes the family ripe for a ritual which may help to solidify some of the positive changes which come about.

REFERENCES

Sher, B. (1979). *Wishcraft: How to get what you really want*. New York: Ballantine Books.

Visher, E., & Visher, J. (1988). *Old loyalties, new ties: Therapeutic strategies with stepfamilies*. New York: Brunner/Mazel.

Ingredients of an Interaction

Michele Baldwin

One of my favorite and frequently used interventions is based on the powerful transformational process, "Ingredients of an Interaction," developed by Virginia Satir in collaboration with Maria Gomori and myself. Some of the elements in this process had been used by Virginia for many years, but were only formalized during the last few years of her life, when many of the theories underlying her work were made more explicit. The basic assumptions of this intervention are that much of what we hear, feel, and react to is based on the past and that the sequence of the internal process of an interaction follows a specific and universal pattern. In this brief presentation, I would like to demonstrate how this process can be used as an instrument to facilitate interpersonal communication. I believe it is applicable to any situation in which the reaction of one family member to a verbal or non-verbal message of another family member does not seem to fit the message received or seems upsetting to the recipient.

Spoken words and behaviors represent primarily the external aspect of a communication. They are the result of complex internal transactions, which, if they are not acknowledged or are misunderstood, contribute to dysfunctional communication patterns. These transactions go at a computer-like speed and occur in an instant, out of awareness. Therapy often consists of bringing them to the surface. In fact, the audible (or visible) part of the communication can be compared to the tip of an iceberg, with the major impact of the communication being buried beneath the water. A great deal of miscommunication and stress occurs because of a failure to recognize the internal processes of communications from others. Understanding these internal processes can help to clarify behaviors or reactions that would otherwise be misunderstood and gives family members a useful tool that they can use in their home setting.

Before explaining the intervention, I would like to briefly describe the internal pattern of a message which induced stress in the receiver and caused her to react in a dysfunctional manner. In dysfunctional families, the level of stress is usually high for all members and is constantly reinforced by communication patterns which fuel further stress. Once this vicious circle is established, a family lives in pain unless its members find new ways of communicating and coping. We will follow this message through the complex internal process that occurs, pointing out how the stress is created and how the inability to deal with it results in ineffective coping, usually followed by a response which tends to escalate the stress. This internal route is similar to an obstacle course, where something can go wrong at every step of the way.

1. The Sensory Input Level

We could compare what happens at this level to a video camera which takes a picture and records the sound. What was seen and heard? Unfortunately, most of us are poorly trained to be objective observers, yet we assume that we are. As a result, the internal process can be derailed at the start.

2. Making Meaning

As humans we are driven to make sense and give meaning to everything we hear and see. The meaning we assign to what our senses have taken in results from making an interpretation, based on all our past experiences, beliefs, values, and feelings of self-worth. The whole background that we use to attribute meaning can contribute to distortion of the message received. For example, a mild criticism from my boss may reawaken the memory of my father telling me that I can never do anything right and of the ensuing punishment. From that point on, I will not be responding to my boss's statement, but to the old memory.

3. The Feeling About the Meaning

How do I feel about the interpretation I have just made? Using the above example, I may feel afraid and/or worthless.

4. The Feeling About the Feeling

The first three steps described thus far are probably familiar to most therapists. For Satir, however, more critical than the feeling itself is the feeling that a person has about the feeling. A person with high self-esteem can usually accept the feeling, whatever it is. A person with low self-esteem, on the other hand, will react to the feeling by making a decision as to whether the feeling is acceptable or not (and will have to find a way to protect himself or herself from the feeling, if it is unacceptable). For instance, I may feel stupid about feeling afraid or worthless and either deny or reinforce the feeling.

5. The Defenses

My reaction to my feeling activates my survival and coping behaviors. Having told myself that I should not experience what I am experiencing, I nevertheless need to find a way to deal with the internal discomfort which I experience. I will do that by eliciting the survival defenses which I have learned to use when I get into such a spot. I can deny that I feel afraid or worthless, telling myself that I do not feel that way. I can put the responsibility of my feeling on someone else and, in the example above, feel blame towards my boss. Or, I can put an internal barrier between myself and the feeling and ignore it.

6. The Rules for Commenting

My reply or my behavior will depend on the rules I have about commenting. Those are also based on the past and will lead to the answer I will make. Although I may feel like blaming my boss, I may have a rule which says, "Be nice to those more important or more powerful than you." I will then ignore the criticism and my feelings.

The response — the observable phase of the communication — although immediately expressed, is the result of the above process, whose steps will remain at an unconscious level, unless an attempt is made to identify them. This internal route is not always followed, of course, in such a linear way. In fact, the model is holographic, but serves as a useful guide for the family therapist in helping a family towards better communication.

An example of how I use this intervention in therapy occurred with Mary and Charles, who came to see me because Mary was not sure that she wanted to stay married to a man who appeared to be more interested in his work than in her. After we had worked together for about a dozen sessions, they reported a bad argument. They were both baffled at their inability to come to terms with the issue at hand: A few days ago Charles had called home at about 6 p.m. stating that he was delayed, but would be home as soon as he could. Mary asked him where he was and he responded rather angrily, "Here you go again." This response led to an angry exchange and to a lengthy argument when Charles returned home that night.

I processed Charles' response through the "Ingredients of an Interaction." What follows is a slow motion rendition of the internal bullet-speed process which had taken place for Charles.

1. My first question to Charles was: "What did you hear?" Charles had correctly heard Mary's question about where he was, but because they were on the telephone, Charles did not have the visual cues which might have given him a more complete message.

2. My second question was: "What meaning did you give to what you heard?" The meaning he gave to that question was that Mary was upset at him for being late. As we explored how he came to make such an interpretation, he recalled past situations when Mary had been upset because he was late.

3. I then asked him, "How did you feel?" and he stated that he had felt angry.

4. My next question was, "How did you feel about your anger?" He felt entitled to his anger because the reason for his delay was that he intended to buy her a birthday present and Mary's question had spoiled his pleasure.

5. Finally I asked him, "In what way did you deal with your

anger?'' Having put the responsibility of his feeling onto Mary, he had followed his usual pattern of blaming her.

6. Since he had no rule about expressing anger, he responded by expressing his blame. Mary was completely baffled by Charles' reaction to her question. She felt hurt and angry.

Indeed, all she wanted to know was if Charles was still in the office, so that she could ask him to pick up a quart of milk at the market located next to his office.

This first round gave Charles and Mary an understanding of how they had gotten into difficulty. I now needed to show them a way to work through such a misunderstanding. In order to do so, we needed to figure out what he could have done differently at the key point(s) of derailment.

I asked Charles if he could have interpreted Mary's question in a different way. He realized how easy it was for him to interpret Mary's questions as controlling and that this interpretation was based on feelings from the past when he strongly resented the control of his mother. I suggested to him that he might try to check the meaning of a question before reacting. Of course, he might not be aware of a possible derailment of meaning until he is aware of a feeling of anger. So when he becomes aware of the feeling, he needs to say to himself, ''I am feeling angry. What is this about? Does it have to do with something happening right now or could the meaning be based on the past?'' This intervention had a lasting effect on Charles' and Mary's relationship. They were able to be supportive of each other in their effort to become responsible for their internal processes and to communicate their truth to each other, rather than responding in ways which escalated the conflict.

This intervention, so simple on the surface, can produce lasting changes in relationships where there is goodwill and a sincere desire to understand what goes on in the mind of a partner or family member. Once the steps are understood, they can be easily applied when a person is experiencing feelings in himself or herself or in others, that they do not understand.

6

The Tug-of-War Toilet

Joyce K. Gilkey

THEORETICAL ORIENTATION: STRATEGIC

In a group home for adolescents, the staff and residents often form a family-like unit. There is the usual bickering among the kids; the staff pitches in with its share of gripes. Frequently, the staff finds itself in a symptomatic "tug-of-war" with the residents, and the administrator, as the surrogate parent, must officiate. In the following case, this coed group home was filled to capacity with 16 boys. The staff was particularly tired and grumpy and entered into a war of wills with the residents around the problem of their stopped-up toilets. The restroom and toilets were overflowing with clothes, tissues, and unflushed material. The odor and resident refusal to clean their bathroom led the staff to write volumes of discipline reports. The tug-of-war became too much for either group and a weary administrator on emergency call was paged for assistance.

The administrator had minutes to prepare a response. At 5'5", 125 pounds, she reasoned that the male residents required a power source—or at least a person that pretended to be powerful. Approaching the group home, she threw open the front door, angrily pushed by the clerical and housekeeping staff and ordered the residents to meet in a downstairs office. Her language was spiced with the residents' usual choice of four letter words. Seating them at her feet so that no one was taller than she, she explained the legal meaning of "malicious damage." When everyone was asked if they wished to have a special invitation to get a better understanding of this charge from the juvenile judge, all declined. They were asked to devise a solution to their useless toilets—a solution that by definition included a design of their own discipline. The residents outlined several alternatives for their discipline, including: no recreation, loss of allowance, and cleaning the bathrooms. All opted to clean the bathrooms. The administrator agreed and climbed the stairs with the residents to begin the digging-out process. Resident attitudes had calmed considerably but the administrator wanted to be sure the toilets and resident hygiene were restored. All sixteen residents and the administrator piled into the filthy bathroom with the administrator claiming the odor was "stimulating" and "improving" every minute. Each resident followed the administrator as they shoveled the toilets clean. Resident attitude continued to improve; the sixteen residents proposed then to clean the walls, floors, and showers. The staff, in turn, became calm almost immediately but asked the administrator never to pretend that way again.

This intervention was indicated when the resident population was largely made up of fatherless boys and the administration previously sought to persuade and plead with them into compliance with daily rules. Both staff and residents needed an "in-charge" figure, which the administrator adopted as a role at once. Using client language and allowing the use of choices in discipline permitted residents a voice in how their situation was handled. Cleaning the bathroom as a team and calling attention to the pungent odor left a lasting anchor of good hygiene in their minds. It also pushed the symptom to the point of absurdity — allowing paradoxically for the residents to correct their situation and feel better about themselves at the same time.

7

Metaphors on Space

Gregory Brock
Charles P. Barnard

Family therapy often involves helping the entire family or a portion of it to meet outside the therapy session and discuss how to deal with some situation. Therapists are well advised to learn how to capitalize on the 167 hours in the week beyond the weekly family session. For example, treatment of child behavior problems commonly consists of helping parents find the time and place to decide together how they will handle a particular child behavior problem. Dr. Anton Smets (Brock & Barnard, 1988) has parents meet in their bathroom. This meeting serves to physically define the adults in the family as a parental dyad. Similarly, treatment of marital difficulties often requires that the spouses meet and come to a shared understanding of an event in their day-to-day lives or how they intend to handle some situation. In our experience, the potency of these out-of-session meetings can be intensified when the power of the metaphor related to the problem is linked with a physical context for addressing it.

The power of the metaphor has been capitalized upon by all the great teachers. From Plato's allegory of the cave, to the teachings of Jesus and Buddha, metaphor has changed thinking and subsequent behaviors. We believe the use of living space as a metaphor is all too often overlooked as a therapeutic adjunct.

Applied in the home setting, we encourage families and couples to use the living space most closely related to the relationship difficulty they must address. For example, if a couple argues about or needs to discuss an issue that is at the foundation of their relationship, we encourage them to conduct the discussion in the basement. Other constraints are placed on their discussion of course, but we ask that they hold their meeting in the basement. Or, if a parent wants to confront a child on bed-wetting/defecating to clarify what will happen if the soiling recurs, we suggest the interaction occur in the bathroom or the bedroom depending upon the details making up the issue.

Naturally, clients with larger homes have more flexibility in using space for this procedure. In our experience, however, even the simplest environment can be a rich resource for family development if the therapist takes the extra step of assigning specific activities to the physical space where those activities are to take place.

Below is a list of spaces and examples of related topics a family might address in each:

Bedroom

Sexual issues, personal attractiveness, sleep disorders, marital issues.

Kitchen or Dining room

Eating disorders, family unity, roles as they relate to chores.

Family room

Family boundaries, issues addressing cohesiveness.

Attic

Religious concerns, values, and attendant differences. Issues present since premarital days that have prevented couples from progressing beyond the "threshold" level.

Hallways

Intergenerational issues such as parents dealing with their parents (issues that connect the generations).

Garage

> Issues that constitute interface with family and outside world such as work related.
>
> Issues that "clutter" their relationship and prevent them from getting closer (garbage generally in garage).

A fundamental characteristic of effective verbal metaphors is that the characters and events are symmetrical or isomorphic with the clients' situation or problem. If a metaphor has no apparent similarity with the clients' circumstances, it likely will be ineffective. In using this intervention, the therapist must establish for the clients the isomorphic connection between the space suggested in which to complete the assigned task and their world view of current circumstances.

Gordon (1978) states, "A metaphor, then, is a novel representation of something (the old saying that 'there is more than one way to skin a cat' comes to mind). . . . metaphors are a way of talking about experience" (p. 8-9). When discussing therapeutic use of metaphors, most often we refer to the construction of experience with words. Metaphor, as described in this intervention, is using space in the family's living environment as a tool for defining and contextualizing an experience.

As the family, couple, or some other subsystem engages in whatever they are asked to do in a new, physical context metaphorically related to their problem, we find that they identify options never previously considered. The new context seems to serve to incubate new possibilities and increase their sense of hope and optimism. In *Therapeutic Metaphors* (1978), Gordon states, "Often individuals have a problem coping within a particular situation, not because of a lack of choice about what to do but because of a lack of choices about how to do it" (p. 76). The application of this intervention seems to dislodge clients and increase their choices. Further, clients report that they rediscover a playful quality the family or couple lost in the struggles that brought them into therapy.

We have yet to encounter a situation made worse by this intervention. At the very most, no change results. Fisch, Weakland, and Segal (1982), in describing their form of brief therapy, suggest that theory and related interventions should ". . . be judged primarily by the results of use" (p. 7). As we have used this intervention over several years, the results continue to validate its effectiveness.

REFERENCES

Brock, G., & Barnard, C. (1988). *Procedures in family therapy*. Boston: Allyn and Bacon.

Fisch, R., Weakland, J., & Segal, L. (1982). *The tactics of chance: Doing therapy briefly*. San Francisco: Jossey-Bass.

Gordon, D. (1978). *Therapeutic metaphors*. Cupertino, CA: META Publications.

8

The Treatment of Postdivorce Adjustment Problems Through Cognitive Restructuring

Donald K. Granvold

Cognitive restructuring methods have been applied to an extensive array of problems (Ellis & Bernard, 1986; Ellis & Grieger, 1986; Grieger & Grieger, 1982). Comparatively recently a number of practitioners have applied cognitive methods to treat postdivorce adjustment problems (Broder, 1985; Ellis, 1986; Graff, Whitehead, & Le Compte, 1986; Granvold, 1989; Granvold & Welch, 1977, 1979; Huber, 1983; Johnson, 1977; Walen & Bass, 1986; Walen, DiGiuseppe, & Wessler, 1980). The divorced client is highly subject to errors in cognitive functioning as s/he experiences the crisis of divorce and addresses pervasive change demands related to: (1) redefinition of self and object loss trauma; (2) role loss, disorientation, and restructuring; and (3) lifestyle adjustment. The process of postdivorce adjustment is marked by high stress, extreme and oscillating emotions, and both positive and negative experiences.

The application of cognitive restructuring methods to promote adaptive postdivorce adjustment involves the determination of irrational beliefs, faulty expectations, and faulty causal attributions regarding the divorce as an event, the ex-spouse, and the divorce adjustment process. These faulty cognitions are considered to be largely accountable for extreme negative emotions, low self-esteem, interpersonal problems (Broder, 1985; Granvold, 1989), inhibited goal attainment, and the like among the divorced. Once identified, the active set of faulty cognitions is targeted for change.

Ellis (1962) has identified eleven irrational beliefs which serve as the basis for dysfunctional thinking and faulty expectations. These beliefs incorporate such imperatives as: (1) the demand (as opposed to the desire) for love and approval, perfection, and control over one's world; (2) freedom from self-responsibility for one's own emotions; (3) extreme dependency on others; (4) irrefutable right to blame others for one's own and others' imperfections and short-comings; and (5) the indelible effect of history on current behavior and emotions. Evidence of each of these imperatives as active in-gredients in postdivorce maladjustment has been presented else-where (Granvold, 1989). Below are examples of irrational beliefs that are common among those who maintain strong negative feel-ings regarding self, the ex-spouse, and their postdivorce circum-stances:

Demandingness
"I am nothing without him/her."
"I'll never be happy again."
"I should have prevented the divorce."
"I am no good because I am divorced."

Placing responsibility for one's own emotions on others
"I have been depressed for two years because of him."
"My ex makes me so mad."
"I am emotionally disturbed because of her."

Dependency
"I *need* another (my ex-spouse) in my life to help me."
"I am too insecure to make it alone."
"I can't make decisions alone."

Blaming
"He taught me how to hate."
"I was kind and sweet before him/her."
"I'll never be able to trust again; s/he took that with him/her."

I can't change—this is the way I am
"I'm shy and always will be."
"I have always had a problem with anger/depression/worry."
"I'm a failure—all divorced people are losers."

After targeting the rigidly held set of irrational beliefs which have been promoting the client's emotional disturbance and associated maladaptive behavior, the therapist and client collaborate to: (1) establish the relationship between thoughts, emotional disturbance, and behavioral dysfunction; (2) search for sound, logical evidence for targeted beliefs; (3) modify the beliefs on the basis of the evidence (substitute more logical, reality-based beliefs for the distorted cognitions); (4) appraise gradual changes in maladaptive emotion and self-defeating behavior since rational thinking is more consistently and penetratingly applied to the client's circumstances.

EXAMPLE

Bill approached Mary for a divorce saying that he no longer felt "anything" for her. He filed for divorce, and a year after the divorce was final, Mary sought therapy for depression and social withdrawal. The assessment revealed that while Mary, too, had lost her feelings of love for Bill and wanted the divorce, she continued to feel hurt and depressed over his rejection of her. Furthermore, it was determined that she was operating with conditional self-regard contingent on Bill's love, his acceptance of her, and continued marriage.

Mary:	I don't understand it. Even though I, too, wanted the divorce, I feel so bad as a result of it. I'm depressed and I've even shut myself off from my friends.
Therapist:	What is it about the divorce that prompts you to feel this way?
Mary:	I think that it is mainly Bill's rejection of me. I feel so upset by it. I feel I'm no good, that if he rejected me I must be some awful human being.
Therapist:	So Bill's rejection is a main source of your feeling emotionally upset. Suppose we explore your thinking in relation to Bill's rejection of you to see if it is logical.
Mary:	All right.

Therapist:	How does Bill's rejecting you make you no good, an awful human being?
Mary:	I guess it really doesn't. But it doesn't feel good.
Therapist:	I agree that it doesn't feel good to be rejected. But to conclude because of it you're no good is faulty thinking. And if you continue thinking "I'm no good" in response to the rejection, how will you continue to feel?
Mary:	Bad, depressed.
Therapist:	What could you think in order to feel better?
Mary:	That I'm okay without Bill's acceptance of me.

USES

Cognitive restructuring is particularly appropriate when the client's emotional disturbance is in response to events which are either irreversible or unlikely to change and when rigidly held beliefs are the basis of extreme emotional upset and behavioral maladjustment. As noted earlier, the pervasiveness of the change demands concomitant with divorce expose the divorced individual to ample opportunity for cognitive distortions. Divorced individuals find cognitive restructuring to be a rapid, straightforward, and portable approach to the treatment of emotional distress. While applicable to most adults, the more highly educated and cognitively complex clients appear to most efficiently and effectively apply the method.

REFERENCES

Broder, M.S. (1985). Divorce and separation. In A. Ellis & M.E. Bernard (Eds.), *Clinical applications of Rational-Emotive Therapy*, (pp. 81-99). New York: Plenum Press.

Ellis, A. (1962). *Reason and emotion in psychotherapy*. New York: Lyle Stuart.

Ellis, A. (1986). Application of rational-emotive therapy to love problems. In A.E. Grieger (Ed.), *Handbook of Rational-Emotive Therapy, Vol. 2*. New York: Springer Publishing.

Ellis, A., & Bernard, M.E. (1986). What is rational-emotive therapy (RET)? In A. Ellis & R. Grieger (Eds.), *Handbook of Rational-Emotive Therapy, Vol. 2*. New York: Springer Publishing.

Ellis, A., & Grieger, R. (1986). *Handbook of Rational-Emotive Therapy, Vol. 2.* New York: Springer Publishing.

Graff, R.W., Whitehead, G.I., & Le Compte, M. (1986). Group treatment with divorced women using cognitive-behavioral and supportive-insight methods. *Journal of Counseling Psychology, 33,* 276-281.

Granvold, D.K. (1989). Postdivorce treatment. In M. Textor (Ed.), *The divorce and divorce therapy handbook* (pp. 197-223). Northvale, NJ: Aronson.

Granvold, D.K., & Welch, G.J. (1977). Intervention for postdivorce adjustment problems: The treatment seminar. *Journal of Divorce, 1,* 81-92.

Granvold, D.K., & Welch, G.J. (1979). Structured, short-term group treatment of postdivorce adjustment. *International Journal of Group Psychotherapy, 29,* 347-358.

Grieger, R., & Grieger, I.Z. (Eds.) (1982). *Cognition and emotional disturbance.* New York: Human Sciences Press.

Huber, C.H. (1983). Feelings of loss in response to divorce: Assessment and intervention. *The Personnel and Guidance Journal, 61,* 357-361.

Johnson, S.M. (1977). *First person singular: Living the good life alone.* New York: Signet.

Walen, S.R., & Bass, B.A. (1986). Rational divorce counseling. *Journal of Rational-Emotive Therapy, 4,* 95-109.

Walen, S.R., DiGiuseppe, R., & Wessler, R.L. (1980). *A Practitioner's guide to Rational-Emotive Therapy.* New York: Oxford University Press.

9

Termination as a Therapeutic Technique

M. Ellen Mitchell

Recently, a great deal has been presented and written (e.g., Stanton & Todd, 1981; Todd, 1984) on treating the difficult family/client. Many of the problems revolve around lack of compliance and/or motivation to change. Families may appeal for sessions with one or more members missing; homework assignments may go uncompleted with vague or superficial explanations for the lack of execution; clients may agree to implement directives only to later report that they "forgot" or met with a trivial impediment. The following technique was developed for use with difficult cases and should be employed with caution.

The use of termination as a technique has strategic theory (Haley, 1976; Madanes, 1981; Stanton, 1981) as its origins but differs insofar as it is not necessarily designed to bring about change per se. It also has some similarity to paradoxical interventions (Madanes, 1980; Weeks & L'Abate, 1978) because change may arise when the client does *not* follow the therapist's directive. It is a last resort intervention to be utilized carefully after all else has failed. Therapists are often reluctant to end therapy and instead engage in an endless, frustrating cycle of attempts to get the clients to do something. This intervention serves to stop this unproductive process which ironically often mirrors a pattern of defeat reported by the family.

The intervention is simple, powerful, and straightforward, albeit perhaps extreme. The therapist must fully assess the degree to which compliance and change have occurred. If the conclusion from that assessment is that there has been little or no cooperation or reorganization, and if the therapist is unable to identify other potentially useful methods, then termination must be considered. In addition, the therapist must be certain this intervention is not being employed simply because the therapist feels angry and frustrated about the lack of progress. Consultation may be indicated.

Ethical guidelines for psychologists (American Psychological Association, 1981) dictate that in the absence of benefit to the client, one must contemplate ending therapy. The decision to embark on this intervention must include this consideration. The difference, however, is that termination is not sought as an end for its own sake but is formulated as a critical intervention designed to communicate something to the client of the utmost importance, namely, that the client must decide to make a commitment to change or to abandon the charade of therapy with which the therapist will not collude. The intervention serves to exemplify the essential role of decision making and self-determination. The following cases illustrate the use of this intervention.

CASE #1

Mary was a 27-year-old single woman who presented for depression with, and at the behest of, her parents, with whom she lived. Sessions were split into family and individual components as it was readily apparent that individuation was an issue. Mary wanted no part of treatment but would tell her parents about her misery and suicidal thoughts. Further, she began to complain that therapy was just another way her parents persecuted her. Mary managed to maneuver her parents into doing all the therapeutic work while she remained essentially uninvolved. After many unsuccessful attempts to intervene, therapy was strategically terminated. She was told that her lack of interest and commitment were evident. Her parents were told that Mary was an adult who needed to make her own decisions and who obviously did not want therapy. The parents were informed of legal commitment procedures in front of Mary in the event that she became actively suicidal. Further appointments were refused despite protestations of the parents. Mary was invited to return when she felt ready. Alone, unknown to her parents, and of her own volition, Mary returned to treatment five months later and made remarkable, rapid progress.

CASE #2

The Smiths presented with complaints about their adolescent son acting out in the form of staying out beyond curfew, verbal fighting, and failure to comply with parental directives. After a few sessions it was clear that the parents wished their son would simply behave without their supervision or involvement and that the adolescent was not going to take responsibility for himself or change in the family. Consequences were not applied, behavior was not monitored, plans were formulated and not followed. Not surprisingly, the problem behaviors continued. Each weekly session brought with it a new start rather than a gradual progressive move toward agreed-upon goals. The family was confronted about their apparent lack of interest in real change and terminated. At the final session, it was evident that despite some general unhappiness, the family situation was essentially comfortable for all and certainly preferable to the effort required for real change to occur. The imposed decision to stop appeared to be a relief to the family.

DISCUSSION

Both cases illustrate that ending treatment before goals are achieved can represent a successful outcome. Despite major differences, the cases share several commonalities. Confrontation was central and in each case, clients were told that their behavior appeared unmotivated and disinterested despite adherence to scheduled appointments and protestations to the contrary. Both families presented legitimate complaints that were within the purview of therapy. Interventions were unsuccessful because of apparent (albeit covert) lack of compliance. In both cases, the families conveyed the hope that change would happen spontaneously and effortlessly. In both cases the termination was an intervention designed to either force the family to redefine the problem and identify the present situation as acceptable or to promote change.

Continuation of therapy was offered to each but made contingent upon a break in sessions to rethink goals and an overt resolution to approach the task of therapy in a new manner as evidenced by concrete behavior, not simply as new exhortations to the therapist for prescriptions they had no intention of following. In both cases it was impressed on the families that the decision to be in therapy was just that, a choice, and that planned nonattendance was not failure.

REFERENCES

American Psychological Association. (1981). Ethical principles of psychobiologists. *American Psychologist, 36*, 633-638.

Haley, J. (1976). *Problem solving therapy*. San Francisco: Jossey-Bass.

Madanes, C. (1980). Protection, paradox, and pretending. *Family Process, 19*, 73-85.

Madanes, C. (1981). *Strategic family therapy*. San Francisco: Jossey-Bass.

Stanton, M.D. (1981). Strategic approaches to family therapy. In A.S. Gurman & D.P. Kniskern (Eds.), *Handbook of family therapy*. New York: Brunner/Mazel.

Stanton, M.D., & Todd, T.C. (1981). Engaging "resistant" families in treatment, II: Principles and techniques in recruitment. *Family Process, 20*, 261-280.

Todd, T.C. (1984). Strategic approaches to marital stuckness. *Journal of Marriage and the Family, 10*, 373-381.

Weeks, G.R., & L'Abate, L. (1978). A compilation of paradoxical methods. *American Journal of Family Therapy, 7*, 81-76.

The Communication Stone

Lorna Hecker

TARGET POPULATION

This intervention is useful for couples or families who consistently talk in the therapeutic session at the same time. It is most useful for those who seem oblivious to any structuring moves the therapist may suggest to change the interruptions.

DESCRIPTION OF THE INTERVENTION

For couples or families who talk at the same time and do not listen well to the therapist's request for them to speak one at a time, I have a "concrete" example I use, which I call my "Communication Stone." I have a handsome rock I keep in my office, and when clients consistently interrupt each other, I ask them to take hold of my "Communication Stone." I instruct them that when one of them is holding the stone, the others are forbidden to talk until that person is done. Meanwhile, they can simply listen attentively until it is their turn to talk. I instruct the person who is holding the stone that when he/she has said his/her piece, he/she may pass the stone to someone else.

RATIONALE

This intervention restructures communication in a nonthreatening way, enhances listening behaviors, and puts the clients in charge of their own communication behaviors.

Most clients catch on quickly and the "Communication Stone" can then be shelved for future use.

Termination Rituals

Janine Roberts

Termination in family therapy has been the least examined treatment phase. If anthropologist van Gennep's (1960) three stages of ritual process (separation, transition, and reintegration) are applied to families in therapy, it is evident that significant work has been done in looking at how families separate from their old organization and join with the therapist(s) to create a new system. Meeting in a special place (therapist's office) with particular paraphernalia (e.g., phone, one-way mirror, video), and at a fixed time all help to mark that the family is outside of their day-to-day context (Kobak & Waters, 1984). Similarly, the mid-phase of treatment (which van Gennep calls the transitional stage) has been well-explained. Through various questioning techniques, homework interventions, and in-session tasks, the family experiments with new roles and rules and tries different interactional patterns. They are "betwixt and between" their old and new identities.

However, the third phase (reintegration), where the family is connected back to their day-to-day life with their new roles, rules, and status, is often not discussed. Yet, integration back into their daily context is crucial to mark family strengths and problem-solving capabilities, to highlight their changed relationships with the therapist(s) and other social service professionals, and to bring closure to the therapy. And therapists need a chance to step back and hear from families about what therapy has been like for them. We are making too many assumptions in the field of family therapy about how families view treatment and we need to hear more clients' voices.

My colleagues, Drs. Richard Whiting and Evan Imber-Black, and I routinely use several termination interventions. First is the therapist's ritual where clients are asked to comment upon the therapy process with questions such as: What was most useful or helpful in therapy? What was least useful or helpful in the treatment process? What advice would they give to us in working with other families with similar problems?

If there have been any team members working behind the one-way mirror, they come into the room. This physically marks the shift to moving collaboratively out of treatment. At the same time, the questions mark the change as the family is being asked to give feedback to the therapists. As a part of this ritual, food can be brought in both to highlight the move toward a more social, everyday relationship (you don't usually eat in a therapy session) as well as to symbolically note family resources. For instance, for lesbian couple Eva and Delores, I brought in Baklava (a honey drenched, many-layered Greek pastry) and talked about how multi-layered their relationship was with its different levels of care/connection/humor and attention to each other. Richard Whiting and I have even gone so far as to wrangle ourselves an invitation for potluck supper at families' homes when they have called and said things were going so well they did not want to come in for more sessions. Around the dinner table we talk about what did and did not work in the therapy process, highlighting the family's problem-solving capacities.

Another common ritual that we do at the end of treatment is to ask families to bring in *symbols* of what therapy has been like for them and/or the therapist/team can give the family a symbol to take home. For instance, with the Hayden family, where the father was found by the Department of Social Services to have been inappropriately disciplining his children (including hitting them with a broomstick), the team took another broomstick and with brightly colored markers wrote messages to the family about strengths they had demonstrated in treatment. (For instance, the therapist wrote, "Positive rewards, limits on favorite things, curfews—you have shown that you don't need to use the broomstick.") The team then shellacked the stick and wrapped it up for the last session. The family put the broomstick on the fireplace mantlepiece in the front room and Ralph Hayden told the therapist on a follow-up call, "When I get the urge to pick up a stick, I go and read your stick and think about other things I can do."

With the Sterling family, the parents were asked to bring symbols of the therapy to the final session. They entered the room laughing with a laundry basket full of clean, folded clothes, a copy of *The Velveteen Rabbit* and an imperfectly special box that had all hand-made joints but was not quite finished. Mr. Sterling talked about how the laundry basket represented for him a key shift in therapy, that the housekeeping things they had been squabbling over were not so significant. Mrs. Sterling shared how the imperfectly special box represented that she could not get her husband to do things only in a particular way, that she needed also to see his ways of caring for her. *The Velveteen Rabbit* was brought in "not only because of its theme of imperfectly being special, but because you (Janine) gave it to us. It was a nice connection. That was special." We brought two inscribed T-shirts for them, one of which said, "Celebrate imperfectly special mothers," and the other, "Celebrate imperfectly special fathers."[1]

Symbols shared or exchanged at the end of treatment can be used to visually trigger new interactional patterns at home, thus anchoring changes made in treatment. With the Sterlings, they talked about how, when they were becoming too self-critical and uptight with their children, they could put their new T-shirts on or put them on the kids or throw one to the parent who was upset and give them a hug. Another couple, Rhonda and George, brought in a teddy bear as a symbol of the vulnerability that they were having difficulty sharing with each other. At home, they then used the bear as a cue that they needed to sit and talk with each other as they had done in therapy, rather than distancing out their own fear.

Use of symbols, therapists coming out from behind the mirror, and giving of small gifts can also facilitate closure in treatment when work has been done with different subsystems. The Marks family, a single-parent father with four daughters, originally came in for therapy because he thought one of the daughters was depressed. She claimed she was feeling fine and as she was doing well in school and in her job and had many friends, more attention became focused on her father's sadness and shame over career choices he had made, his divorce, and current isolation from intimate sexual relationships. He felt particularly that perhaps he should have pursued a more prestigious career, instead of devoting the kind of time he had to being a parent. We worked primarily with the father for five months and as he became clearer about future choices in his life as well as past decisions he had made, he started to feel more comfortable with his life style.

For the termination session, we invited the daughters back and asked Mr. Marks whether he would like the four team members behind the mirror to come in. He said "Yes" very strongly and so all ten of us met in the room. The team gave him a gift-wrapped copy of Watzlawick's book *How Real is Real?* because it related to much of the work he had done on going back and looking at his life differently (being the same differently). In the front of the book, the therapist wrote, thanking him for all he had taught us about the many ways there were to reconstruct a floor/view the world. This came from an extended metaphor that had been used in treatment after Mr. Marks told the story of how he reconstructed the floor of a house he was working on when the floor boards did not come out even. (By small imperfect adjustments, the boards were able to be fitted into a solid whole.) The other four team members had each also drawn in the front of the book a picture of themselves in chairs in the same positions that they had taken in the room when we had a reflective debate about the different ways to look at Mr. Marks' life. Each chair was then autographed. The daughters got a flavor from this gift-giving of the work that their father had done in therapy without hearing all the details.

The rest of the session was spent talking about people's future plans and how the ways in which the daughters were leading their lives represented a validation of Dad's values and choices. (One was going off to Europe on a study exchange and another had just been accepted to a prestigious college on scholarship.) We ended the session out of therapy. We were not talking about problems or presenting ourselves as helpers but rather were discussing present and upcoming events in their lives and ours.

Numerous possibilities to give closure to the unique intimate relationship of therapy are provided by having clients comment on the therapy experience, with the exchange of symbols about the process, and sharing food. As one client said, "The symbols hold all those ideas floating around and help you to put them into words." These types of termination rituals, while providing some structure (with particular questions or requests for things to be brought in) to handle the mix of ambivalent feelings that most people have about endings, are also open enough to fit with each family's and therapist's needs to personally express what their encounter together meant. Treatment is connected with day-to-day life and moves out beyond the confines of the therapy room.

NOTE

1. See Roberts (1988) for a complete description of this case.

REFERENCES

Kobak, R.R., & Waters, D.B. (1984). Family therapy as a rite of passage: Play's the thing. *Family Process, 23*, 89-100.
Roberts, J. (1988). Mythmaking in the land of imperfect specialness: Lions, laundry baskets, and cognitive deficits. In S. Anderson & D. Bagarozzi (Eds.), *Family myths: Psychotherapy implications*. New York: Haworth Press.
van Gennep, A. (1960). *The rites of passage*. Chicago: University of Chicago Press.
Watzlawick, P. (1977). *How real is real?* New York: Vintage Books.
Williams, M. (1983). *The velveteen rabbit*. New York: A.A. Knopf.

12

Growthful Touch

Connie J. Salts

The use of touch in the family therapy session and incorporating touch as part of client homework can serve as a very powerful communication medium.

The importance of touch in the early stages of human development and throughout the life cycle has been reported in the research literature (Borenzweig, 1983). Touch is considered essential for our physical and emotional well-being. Touch can provide a sense of reassurance and comfort, particularly to those who are distressed. However, members of couples and families who present for therapy have often distanced themselves from one another, thereby eliminating the opportunities for increased communication and understanding through growthful touching.

Incorporation of touch as an intervention in couple and family therapy is not identifiable with a specific theoretical orientation. The therapist does need to be directive regarding the use of touch and perceptive of the client's responses to being touched. In-session observation of clients' touching (or absence of touching one another), coupled with direct questions regarding the type/amount of physical contact between family members can provide the therapist with data to determine if positive touching is missing from the family interactions.

Use of touch in session can be incorporated as part of other interventions or may be a primary intervention. It may be as tentative as asking a client if she could lightly touch her husband's forearm while she tells him one thing she would like to keep in their relationship. It may also be as bold as directing a family to practice, in session, several types of hugs (Keating, 1983, 1987) and then sending them home with the homework that everyone must hug everybody else at least twice a day for the next week. While clients discuss an important issue together at home, they can be directed to hold hands across the table or sit side by side on a couch or the floor. Young children can be held on an adult's lap, and a parent-adolescent agreement can be confirmed through a handshake or a hug. The possibilities for touch interventions leading to positive family interaction are immense, and when introduced appropriately, are readily accepted and followed by families.

In order for a touch intervention to be experienced positively by the clients, it must: (1) be appropriate to the situation, (2) not impose a greater level of intimacy than the clients can handle, and (3) must not communicate a negative message (Fisher, Rytting, & Heslin, 1976). As the same physical act can be executed and perceived very differently by different people, it is wise to directly assess whether clients would be comfortable giving and receiving the touch intervention. Power can be perceived as being in the hands of the toucher. Touch may also be manipulative and paternalistic as in a pat on the head for being a "good" spouse or a "smothering" embrace given to a teenager by a parent (Willison & Masson, 1986).

Another aspect of touch in session is that of the therapist touching the client. A gentle touch from the therapist can place emphasis on a verbal directive, focus the attention of clients who tend to lose contact with the therapist, model a caring form of communication, and help express feelings. Sometimes, however, the therapist may find it more appropriate to hold a small child on his/her lap, and to give older children and adults a non-sexual caring or comforting hug. Therapists, however, must be clear about their own attitudes toward touch and sensitive to the needs of the client and the impact physical contact may have on the therapeutic relationship. The author has found touch (including hugs) to be the most consistently used intervention in her predominately structural/strategic therapy approach. But, for touch to be positive and consequently therapeutic, the nature and duration of the contact should not generate discomfort in the therapist or the family members. The physical contact should be consistent with the needs of the family members. A person's need for privacy and space must be respected; therefore, always be certain you have permission before using touch.

The contraindications of the therapist's touching the client have been addressed by various authors. Sexual issues, especially for the male therapist with both male and female clients, are of major concern; therefore, appropriate caution should be exercised (Alyn, 1988; Borenzweig, 1983; Brock & Barnard, 1988; Willison & Masson, 1986).

REFERENCES

Alyn, J. (1988). The politics of touch in therapy: A response to Willison and Masson. *Journal of Counseling and Development, 66*, 432-433.

Brock, G., & Barnard, C. (1988). *Procedures in family therapy*. Boston: Allyn and Bacon.

Borenzweig, H. (1983). Touching in clinical social work. *Social Casework: The Journal of Contemporary Social Work, 64*, 238-242.

Fisher, J., Rytting, M., & Heslin, R. (1976). Affective and evaluative effects of an interpersonal touch. *Sociometry, 39*, 416-421.

Keating, K. (1983). *The hug therapy book*. Minneapolis, MN: CompCare Publishers.

Keating, K. (1987). *Hug therapy 2*. Minneapolis, MN: CompCare Publishers.

Willison, B., & Masson R. (1986). The role of touch in therapy: An adjunct to communication. *Journal of Counseling and Development, 64*, 497-500.

13

Using a Funeral Ritual in Therapy: Changing Rigid Interaction Patterns

Amy D. Frankel

The use of prescribed symbolic acts within the therapy process can facilitate a number of changes for both families and for couples. Rituals can serve as markers for entrances into and exits out of a system, to delineate boundaries within and around a system, and to redefine the membership of a system (Imber-Black, 1989). Rituals are useful in helping families to adopt new roles (Imber-Black, 1989) and to let go of the familiar yet rigid interactive patterns they tend to cling to tenaciously. Since rituals are able to address a large variety of issues, they are applicable across a wide range of therapeutic orientations.

While rigid interactive sequences may, in part, maintain the problem that brought the family into therapy in the first place, the prospect of modifying these behaviors may be a frightening one for the family. These sequences often have become the glue that holds the precariously balanced system together. A sense of loss and of fear may accompany the thought of abandoning these destructive yet familiar patterns. Rituals, such as funerals and wakes, are very much a part of the societal response to loss, and these grief rituals mark the loss as well as sanction the expression of grief over the loss (Imber-Black, 1989). Families and couples who are experiencing fear and a sense of loss when faced with the challenge of adopting more adaptive patterns of interaction may be helped to deal with loss through the use of a grief ritual.

DESCRIPTION OF THE INTERVENTION

The specific intervention involves asking the family or the couple to write down on small slips of paper the elements of the targeted interaction sequence that they now find reinforcing yet that will require modification for healthier functioning of the system. These elements are systemic in nature and will tend to consist of abstract concepts such as beliefs or needs. Family rules pertaining to emotional expression, leadership and influence, or closeness and distance may be alluded to on these slips of paper. By using these slips of paper as symbols of the elements maintaining the sequence, abstract ideas tend to be made more concrete in nature.

Clients are then asked to select the one piece of paper that they feel most ready to give up. This choice allows each person to begin to change at the level with which s/he feels most comfortable, yet eliminates the choice of not changing. That person is then asked to recite a eulogy which s/he has prepared for that choice. The eulogy can address not only the loss that person will feel but how that choice has served each of them and how each is now ready to let go of it. The slip of paper is then burned while the other members of the system respectfully watch the flames eradicate the symbol of the speaker's loss. This burning not only gives a sense of finality to the choice, but the use of flames may lend a hypnotic quality to the ritual. This may allow the client to lend more credence to his/her experience or to attribute spiritual and religious connotations to the ritual (Bergman, 1989). This ritual may be repeated at a later stage of therapy when the system has consolidated the change facilitated by the initial ritual and is ready to look at either different elements of the same sequence or at a different maladaptive interaction pattern. In this case, the funeral ritual also serves as a marker for change.

GUIDELINES FOR USE

The use of this intervention requires that the family members have already come to some understanding of the systemic nature of the problematic sequence as well as of the systemic consequences of modifying this sequence. Therefore, it is expected that this intervention will not be useful in the initial stages of therapy. This intervention was specifically designed for use in systems where the interactive patterns have been long-term and are highly rigid in nature.

EXAMPLE OF THE INTERVENTION

This intervention was originally designed for use with a couple who had been working on marital issues of control and of anger common to alcoholic marriages. They were both adult children of alcoholics. The wife had taken care of her alcoholic mother her entire childhood and had been previously married to three men, all of whom were chemically dependent. The husband had been asthmatic as a child and had been constantly watched over and cared for by a grandmother. He had been drinking heavily when the couple first met but she had been able to turn him around and help him to stop drinking and to find a job.

The couple's presenting concern was the husband's inability to stop spending money while the wife tried to maintain a strictly controlled budget. Although he was not drinking, the dynamics of an alcoholic system were stuck intact.

During the course of therapy, the couple had been unable to modify their relationship yet they had become aware of personal issues arising from their individual histories that propelled them into their one-up/one-down, or caretaker/care-needer dynamics.

Prior to assigning the task of writing their paper slips and eulogies, a brief discussion was initiated on how any change as large in magnitude as the one they were facing is bound to trigger feelings of fear and of loss. The discussion progressed to how societies and religions have given us ways to deal with loss and to adapt to our grief. This not only lent a frame to the impending task but validated their fears and introduced the sense that change, like death, was inevitable.

The next session was the ritual burning. The wife chose from among her slips of paper one on which she had written, "Taking care of myself by taking care of everyone else," while the husband chose, "Acting helpless and incompetent to hide my real self which people won't like." After the ritual, the couple was helped to find a way in which to begin to implement their choices.

OUTCOME

The successful performance of a ritual may be accompanied by both a change in attitude (Van der Hart, 1988) as well as a feeling of completion of the act within the individual (Jackson & Donovan, 1988). Ritual burnings of elements associated with past histories and experiences serve as boundary markers delineating the past from the present (Sanders, 1988). This was the outcome of the funeral ritual with this couple. They both reported feeling an increased sense of empathy and of respect for their partner's plight as well as a sense of their own need to change behaviors based on past experiences. They began, for the first time, to relate to each other in different ways. The wife began to relinquish her caretaking role while the husband was able to stop his compulsive spending and to begin to act in a manner which defined him as competent. This ritual, in various forms, has been a factor in helping numerous families change belief systems and behavior patterns that are expressions of the beliefs.

REFERENCES

Bergman, J. (1989). The family shrine. *The Family Therapy Networker, 13*, 48-51.

Imber-Black, E. (1989). Creating rituals in therapy. *The Family Therapy Networker, 13*, 38-46.

Jackson, B., & Donovan, R. (1988). Therapeutic ritual in divorce. *TACD Journal, 16*, 5-15.

Sanders, G.L. (1988). Systemic rituals in sexual therapy. In E. Imber-Black, J. Roberts, & R.A. Whiting (Eds.), *Rituals in Families and Family Therapy*, (pp. 257-275). New York: Norton.

Van der Hart, O. (1988). An imaginary leave-taking ritual in mourning therapy: A brief communication. *International Journal of Clinical and Experimental Hypnosis, 36*, 63-69.

14

Neuro-Linguistic Programming in One-Person Family Therapy

Bruce D. Forman
Edmund Cava

Although some family therapists insist on having all members of a family present to conduct therapy, this is not always possible. Family members are frequently unavailable or unwilling to participate in treatment. Therapists who lack the flexibility to modify interventions to treat clients whose views of the world differ markedly from the therapist's own, limit their clientele and thereby diminish their therapeutic impact. Family therapy with one person has been advocated by Bowen (1978). In addition, there is empirical evidence pointing to the effectiveness of treating one person within a family therapy conceptual paradigm (Szapocznik, Kurtines, Foote, Perez-Vidal, & Hervis, 1983).

Pattern interventions are frequently used by strategic therapists to assist couples and families to modify their modes of interacting. The interventions are usually at the level of overt behavioral patterns. Similarly, interventions with individuals may be achieved by altering strategic sequences or internal patterns. One of the schools of therapy that has demonstrated effectiveness in altering internal strategies is Neuro-Linguistic Programming (NLP). NLP is a method for organizing, understanding, and guiding the internal structure of subjective experience and is thereby concerned with the sequences and patterns through which people receive and process information (Einspruch & Forman, 1985). NLP has been described as a cognitive behavioral therapy in view of both its specificity and its reliance on conditioning constructs (Forman, Cava, & Powell, 1986). In addition, NLP has been considered a systems therapy in that the interventions are aimed at modifying the client's constructs of reality with regard to their perceptions of the greater social reality in which they operate (Forman, 1986).

The intervention we find useful in many cases is called the Visual-Kinesthetic Dissociation technique (VKD) (Cava & Forman, 1985; Lankton, 1980). The procedure is commonly used for treating phobias, since their origin is typically the result of a traumatic and consequently distorted learning experience. Whenever a client is encountered whose range of choices is limited because of an irrational fear it is appropriate to employ the VKD technique. The technique involves a sequential recipe of steps that begins by establishing rapport. For the NLP practitioner this means matching the client in a number of behavioral systems (e.g., breathing rate, body posture, tonality, tempo and cadence of speech). The following steps are then followed:

1. Have the client recreate the uncomfortable state in real time* and anchor it. Ask the client to enter into the feeling experienced when in the dreaded situation. It's helpful to imagine a scale in which "10" is the most uncomfortable s/he can imagine her/himself ever feeling and to visualize the phobic circumstance uninterruptedly, so as to generate the uncomfortable feeling to the point that a subjective intensity of at least "8" is reached. Once that level of feeling is attained, "anchor" (one-trial condition) it by simultaneously touching a spot or holding one finger or thumb of the client (with permission, of course).

2. Lead the client back in time to the original traumatic experience. We like to suggest that after closing their eyes, clients imagine metaphorically they are riding a beam of light or sound through space and time until the source is reached.

3. The client is then asked to associate with the original experience so s/he feels, sees, and hears now just what s/he did then.

---

*Real time refers to a state wherein a person accesses an experience in an associated state — i.e., as if s/he is actually inside the situation rather than recalling it from an uninvolved observer position.

4. Release the anchor and instruct the client to remember where s/he went as s/he returns to the present time. To interrupt the negative kinesthetic experience, it is helpful to lead the client to some innocuous experience such as what they had for breakfast.

5. Create a positive kinesthetic experience and provide an anchor for comfort and security. This is commonly done by asking the client to remember an enjoyable experience, revivify it, and anchor it with a hand hold.

6. Give the client instructions to close her/his eyes and imagine the original experience was filmed or videotaped and it is now possible for another self, sitting in front of the client, to view this on an imaginary screen across the room.

7. Have the client visually review the original episode in the dissociated (observer) state while maintaining a comfort state. Repeat this step if the client experiences discomfort until a separation is fully accomplished.

8. After the scene is completed, invite the younger self to step off the screen to a chair in front of the client or onto the client's lap if a small child. Have the client comfort the younger self and reassure her/him that the experience was survived and life continued. Suggest that appropriate explanations and reassurances be offered to the other self until the client is comfortable.

9. Re-associate younger self and present self by asking client to imagine embracing younger self and squeezing until they merge into one self.

10. Ask the client to again imagine being in the same or similar situation that was previously described as fearsome to demonstrate to the client that discomfort is greatly diminished or extinguished.

CASE EXAMPLE

A couple sought treatment to determine if they should remain together or sever their relationship. They had been "engaged" for 2½ years. Sally, 28, desperately wanted to get married; Bart, 36, was intensely ambivalent. Both had previous marriages ending in divorce. After cohabiting for a year Sally moved out abruptly four months prior to therapy in an attempt to coerce Bart to the altar. The initial phase of treatment focused on relationship qualities and the family-of-origin issues that kept Bart from committing himself. The stalemate continued so the treatment focus shifted to what keeps Sally in a relationship where she is not getting what she wants. She revealed a debilitating fear of abandonment and loneliness. An individual session was scheduled and a VKD procedure was used to recover the earliest remembered formative circumstances after the most intense part of her fear was accessed and anchored kinesthetically. In a matter of a minute or so a significant experience was recovered from the age of five when Sally was separated from her father during a carnival. She reexperienced a sense of dread that she might never rejoin her father or see the rest of her family. She was guided through a double dissociative procedure (i.e., watching herself watching a movie documenting the reclaimed anxious memory). She then gave the younger self reassurance and clarification of the contextual issues and brought the younger self to a state of comfortable resolution of her fears before reassociating the younger self by imaginatively pressing her against her chest. A session two weeks later found her willing to become more autonomous. Four months later Sally reported dating others and feeling confident about her ability to develop a relationship in which she could gratify more of her needs.

The VKD procedure is one of many techniques utilized by NLP practitioners. NLP-based techniques are easily adapted for use with couples and families regardless of the therapist's theoretical framework or favored school of treatment.

REFERENCES

Bowen, M. (1978). *Family therapy in clinical practice*. NY: Aronson.

Cava, E., & Forman, B.D. (1985). Neuro-Linguistic Programming: An instrument for managing the doctor/patient relationship. *Miami Medicine, 56,* 15, 17.

Einspruch, E.L., & Forman, B.D. (1985). Observations concerning research literature on Neuro-Linguistic Programming. *Journal of Counseling Psychology, 32,* 589-596.

Forman, B.D. (1986). Neuro-Linguistic Programming in couple therapy. Paper presented at the 44th Annual Conference of the American Association for Marriage and Family Therapy, Orlando, FL. ERIC Document Number 285 068.

Forman, B.D., Cava, E., & Powell, E.A. (1986). Neuro-Linguistic Programming: An adjuvant to cognitive and behavior therapy. *Corrective and Social Psychiatry, 32*, 117-123.

Lankton, S. (1980). *Practical magic*. Cupertino, CA: Meta.

Szapocznik, J., Kurtines, W., Foote, F., Perez-Vidal, A., & Hervis, O. (1983). Conjoint versus one person family therapy: Some evidence for the effectiveness of conducting family therapy through one person. *Journal of Consulting and Clinical Psychology, 51*, 889-899.

15

Clare's Sonata

Sandra Diskin

Picking a favorite intervention is rather like asking a parent to choose a favorite child. Each is precious, but the unique qualities of one or another in a particular situation are more useful to the task at hand than others.

As a family therapist, I find myself often working with individuals, especially those who exhibit early traumatic imprints from their family of origin. The themes from these childhood dramas often surface to interfere with the normal flow of life events and with the formation of satisfying relationships in adult life. Problematic to therapy is that these early memories are often obscured by a protective cloak of forgetfulness.

The client will present with vague symptoms, often accompanied by disassociation and/or depression around a certain event. They complain of being "stuck," feeling empty or blocked. When queried, the client will often say of early family life, "It was pretty much like everybody else's."

One method of gathering information pertinent to the problem at issue was developed by David Grove.[1] Use of his technique can access early trauma that is usually consciously unavailable, bringing it to a conscious level and available for intervention. This method uses linguistic metaphors and internal imagery unique to the client to facilitate work. Moreover, because it is uniquely personal and individual, it is the magic bullet that targets the *specific* happening and the *specific* block to further learning.

---

1. David Grove Seminars, Edwardsville, IL 62025

Although there are many permutations of his techniques, the one I use most often is in tracking the origins of some painful symptom. It can best be illustrated by the following example.

Clare was an eighteen-year-old piano student who loved to play for her own enjoyment in the music room of her family home. Unfortunately her piano teacher insisted she play in the piano recital every year, at which time Clare's hands shook so uncontrollably she was barely able to play. With time, this problem generalized to incidents unrelated to music. For example, when at school her hands would begin to shake. Her symptoms progressed to a point where she could not eat lunch at school because she said she felt unable to comfortably feed herself.

Tracking symptomology within a family session filled with high achieving members that included a practically perfect sibling (an older brother who was also a piano player) made the intervention clear. Support Clare, back off criticism, allow her personhood and appreciation for her talents—all of which the family pledged to do, and which they carried out. Theoretically, with the pressure off, she could gain control of her hands' shaking.

There was some symptom remission but not extinction. Clare also disallowed the impact of their efforts by disdaining her family's effort because "you told them to do that." Clearly the problem was not as simplistic as it had originally seemed.

Sabotage is another word for "just new information" in the skill book of the chronically optimistic therapist, so I began to generate other hypotheses that incorporated the new information and suggested another intervention.

Knowing that you cannot convince a person with low self-esteem that they have done something well, I began to conceptualize the origins of the symptoms as possibly relating to some traumatic problem in her past. This possibility was reinforced by the immediate experience of this young, attractive, competent, sensitive, intelligent woman sitting with me in the therapy room.

I asked Clare to remember the time when her symptoms were the worst (at a recital), then to close her eyes and tell me the part of her body of which she was most aware. Using Grove's intervention technique enabled me to then guide Clare to describe and expand on what she was experiencing in memory recall.

Clare described an empty space where her heart should be; she described it as a vacuum, filling her chest cavity. It felt like a black hole. Then the tension crept up to her shoulders and her arms and her hands began to shake.

Using her words and description I asked her to remember other times in her life when she had that feeling and asked her to silently group them according to commonality. I then asked her to remember the first time she had the feeling of "a vacuum where her heart should be, filling her chest cavity, feeling like a black hole, with the tension building, causing her arms and hands to shake." I told her it would probably be a very early experience, perhaps about age five or seven, and that she should not intellectualize but allow the feelings to take her back to help her remember that time.

She said, "It was earlier than that, it was when I was three!" Clare than related the incident. She had been dressed to go out with her parents and she had wet her pants. (Clare had an endocrine problem as a child that had made training late and difficult.) Her father had beaten her (saying it was a spanking), berated her, and held off an emotionally overwrought mom by telling her he had to do it for Clare's own good because she would "never learn" otherwise. Clare remembers him walking out leaving her trembling on the bathroom floor.

As with any memory, this scene was imprinted with all of the emotion of the particular age at occurrence. It resurfaced with recall, as in this case, with the unbridled fear and primitive anger of a three-year-old.

The shaking later surfaced upon any occasion permeated by parental expectation, whether it was academic, social, or performance related. She believed what had happened was her fault, proof that she was bad and unworthy. But before she could resolve these feelings, she had to unearth the secret shame.

In restructuring the past for her, together we created a "snapshot" from her mental image that froze the scene in time. Clare was then called upon to examine this picture and comment on the scene and the players. Now safely "outside" of the emotional content of the incident and seeing the event from the perspective of fifteen years of wisdom since it transpired, she came to a new understanding. Clare began to realize that what had happened when she was three was about her father, not about her. It was not Clare but rather Clare's father who had acted in a shameless manner. After a while we rewrote the scene so Clare could begin to heal herself.

I still see Clare occasionally. Her hands have lost their tremor. Now we talk about her boyfriends and her plans for college, something she thought she would never be able to do. She insisted on quitting piano lessons, but continues to play for her own enjoyment in the music room of her family's home.

-16-

Hanging Out:
An Intervention for Random Families

James L. Hawkins

Previously, the literature has avoided, misnamed, or failed to understand random families. There were some references to "chaotic" families, but they were described as if they were failed versions of the closed type. The preferred treatment, therefore, was to empower the executive team and "reestablish" a workable hierarchy of power, etc. There was no notion that random families might have a functional version or even that they represented a distinct type with their own dynamics.

Now we know better—and work has progressed well beyond the Kantor and Lehr (1975) beginning. But we still have not developed a wide variety of interventions tailored to the random system. "Hanging out" is one technique I have used that seems to have considerable effectiveness.

The sample of kids with whom we have had the most experience is that group collected by programs designed to divert first time offenders and status offenders from the juvenile justice system. This group includes a high frequency of truants, runaways, etc. Most of these kids would be classified in DSM-III-R terminology as Oppositional Defiant Disorder, some as Conduct Disorder.

If the closed-type family honors hierarchy and authority, random families are enamored of anarchy and divergence. Random families require no joint problem solving, valuing individual initiative above

Author Note: I would like to thank Elinor M. Adams for critical comments on the original draft of this intervention.

all. At their best, they are creative, vibrant, joyfully disjointed affairs. At their worst, chaotic is not too strong a term. Always, the preferred psychopolitical style is oppositional. The trick is to figure out how to turn chaos into creativity—to get the family system to get the kid back to school or to stop running away.

Random systems fail by losing significant information in the overload of information often found here. They fail by not passing relevant information along. They fail by not having enough connections between people, by not being in the same place enough. They fail by having too many acceptable solutions to problems. They fail by including too many people in the family. They fail by being too often oppositional. But each of these is a strength as well.

The "hanging out" technique requires that the worker be free to drop in on the family at odd hours of the day. This leads eventually to knowledge about who is at home and more or less approximately when, for some regularities can be found in even the most chaotic system. After that, the task is to drop in at the times most likely to find family members at home, especially the IP.

In random families one often finds it hard to know who is actually a family member. Often there is a drifting in and out of people as activity ebbs and flows. There may be two TV sets and three boom-boxes blasting with nobody or everyone-and-then-some about. You may be invited in or more likely simply not invited to go away. Your presence will likely not cause much of a stir if you can be unobtrusive. Go help yourself to coffee if some is brewing it in the kitchen.

The goal is to be non-reactive, non-directive. Let yourself be led and avoid the trap of being official or even goal oriented. The last thing you want to do is bring up the truancy. It is *Verboten* to propose a solution. It is important to focus on helping the system to find its own way to its unique individual non-group solutions.

The popping in unannounced and leaving before anything happens apparently marks the therapist as "one of us." The therapist is allowed to join the family, thereby gaining access to information not previously available.

But the technique is more than a joining technique. It is a way for the therapist to avoid trying to bring about a "group" or "joint" solution to some problem. For even when the therapist has the information that permits solution, s/he cannot use it in the conventional way. To do so is to invite the system to oppose an authority, something the system is probably doing too much of already anyway.

This work style is difficult for therapists as they often feel that they have so little control of things. For most of us raised in hierarchical closed systems it is a feeling of being out of control, of the anchor dragging. After all, therapists usually represent some institution that wants to see action.

Moreover, it is hard to write convincing case notes. Supervisors who do not understand random systems may not view hanging out as true therapy. If they support home visits though, you'll get a raise.

To do this work well, one must believe in systems. One must respect random systems and believe that they actually do get work done.

The therapist looks for functioning dyads, any two or three people, regardless of their status, who can connect and who have some of the ingredients of a possible solution to the problem. Sometimes these groupings include a parent, often a cousin or an aunt. In some cases the first task is to try to get even one pair of souls in contact. But when you've got one or two categories of relationship identified, spend some time hanging out with them.

The adults in one family all had full-time employment with no particular hours so were actually around home a lot. Indeed, it was a rather pleasant place to be. After two weeks of uneventful hanging out, the worker joined a pair of people that included one of the parents. The parent became quite opinionated about school, stating that school was too rigid about attendance and tardiness. Besides, he said, the teenager was bright and could learn on her own.

The teenager, staring at the TV on the other side of the room, was asked her opinion. Taking an oppositional stance, she claimed that the only reason she didn't get to school on time was that she got up late and had no ride because the bus comes too early. In another type of family, the therapist might have seen the response as a mere emotional ploy, a denial, a minimization, blaming. It was probably all of those things here, too, but in a random family, opposition is the basis for action so she paid attention. A few days earlier, the worker had been in on a conversation that included the teenager's favorite cousin who drives past the house each morning at about school time.

The worker now had two puzzle pieces in hand that might get the kid back in school: (1) The teenager was willing to oppose her parents' concept that the school was too rigid; and (2) the favorite cousin is in the right place at the right time. On her way out of the house the worker simply asked if the teenager had seen her cousin lately. That was it. Nothing more.

In less than a week, the truant had resumed going to school and on time. She was telling everyone that her cousin gave *her* a ride to school every morning! It turned out that the girl had made a point of contacting her cousin and "he just started stopping to pick me up on his way to work." Later in the year, the cousin was replaced by a boyfriend, but attendance continued.

REFERENCES

Kantor, D., & Lehr, W. (1975). *Inside the family: Toward a theory of family process*. San Francisco: Jossey-Bass.

See also Constantine, L.L. (1986). *Family paradigms: The practice of theory in family therapy*. New York: Guilford.

Functional Dysfunctions

Jannah J. Hurn

There has been extensive discussion in the last several years regarding the "dysfunctional family" and the resulting psychological effects on individuals within these families. As more popular psychology books and TV programs cover this issue, therapists will continue to have families walking in with this information out of context. A familiar question that is appearing more in early family therapy sessions reflects the client's self-diagnosis of coming from a "dysfunctional family" and their concern over subsequent negative effects. Recent data suggest that the idea of dysfunctional families may be based more on the typical American family rather than the atypical family. Several studies have estimated that as many as 96% of American families can be classified as dysfunctional according to the current definition being given the term.

While the negatives of coming from or being in a dysfunctional family are well known, very little is understood about the impact of considering yourself from a dysfunctional family. Helping the client to recognize that not all of his/her issues are because of personal faults is effective in allowing each member of the family to refocus on interactional familial issues. However, there is often an overwhelming negative response to clients' classifying their families as "dysfunctional."

When families bring this identification with them, it becomes important for them to understand that not all aspects of their family may be dysfunctional. Reframing many of the components of a family as "functional dysfunctions" can aid a client or family in perceiving themselves as well as their families in a more favorable light. This process provides hope and humor in what are very probably normal dysfunctional family situations. An example of this can be seen in the following descriptions of a family therapy situation.

A young dual career couple entered family therapy due to their difficult family situation regarding adjustments of roles within the home and workplace. Each recounted a history of positive interaction for approximately the first ten months of their marriage. At about this point, the husband experienced the death of his father. Following this event, arguments over responsibilities in the home began to ensue. As each recounted individual family history, the wife mentioned the fact that she is from a dysfunctional family as is her husband. When inquiry about this definition was made, the wife explained that she has been pursuing causes of their problems through popular self-help books. Her discovery and her husband's subsequent pursuit of the literature had convinced them that their family backgrounds had helped produce similar dysfunctional family patterns in their own family situation. They both noted, however, that although the books helped identify their problems, they had not really found them helpful in changing the patterns.

As the family therapist listened, each recounted how their arguments were caused by their own critical parental upbringing and the high expectations their parents placed on them. The therapist acknowledged their descriptions of the expectations placed on them and encouraged the husband as he began to describe how he emulated his father's role with his own wife. The theme of their description was one of negativism and despair as the couple painted a hopeless situation of continued dysfunctional patterns.

In response to this picture, the therapist requested the couple to begin to reframe some of what they perceived as dysfunctional patterns into functional aspects. The husband acknowledged his own thoughts of how he saw his high expectations of himself as self-punishing but also very productive at work. The wife acknowledged the fact that although she felt her mother may have pressured her, she was glad she did in certain situations such as educational pursuits. The therapist again acknowledged the couple's concern over family dysfunctional patterns but pointed out that these dysfunctions may be such that they relate to particular aspects of the couple's life rather than all aspects of their lives. The term "functional dysfunctions'' was then presented as a humorous way to acknowledge the normalcy of certain patterns that are negative in some contexts and functional in others. The couple's response was one of relief as they began to view their lives as more functional than they had previously believed.

This kind of reframing for families becomes vital as more and more popular psychology books and programs present information that many families will take out of context and frame into hopeless experiences and memories. Remembering that people need hope as well as understanding will offset the negative effects of misconstrued information.

−18−

The Absent Expert: A Method of Indirect Confrontation

S. Allen Wilcoxon

THEORETICAL ORIENTATION

This intervention is based primarily on experiential and communicational conceptual models of family intervention. The intended emphasis is upon aiding both individual and collective members of the family system in monitoring and confronting self and others regarding hidden agendas, manipulative tactics, mystification, and similar forms of interaction that promote nonproductive, repetitive patterns of communication and behavior (Whitaker & Keith, 1981). Once confronted with discrepancies between their literal and metacommunicative interchanges, members can pursue more productive forms of dialogue and problem solving (Napier & Whitaker, 1978). Such opportunities are not unlike Perls' (1969) notion that once one has had an experience, one can no longer behave as though the experience never occurred; one must therefore accommodate and change or consciously deny and rationalize to avoid the impact of the experience.

DESCRIPTION OF THE INTERVENTION

The intervention may be employed with almost any modality (e.g., individuals, couples, families, multiple family groups, etc.). The intervention is typically introduced in a manner that can depersonalize the observation and confrontation and thereby continue

the supportive alliance between therapist and client(s) without assuming an adversarial position. The introductory remarks are typically made in the following manner:

> I'd like to tell you about an experience I had in my school
> years and then ask you to respond to a question. When I was
> involved in my graduate training, I had a supervised internship
> where I and other student interns were regularly observed by
> our supervisors watching and listening from behind a one-way
> mirror. Much of the time, the supervisors and other students
> were busy discussing what they saw and heard as they watched
> from the observation room. We would discuss what the intern
> was saying and doing, but most of the time we would com-
> ment on what we believed about the clients' interactions.
> Sometimes the observers would even pose questions about the
> clients as though they wanted an answer from them about
> something the clients were saying or doing. If we were in that
> situation right now, there might be someone on the other side
> of a mirror who might say/ask "(insert confrontation here)."
> If that was the case and you could answer them, what would
> you say?

In this way, the confrontation is made from a somewhat con-
trived vantage point and in a rather impersonal manner without
threat to the client(s)' affiliation with the therapist. In addition, the
therapist may employ any number of variations such as:

> If the microphone connection between the two rooms was not
> working, what do you think those people behind the mirror
> might think you are trying to get across to each other by the
> way you are behaving, the look on your faces, your gestures
> and so forth? (focus on behavioral metacommunications). If
> there were curtains drawn across the mirror so they could only
> hear what you were saying, what do you think they might sus-
> pect about the way you are talking to me/each other? (focus on
> verbal communicational style).

INFORMATION NEEDED TO DETERMINE
THAT INTERVENTION IS INDICATED

This intervention affords only minimal risk to the client-therapist relationship or any hazard to self or others. Therefore, the principal indicators for using the intervention seem to be that there is either a deficit in self-monitoring and appraisal of one's behavior or a lack of sensitivity for the literal and/or metacommunicative messages one communicates to others, especially to one's spouse or family members. The only instances for which the intervention might be inadvisable would be with clients who were highly defensive, potentially combative, or demonstrating characteristics of a thought disorder. Otherwise, the intervention seems to be appropriate for use with most any client.

BRIEF EXAMPLE OF APPLICATION AND OUTCOME

In working with a family in which the mother was clearly aligned with the older son to triangulate the younger son as the identified patient, I introduced the intervention and noted:

> If we were in that situation right now, someone in the observation room might say "I think the mother really favors the older son and even overlooks some of the really good qualities of the younger son. I bet she couldn't even list some of them." If that was the case and you could answer that person, what would you say?

After a few moments of silent thought, the mother responded with some defensiveness, gave a brief list of rather unimpressive qualities, and, after becoming uncomfortable with that maneuver, turned to her husband to demand that he add to the discussion. Following the husband's half-hearted participation in the "listing" activity, the older son began criticizing the list and noting more serious problem areas. To this, the father responded:

I believe that's what that imaginary person would be talking about. You're not the other parent in this room and I'm tired of your thinking you run things in the family. This is for me and your mother to discuss.

Since the session was nearing its end, I suggested a follow-up session with the spouses to continue this discussion. In that session, the husband and wife returned with great animation, noting a discussion between sessions about "the absent expert's" observation and the ways in which it was both accurate and intrusive. They discussed incidents in which the mother aligned with the older son as well as how the father offered tacit support for the triangulation by remaining uninvolved. Subsequent family sessions featured a unified executive subsystem and much lessened familial antagonism. Similar outcomes have been reported from using this technique to confront repetitive patterns of nonproductive, manipulative behavior and styles of communication that promoted emotional disregard and alienation.

REFERENCES

Napier, A.Y., & Whitaker, C.A. (1978). *The family crucible*. New York: Bantam Books.
Perls, F.S. (1969). *Gestalt therapy verbatim*. Moab, UT: Real People Press.
Whitaker, C.A., & Keith, D.V. (1981). *Symbolic-experiential family therapy*. In A.S. Gurman & D.P. Kniskern (Eds.), *Handbook of family therapy* (pp. 187-225). New York: Brunner/Mazel.

19

Safety for the Little Girl

Mary L. Ideran

Ideas for the following intervention have been taken from neuro-linguistic-programming, Jungian theories, and relaxation techniques, particularly Dr. Herbert Benson's book, *The Relaxation Response* (1976).

This particular imagery is used when an adult incest survivor is having difficulty joining with her child(ren) within. It is important that the client has developed trust in the therapist and feels comfortable in the environment.

The purpose is to bring the little girl within the adult to safety. The client is to imagine the place where the little girl is staying. It is important to follow her lead and be there only to assist. The therapist is to help her to go slowly and back up when and if necessary for the concern of the client. The client will experience both fear and relief at bringing her little girl to safety.

For the safety and confidentiality of the clients, the names below are a composite of clients and there is no intention to refer to one specific person.

Gwen is 35 years old and has been married to Tom for 12 years. They have two daughters, Gina, 10, and Laurie, 8. Gwen is an incest survivor. She was abused by her father and older sister. She has been in individual therapy for eight months and in group therapy for two months.

In therapy, Gwen has become more able to talk about her own little girl within. She initially described the little girl as ugly, with a big mouth and terrible disposition. She was repulsed by her. In the past, Gwen has done everything she could to avoid the little girl. In doing this, the demands of the little girl increased and forced her to take notice of the child. This was manifested by periods of depression, anger, excessive needs to be in control, fear, and anxiety when she was not in control.

At one stage, I had Gwen draw a picture of her little girl. Even if the client has very little artistic ability it is not difficult to get a sense of her attitude toward the child. This was certainly true of Gwen. Her picture was a distorted body, large head, and an extremely large open mouth. The mouth looked like a cavern. She viewed the little girl as demanding and rude. Gwen felt ruled by the demands and she was often confused by the power of the child within.

I then asked Gwen how she could care for her little girl. How could she nurture her? A frequent question that I ask of my clients is, "If you're walking down the street and you see a little girl crying, what would you do to comfort her?" The answer I get from many clients and the one I got from Gwen was, "I wouldn't do anything. I'd get out of there as fast as I could."

When we talked about Gwen's child within and how to care for her, Gwen became uncomfortable. She would look down, change the subject, or begin to fidget with her fingers. Finally, she said, "I don't know how to take care of the little girl. I need some help. I don't know what to do or how to do it. I'm afraid."

As we discussed this further, I discovered two things. The first was that there was more than one little girl. This is not unusual for incest survivors. The little girls may represent different stages of the abuse or may even have different abusers.

The second piece of information uncovered was the fact that the little girls were still at the home where the abuse took place. Part of the reason Gwen was having difficulty dealing with the little girls was their anger and/or fear of their environment. This, of course, prompted anger and/or fear in Gwen.

We then discussed taking the little girls, with the use of imagery, to safety. This process needs to proceed slowly. The therapist must never rush the client. There may be things going on in the image of which the therapist is not aware. I take my cues from my clients. I help them get as comfortable as possible. Closing their eyes is helpful for many. I watch for signs of tenseness and ask about it: "What is going on?'' ''What do you see?'' I then ask how I can help and what I can do.

Gwen began by describing what she saw. It was her childhood home. She couldn't go in, because it wasn't safe.

T. How can we make it safe, Gwen?

C. I need someone to check it out first.

T. Shall we send in the police?

C. No, I don't trust that. (Of course not. Her father was a policeman. Try again!)

T. (After several attempts) How about a group of Amazon women?

C. That's good! I like that.

The Amazons checked out the house and came back and gave the go ahead.

C. Can the Amazons go in with me again so I can look around?

T. Of course, they can protect you as we go through.

After Gwen felt safe we began to look for the little girls. Gwen had two that she needed to get out. The first one was frightened and hiding in the closet. Gwen sat down outside the closet and softly talked to her little girl. She reassured her and asked her what toys she wanted to take along with her. Gradually, two large round eyes peered out asking to take her teddy bear and blanket.

The next little girl was just as hard to deal with. She was angry. She had her arms crossed and her lower lip out in defiance. She had been ignored and left behind. She knew it and so did Gwen. Gwen continued basically the same way. She worked hard to talk softly and stay calm.

These conversations may be quite lengthy. The little girl(s) will not quickly trust the adult survivor. They have been abandoned, ignored, and devalued. One client reported the little girl questioning and challenging the whole area of trust. She (the little girl) said, ''You've ignored my feelings and my fears and now you expect me to trust you?'' This is not an unusual internal struggle. The little girl needs to be encouraged and supported as well as the adult survivor.

The next decision was where to take the girls. Gwen realized she **didn't have enough** energy to deal with them 24 hours a day. We decided that they needed to go to a safe place, where Gwen could go to visit when possible.

Gwen decided that the frightened little girl would go to her best friend's house. She felt that her friend was very nurturing and would be good to her. The angry little girl was to come home with me. Both little girls were then available to Gwen when she was able to do more imagery. In between times she knew that both girls were being cared for.

I have condensed this imagery into one session. The client may need several sessions to complete the imagery. It is also important to use the client's name throughout the imagery. This is to help ground the client. She may also need to be reminded that she is safe and in your office and that no harm can come to her now.

It has been my experience that this is the start of the joining that needs to take place between the little girls and the adult survivor.

REFERENCE

Benson, Herbert (1976). *The Relaxation Response*. Avon Publishing.

20

Facilitating Marital Dialogue:
A Few Fundamental Components

Bill Forisha

INTRODUCTION

The following demonstrates how to facilitate effective dyadic communication by reducing it to a few fundamental components. By "effective dyadic communication," I mean "dialogue" as defined by Buber (1958) and Jourard (1968). Undoubtedly, were these scholars yet alive, they would charge me with "nimis simplicandum," or making mole hills out of mountains. However, I tend to view such simplification as justified on the basis of its purely utilitarian or practical value. Married couples in particular have often requested some kind of basic, concise method to improve their communication as soon as possible. Suggesting books to read was all well and good, but most often they didn't get read. I wanted a model, or rather, a compact system of ideas on communication that I could teach to clients rather quickly that could facilitate their using them immediately.

This approach to dyadic communication is particularly designed for use by those who are relatively well-educated and/or somewhat cognitively-oriented and who appear to be deficient in their ability to negotiate their individual differences. It is designed to be used whenever partners find themselves in a crisis and/or at a time when the resolution of some specific area of incompatibility is needed. It may also be used as a diagnostic tool in that couples with relatively more severe dysfunction will probably be unable as well as disinclined to use such an approach.

This structured dialogue encounter is deceptively simple. Inherent in the proposed model of interaction are rather complex and controversial assumptions about human beings and their relationships. These are drawn primarily from tenets of humanistic and existential psychology. In fact, sessions devoted to clarification of values and beliefs will probably be required before clients are ready to proceed. The first person singular is utilized in order to underscore what may be considered the most essential ingredient in effective dyadic communication: making "I statements."

UNDERLYING ASSUMPTIONS: PREREQUISITES FOR EFFECTIVE COUPLE COMMUNICATION

Three Parts to a Relationship

According to Satir (1988), there are three parts to any relationship between two persons: the "you," the "me," and the "us." I am the only one responsible for me. I may choose to be responsible for us, as a way of being responsible for me. In this way, I provide myself an intimate relationship with you. I do this because I want to partially transcend my aloneness in this world by choosing to be in a relationship.

However, I am not responsible for you, and I cannot cause anything to happen or not happen to you. I cannot make you happy or unhappy. I can only make myself happy. I may care what happens to you, but I am not responsible for you. Thus, taking care of self is a fundamental responsibility. What this means, in terms of our communication, is that I am okay when wanting, feeling, and thinking anything — and so are you. This is true despite the fact that there are no guarantees that either of us will get what we want or that anyone — including each other — may know or care what we feel.

Four Basic Feelings

It is useful to categorize human emotions into four basic or "genuine" feelings that spontaneously occur as people respond to one another: fear, sadness, anger, and joy. Of these four, I believe that fear is the most basic and often accompanies other feelings. For instance, I may be scared of being scared, scared of being sad, scared of being angry, or scared of being joyful. It is important to identify feelings that we experience as being a combination of the four basic feelings. For instance, feeling hurt becomes feeling sad and scared and perhaps even angry.

Ineffective Ways of Expressing Feelings and Managing Dyads

In order to take care of "me," people often choose from among four specific ways of experiencing and/or expressing their feelings. These ways are ineffective, however, if a person also desires to take care of the "us." These ways are repression, suppression, manipulation, and accusation. An appropriate task of marital counseling is to suggest alternative, effective ways of expressing feelings.

At lower levels of emotional intensity, fear, sadness, anger, and joy are often more or less well-managed in a relationship even when experienced or expressed in the above-mentioned ineffective ways. However, in order to manage increased intensity, not only do we escalate our use of such ways, but, acting in collusion, we may also attempt to triangulate a third person into our dyad. We choose to do this in order to reduce the intensity between us.

Disclosing Shifts in Three Internal Processes

According to Rogers (1972), ". . . in any continuing relationship, any persistent feeling had better be expressed" (p. 20). The same is true of what I am wanting and what I am thinking. One way I choose to be responsible to "us" is to take the risk of disclosing my present internal processes to you. Such self-disclosure requires my becoming aware of my internal processes; self-awareness is my responsibility. Whenever I become aware of a shift in my internal processes during discussions, I will disclose that I want you to be available to hear me talk about shifts between wanting, feeling, and thinking. Possible shifts are: wanting to feeling, wanting to thinking, feeling to wanting, feeling to thinking, thinking to wanting, and thinking to feeling.

Since such shifts are common, a contract to be irrational and/or a contract to brainstorm thoughts is very facilitative of effective communication in a relationship. The value of the latter is especially noteworthy when either party experiences one of the basic feelings at a relatively high level of intensity. Such agreements more safely allow the focus of the dialogue to temporarily shift by taking time out from the negotiation of individual differences regarding what is wanted by each member of the dyad. For instance, if I become aware of intense feelings and we have previously negotiated such a contract, I may call time out and then proceed to ventilate or express my intense feelings. I will endeavor to do so, of course, without resorting to any of the aforementioned ineffective ways of expressing my feelings. When I am finished, I will invite you to do the same before we resume our negotiations.

STRUCTURED DIALOGUE:
THREE INTERACTIONAL STEPS

This portion of what could be called a "bare bones" model of dyadic communication is, essentially, a formula for negotiating conflicting wants in a relationship. The model contains three interactional steps that are continually repeated, plus the identification and disclosure of any of the above shifts in internal processes.

Step one involves a *declaration of wants*. Essentially, this is an assertive disclosure of what it is that I am presently aware of wanting. Furthermore, quite often my declaration may take a comparative form: "I want 'x' more than I want 'y.'" In this case, I have clearly established for myself and disclosed to you the relative position of what it is I am wanting in my hierarchy of wants. In other words, I have let you know how much or to what degree I want what I want.

Step two involves providing *confirmation*. This is done by the person to whom the self-disclosure has been made. I would like to stress that confirmation does not mean agreement by the second speaker to provide what the first speaker wants.

Step three is *verification*, which has two parts. In part one, the second speaker requests that their confirmation be verified by asking some such question as, "Am I correct?" In part two, the first speaker simply says "yes" or "no." If the answer is "no," then the first speaker starts over again by expressing what it is that he or she is wanting. If the answer is "yes," then the roles are switched and the second speaker repeats step one.

This three-step process is continually repeated until the incompatibility is resolved. If each partner wants the same thing and if the hierarchical position of what each partner wants is relatively high and similar, they probably will take action together and realize their wants. However, if the hierarchical position of what one partner wants is relatively lower or higher, they will probably take action separately to realize their wants. This is like the old adage, "We can agree to disagree." Such a resolution, nevertheless, constitutes compatibility.

The three steps are quite simple to understand, but they are often not at all simple to implement. A shift in internal processes may occur at any moment within either or both participants. For instance, she may shift to thinking about information that she deems to be relevant to what he wants. If she spontaneously shares her information, he may, in anticipation of not getting what he wants, shift to feelings of fear. Either or both need to declare that they want to take "time out" to share such thoughts and/or feelings. With her awareness of his vulnerability plus his permission to continue, she might expand on some of her ideas and he might talk about his fear or get held by her for a few minutes. Additional shifts may occur as this time out to brainstorm and/or be irrational continues. Each such shift in internal processes needs to be self-disclosed.

The negotiation of wants and the resolution of individual differences involves the three steps plus the identification of any shifts in internal processes. Regardless of how much or how little shifting goes on, it is important to eventually return to the original expression of wants. What I'm wanting and what you're wanting constitute the real issues between us. What we are thinking about in relation to such wants constitutes information or data which might shed light on the issues. What we are feeling reflects the unique meanings that our wants have to each of us. By building an interpersonal climate based on mutual respect and acceptance and by sharing our feelings and thoughts in a straightforward manner, we learn more about ourselves, our significant other, and our relative degree of compatibility.

STRUCTURED DIALOGUE:
A CASE EXAMPLE

Tom and Sue sought marital therapy because, as Sue put it, "We seem to have trouble communicating." They had been dating for a couple of years and had, until recently, planned on getting married. They had both been married before. Sue had custody of her two children, ages ten and twelve; Tom had no children. During the second session, Tom complained that Sue was never available; Sue complained that Tom was too demanding of her time. The therapist congratulated the couple for having isolated and identified a particular area of incompatibility – namely, togetherness time. He then invited them to further explore this incompatibility while at the same time learning a few principles and techniques of effective communication. They both agreed to do so.

During the third and fourth sessions the therapist went over the assumptions. These were elaborated upon by using examples from both the clients' lives as well as from the therapist's own life. The therapist was careful to both use and encourage the use of "I statements" throughout. Fortunately, there were no major philosophical or religious disagreements between the three participants. Had there been such disagreements, resolution would have been necessary before proceeding with the facilitation of a structured dialogical encounter.

The following was taken from a structured dialogue between Tom and Sue. It represents a portion of their fifth therapy session.

Tom: I want to see you at least two or three weeknights a week as well as Friday and Saturday nights. And I want to talk to you on the phone every night.

Ther: Tom, I want you to negotiate one issue at a time. So, I want to know which one is more important to you?

Tom: When we see each other. (Tom then repeats the first part of his declaration of wants.)

Sue: I'm feeling really angry. I want to take time out just to be mad.

Ther: I want you to do that – but after you have confirmed that you have heard what Tom has disclosed to you.

Sue: I hear you saying that you want to see me at least two or three weeknights a week as well as Friday and Saturday nights. Am I correct?

Tom: Yes.

Ther: Now, I want to know if you (to Sue) still want to take time out to be angry. (Sue answers in the affirmative.) So, I want us to stop negotiating and listen to Sue.

Sue: (proceeds for about ten minutes or so to ventilate anger; makes a lot of statements about having so much to do and Tom's lack of support and understanding; agrees with therapist that much of what she is feeling is also fear and sadness and is asked to identify when she is finished and does so.)

Ther: Tom, I'm wondering what you're feeling right now? I think you may want some time out also?

Tom: Yes, I guess so. At first I was feeling scared, but now I feel sad for Sue.

Ther: I think you're feeling sad because one thing that you want that you're not getting is for Sue to feel less angry and less sad. Is that correct?

Tom: Yes, and I'm just as sad that we're in such different places. (continues for about ten minutes or so; cries briefly. Tom is asked to identify when he is finished and does so.)

Ther: I'm wanting to know if both of you are ready to return to the negotiation of the amount of time you want to spend together. (both affirm that they are ready; Tom is invited to continue since it is he who is wanting something specific during this portion of the session.)

It took two therapy sessions to reach an agreement on this one issue. Sue took an additional time out to share both her thoughts and her feelings regarding her children's need for her attention. Tom took time out to brainstorm ways he might occupy himself whenever Sue is not available. They subsequently negotiated an agreement to spend one "family" weekend night together, Saturday night without the children, and one other night per week together. When and what activity would be determined by just one of them on an alternating basis.

As their structured dialogue proceeded, it was apparent that relatively high on both of their hierarchies of wants was the desire to find a means to live with the particular incompatibility in question. What they learned can be utilized in future sessions and eventually, perhaps, without facilitation. Hopefully, they may someday engage in such dialogue on a more spontaneous basis, that is, without relying on the formal structure learned in therapy.

REFERENCES

Buber, M. (1958). *I and thou*. New York: Scribners.
Jourard, S. (1968). *Disclosing man to himself*. New York: D. Van Nostrand Reinhold.
Rogers, C. (1972). *Becoming partners: Marriage and its alternatives*. New York: Dell Publishing Co.
Satir, V. (1988). *The new peoplemaking*. Palo Alto: Science and Behavior Books.

21

Multiple Split Opinion

Glenn I. Bronley

The multiple split opinion is an extension of the split opinion described by Papp (1980). The intervention is generally presented through our live-team treatment approach, a team reflecting a systemic/constructivist orientation.

The team usually meets with cases in which the therapeutic process has come to a standstill. A therapist requests a consultation because s/he believes that s/he is no longer providing assistance to the client/family. At other times, the team will set up an initial meeting with new, unassigned cases who demonstrate a history of being treated by competent therapists, using a variety of modalities with no significant difference in presenting problems.

It becomes clear to the team members that some of these client families are locked in a no-change position. The client family would like to make changes with positive outcomes as they perceive them. We call this "changing for the positive." Yet, many client family members believe that any change might also promote negatively valenced outcomes. We call this "changing for the negative." What occurs is an ongoing cyclical continuation of tried and true behaviors of the familiar, resulting in the no-change position. The ambivalence contributes to the extreme difficulty of making differences with these cases. In other words, the client's internal system of beliefs of making changes for the better and worse leads to making no changes (changes for the positive plus changes for the negative equals no change).

The intervention consists of a three way split from behind the mirror given at the end of a session. The information given for the three positions is acquired during the live team therapy session. The client family is informed, by the therapist, that the team is split. One part of the team believes things will change for the better. The most beneficial and positive outcomes, as described by the client family, will be provided. Another part of the team believes change will occur for the worst. The family members' negative outcomes of change are described. Finally, another part of the team takes responsibility for describing behaviors the client family are already performing and believes, as a result, things will stay the same.

We take the position that it doesn't matter what choices are selected by the client family. If they decide to stay the same, that's all right. Not changing is an option. The intervention merely allows the client family to more objectively see the role each member provides in assisting the no-change position. On the other hand, many client families have shown a considerable degree of general response to the multiple split opinion. They smile and nod when presented the positive-change view, nod and frown with the negative-change view, but almost across the board respond to "things will stay the same" with a statement analogous to: "Things can't continue as they are!" Apparently, by placing the views in at least three distinct positions, no-change becomes more negatively valenced than changing for the worst (fears). The positions become relational.

Now, we do not imply that we use the intervention in every case we see, but when applied, do so in the first or second meeting as a statement of some possible choices available. The intervention is one means by which to provide information to some cases locked in therapeutic impasses.

EXAMPLE: THE COUPLE

A couple, having moved to New York one year earlier, applied for the treatment of a marital problem of five years duration. The wife had had numerous affairs, including relationships with a number of her husband's friends. She felt guilty and he felt depressed and angry. They had previously sought treatment out-of-state and now sought treatment at our facility. They complained of daily verbal conflicts that revolved around the husband's accusations of the wife's past wrong-doing, and the wife's apologies and defense of her position, as well as her attack upon his depressive stance.

The couple was assigned a co-therapy team of experienced marital and family therapists. While joining exceptionally well, the therapists found that they could not make a difference in disrupting the couple's daily script. In fact, the couple would not follow through on making any changes in their lives. A consultation was requested and scheduled.

At the end of the consultation, the multiple split-opinion intervention was given: "One part of the team believes some day the husband will exhaust all the anger and disappointment, while the wife will no longer feel a need to apologize. We don't know who will get there first, but whoever does will speed up the time frames, as it takes two to fight. Nevertheless, at that point, they will no longer fight over the affairs and will be able to do things as a couple that are more fun, such as going out on dates." The couple nodded and agreed.

"Another part of the team believe things will probably change for the worse. The fighting will intensify and someone might get physically hurt. The marriage will probably end in divorce." The couple nodded and frowned.

"A third part of the team said that the couple essentially needs to fight. In fact, if they do not fight, what else will they have together? This part of the team believes that things will stay the same. They will not grow closer, nor divorce."

The couple looked at each other, took each other's hands, turned to the therapist and said, "Things can't stay the same, it's terrible the way it is!"

The team never really knows for certain what will happen in response to the intervention, but we do look for repeated coincidences in time and space. In this case, a number of things occurred. First, the couple seemed to stop their arguments regarding the past affairs. Second, they began to discuss with their therapists, in subsequent meetings, issues regarding intimacy and equity in their marriage. Third, they began dating. Fourth, the husband's depressive symptoms dissipated.

The intervention promotes openings; it makes the covert overt and relational. The fear of how bad things can get is directly challenged by how bad things are. Stuck client families seem more willing to take chances to do something different and more often than not, make changes which lead not to negative outcomes but to more positive changes as perceived by client families. The multiple split opinion seems to make a difference.

REFERENCE

Papp, P. (1980). The Greek chorus and other techniques of paradoxical therapy. *Family Process, 19*, 45-57.

22

The Dreaded Transition:
Play Therapy
from a Meta/Isomorphic Position

Susan Toler
Maria Flores
Pat Kessler

This case study deals with a transitional intervention designed to achieve continuity for two young children where changing therapists became a necessity. The previous therapist, a caseworker, felt she had another role other than therapist to play in the unfolding drama of the girls' lives. She might be required to conduct the legal transfer of the children from one home to another. It was felt that the therapy transfer was necessary to keep the boundary issues clear and to possibly mirror for the girls a successful transfer for their future. However, the caseworker planned to continue participating in therapy by observing through a one-way mirror and meeting with the therapist at the end of each session to discuss case issues.

The children involved were two girls, ages 10 and 12, of Hispanic descent. They had resided in a foster home since the oldest was 4 years of age. They were removed from the birth mother due to physical abuse by her and her live-in boyfriend. The foster mother was very cold and distant with the children. She had been threatening to reject the children, was uncooperative with the caseworker, resented the interference by the program, and oftentimes reflected this resentment onto the girls. The foster agency was considering placing the children into another foster home due to the negative attitudes toward the girls and restrictions being placed on them by the foster mother. The girls were not allowed to visit their friends or have them over. They were expected to stay home, doing chores and work suited for teenagers and adults. The children generally appeared sad and fearful. Very few extracurricular activities were planned and the children were found to be lacking in social skills development. Play usually turned to fighting with school friends and with each other.

THEORY

The interventions in this case are based on two concepts taken from family systems theory commonly referred to as metacommunication and isomorphism. Piercy, Sprenkle, and Associates (1986) refer to metacommunication as "Communication about communication. This term usually refers to the covert, nonverbal message (tone of voice, inflection, body language) that gives additional meaning to an overt verbal message" (p. 32). Isomorphism is often thought of as a mirroring or parallel process. Simon, Stierlin, and Wynne (1985) state that "The concept of isomorphism helps generate hypotheses about essential aspects of human thought and communication processes." For the purpose of this paper, we are using the term "metaplay" to refer to playing with play in a therapeutic manner to achieve a specific goal. This process allows one to work at many different levels concurrently.

THE CASE

There were three therapists: the first author, the transitional therapist (an intern); the supervisor/therapist; and the caseworker/therapist. Therapy took place in a large family room with several chairs. The supervisor was present to facilitate the transition from the caseworker to the therapist. The caseworker was not present at the beginning of the session. The therapist began the session by asking the supervisor why we were all present. The supervisor stated we were there because the caseworker had a conflict and was unable to continue in the capacity of therapist for the girls but that she was feeling very strange in this situation. When questioned by the therapist about these feelings, the supervisor expressed that the caseworker felt scared and powerless in the room. Using the systems' concept of isomorphism, the supervisor paralleled the children's emotional state in adult relationships by representing their fear, sadness, and scariness. This enabled us to remove the focus from the two girls and to create a meta play experience.

Immediately, the therapist shifted the discussion to focus on feelings and the energy level in the room, playfully exploring the supervisor's (caseworker's) feelings of strangeness and reinforcing the meta play experience. The children found this to be a delightful and uncomplicated conversation, joining in with their perceptions of what was occurring in the room. They laughed as each shared their feeling state. The therapist then asked the supervisor who had the most power in the room. She responded with, "You do!" Indeed, the therapist had come to the session for the purpose of taking charge. So she suggested that the supervisor exchange seats to see if she would then feel powerful.

Upon doing so, she reflected that indeed my seat seemed to be more powerful and that she was feeling much better. The strategy was to explore how our energy levels affect other people and how we can assume power by changing our attitudes, reflecting on the parallel between physical and emotional states of being. We all decided what kind of energy levels were in the room and began changing seats to feel the influence of that person. Each person playfully spoke about her feelings and/or energy level. After several seat changes, everyone was enjoying the interactions in the room, expressing what they were feeling in each position, and even taking on some of the bodily traits of the person who had sat there before them. These interactions allowed the children to experience change at various levels in a safe way.

The energy level in the room was one of excitement and fun when the case worker entered the room, apologizing for being late. She slumped in her chair and breathed in a pressured manner. I asked her how she was feeling and she responded, "Lost and tired." I asked if anyone noticed a change in the energy level in the room. The children chimed in, "Yes!" When asked what had happened to it, the oldest of the two girls expressed that the energy level had dropped completely because the caseworker had robbed the room of all the energy when she entered. The caseworker was then updated on what had taken place. I asked if she would like to change chairs and get some different energy. She responded that she wanted to be in the happiest chair in the room. When she exchanged seats with the happiest child, the child (now sitting in the caseworker's place) slouched and became quiet. This process continued until a fun experience was created once again. The session ended successfully with the girls' full acceptance and anticipation of future therapy sessions with their no longer "transitional" therapist. As the children waited for their ride they were observed engaging in a play situation with each other for the first time without any fighting.

REFLECTING ON THE SESSION

The therapists stayed meta to the session at all times, constantly aware of what was developing in the room and taking their cues from these interactions. The children were also allowed to remain meta to the therapeutic environment by not being requested to reflect directly upon themselves but on the activity taking place in the room. They were free to interact, to discover therapy could be fun, to join with others in a unique way, and to use "I feel" in a non-incriminating manner. Everyone left the room feeling energized, having learned something about each other, and the transition of therapists had proven successful.

REFERENCES

Piercy, F.P., Sprenkle, D.H., & Associates (1986). *Family therapy source book*. New York: Guilford Press.

Simon, F.B., Stierlin, H., & Wynne, L.C. (1985). *The language of family therapy: A systemic vocabulary and sourcebook*. New York: Family Process Press.

—23—

If It Walks Like a Duck . . .

Fred P. Piercy

Somebody once said that having teenagers is like being nibbled to death by ducks. Many of my clients would agree. When I've been successful with teenagers, it's not because I've stopped their nibbling, but because I've been able to divert their oppositional energies in constructive directions. This is the gist of "my favorite intervention."

THEORETICAL ORIENTATION

Milton Erickson and the Mental Research Institute group have been masters at rechanneling behavior in positive directions. I am indebted to them and other creative strategic therapists for waking me up to the fact that I can't stop a river, but I can hold on in the white water and sometimes even rechannel the flow a bit (and since ducks swim in rivers, there's a connection here somewhere).

THE NATURE OF DUCKS

Teenagers are famous for taking whatever position their parents despise. For some kids, it's just recreation, for others, it's their life's work. One of my colleagues recently circulated a poster that was probably written by some nibbled parent. It captures some of the arrogance that goes with duckhood:

ATTENTION TEENAGERS

Tired of Being Hassled

By Your Stupid Parents?

ACT IMMEDIATELY

Move Out. Get a Job

Pay Your Own Bills

START NOW
WHILE YOU STILL
KNOW EVERYTHING

I showed this poster to my own fifteen-year-old, who saw nothing particularly funny about it. Generally, teenagers don't realize they're reactive. They take a point of view contrary to that of their parents with absolute certainty that their own view is right.

THE PROBLEM

Of course, there's a mutual dance here. Many parents take "reasonable" stands and justify them into the dust. They become broken records and before long everyone is engaged in recursive nibbling or "fowl play." (This is an obscure DSM-III classification. A "V" code, I think.)

THE INTERVENTION

As with any predictable cycle, there are plenty of possible ways to break it. For example, the parents can learn to talk less. Expectations and consequences can be spelled out. House rules can be negotiated. The positive aspects of the parent-teen relationship can be nurtured. All these are credible goals the family therapist can try to facilitate. My favorite intervention, however, is more one of style than substance. I use it to supplement the usual interventions. The following interchange with Mr. and Mrs. Duck about their son, Don, will give you a flavor of what I have in mind.

Father: Don is so unreasonable. He seems to fight everything we say. It drives us crazy.

Therapist: It's a teenager's job to drive his parents crazy, and it sounds like Don's pretty good at his job.

Mother: Yeah, he's a real champ.

In other words, the therapist acknowledges that Don's defiant behavior is par for the course and that the therapist doesn't really expect anything different. The therapist should keep his/her eyes open, though, for a way to use Don's adversarial tendencies. Here's an example:

Therapist (to parents): Congratulations. You've come up with a curfew time and a consequence that will keep both you and Don off each others' backs. What is it again?

Father: Eleven on weeknights and twelve on the weekends, and when he breaks it, he has to stay in for two nights.

Therapist: You talk like you think he'll break it.

Father: Like we've said, he doesn't follow through.

Therapist: Don, your dad doesn't think you can be in on time this next week. In fact, he expects you to fail. What do you think?

Don: If I say I'll be in on time, I'll be in on time.

Therapist: But he doesn't believe you. If you're so sure you'll be in on time, I suggest you bet him a dollar. Of course, you might be afraid to bet him.

Don (smiling): Sounds like easy money. How about it, Dad? Afraid to bet me?

Notice that if a bet is consummated, it puts Don's oppositional tendencies to work in a positive direction. He can win a bet by being responsible – by being in on time. Here the therapist uses the same approach to get Mother and Father to back off a bit:

Therapist (to Don): For it to be a real bet, your coming in on time has to come from *you* and not your parents' reminding you of the **curfew all the time**. Do you think that your mom and dad can keep from reminding you this week?

Don: Maybe Mom can. I don't think Dad can.

Therapist (to Father): OK, Don has given you a challenge. Can you keep from reminding him this week about the curfew?

Father: If I have to.

Therapist: Good. Think of it as an experiment. We are going to find out if Don is as irresponsible as you think he is. We'll also find out if he can be responsible on his own. And Don, do me a favor. Let me know if your father or mother remind you of the curfew. We'll see how well they can back off.

Don: You got it.

A FINAL WORD

I used the "nibbling duck" analogy here, not to make fun of teenagers or to blame them for the family's problems, but to underline a lighthearted theme that the therapist can use to engage and motivate both the teen and his/her parents. Actually, as all family members feel heard, and as mutual agreements are reached, the bickering often subsides.

This intervention style obviously works best when the teenager is contradictory and/or in a power struggle with his/her parents. (Of course, for a lot of teenagers, this is most of the time!) It is really not too difficult to figure out which teenagers to use it with. Look for the nibbling and remember that old saying, "If it walks like a duck, quacks like a duck, and looks like a duck, it's probably a duck."

24

Putting Away Old Loyalties
in Later Life

Sherry L. Rediger

"In an old house there is always listening, and more is
heard than is spoken.
And what is spoken remains in the room, waiting for
the future to hear it.
And whatever happens began in the past, and presses
hard on the future.
The agony in the curtained bedroom, whether of birth or
of dying,
Gathers in to itself all the voices of the past, and
projects them into the future.

–T. S. Eliot
The Family Reunion

Rituals are often a great resource for creating effective therapeutic interventions (Imber-Black, Roberts, & Whiting, 1988). In the
following case study, I combine the use of ritual and intergenerational work with a gentle paradoxical twist.

A couple in their mid-sixties had been referred to the marriage
and family therapy center by a psychiatrist in an out-of-state psychiatric hospital where their son had been admitted. The son (in his late
twenties) held his parents responsible for his poor coping skills and
stress. The son's accusation was terribly upsetting to his parents and
their distress was affecting both their marriage and their work. The
couple attended two family sessions although the hospital was 600
miles away.

The couple decided to begin therapy locally while their son remained in the hospital. During the course of therapy, the couple related that there were many resentments and hurts from the past that impinged on the happiness they desired to have in their present lives and marriage. While exploring these old hurts, the man and the woman began describing incidents in their childhoods that seemed to relate to their present mistrust. I agreed with the couple that childhood experiences often impact present relationships and asked if they would be willing to share those experiences with me more explicitly in future sessions with the goal of addressing their present mistrust and pain. The couple agreed.

We spent four sessions discussing old family roles, rules, expectations, and relationships. Specifically, I asked the man and woman what each had learned from his or her parents about being a husband and father and a wife and mother. I asked what had been helpful to them and what had not been so helpful. It became clear to the couple that the woman had learned that husbands and fathers abandon and wives and mothers sacrifice themselves for their children. The man had learned that husbands and fathers silently provide for the family without showing much affection or approval, and wives and mothers keep charge of the house, the children, and the neighborhood, but also without showing much affection or approval.

The couple also talked enthusiastically about what they had learned from each of their parents that had been helpful to them; many of these "lessons" the man and woman had proudly incorporated into their own marriage and family. This discussion brought warm memories of each of their deceased parents as well as memories of the fun and excitement they had created in their own lives and for each other.

At the end of the fourth session, when the couple had made their own connections of the past with the present, I asked each to bring a box to the next session. I asked that the boxes reflect something about themselves — anything that they wanted — but it should also be a box that they wouldn't need to use again for anything else.

The next week the couple returned with their boxes; the woman brought an old checkbook box and the man brought an empty cigar box. I asked them to carefully consider what they had learned from each of their parents that was helpful and what they had learned that was not so helpful. I asked the couple to write down each of the "lessons" on separate pieces of paper. After they had completed this I asked them to put the pieces of paper that had the lessons that had not been so helpful into their own box. I explained that the lessons belonged in the box because they had not been helpful to them. Then, I carefully warned the couple that they should not bury the boxes or throw the boxes away because the lessons that each had learned that are not helpful are still useful. They need to be able to look at the unhelpful lessons and touch the lessons whenever they want. I asked the man and the woman if they had a safe place to keep each box. The man decided to keep his box in his closet and the woman put her box in her dresser.

Therapy ended a few weeks later when the couple reported that they felt closer to each other than they had felt since their wedding day. They reported that they had been able to parent their son differently as a team; the woman was consulting the man about her decisions and the man was getting more involved with his son. Both thanked me for the special session with the boxes.

REFERENCE

Imber-Black, E., Roberts, J., & Whiting, R. (1988). *Rituals in families and family therapy*. New York: W.W. Norton.

25

Problems with Problem Solving: A Metaphor for Investigation of Problematic Process

M. Ellen Mitchell

Clinicians working with couples and families invariably encounter issues that require active problem solving and negotiation. Often, couples and families either lack skills, insight, or inclination to negotiate in a mutual fashion. Instead, they convey the feeling and belief that bargaining is impossible. They sometimes characterize other family members as unable to understand or as just plain intractable. There are a whole host of interventions designed to help people negotiate. Clinicians may borrow from the problem solving literature (e.g., Jacobson & Margolin, 1979; Guerney, 1977), the marriage enrichment programs (e.g., Davis, Hovestadt, Piercy, & Cochran, 1982) or the communications literature (e.g., Gottman, Notarius, Donso, & Markman, 1976; Haley, 1971; Madanes, 1981). Many of these skill enhancement programs are quite successful (L'Abate, 1981).

The difficulty with these approaches is that families and couples are sometimes unwilling to begin the process of negotiation. The following technique involves the use of a metaphor to illuminate the problem with problem solving. The method has some similarities to a reframe and to the use of metaphor in the strategic sense. One difference is that this metaphor is not utilized to define the problem through analogy but to define the problem with the problem. An illustration may be useful.

Many couples and families present problems that appear readily amenable to negotiation. For example, a child wants freedom in the context of a family that values the demonstration of "maturity" as a contingency. Or a spouse seeks certain behaviors from his/her partner and feels that despite frank discussion, nothing is forthcoming. When the clinician begins the process of identifying individual needs and desires, all goes well initially. When the process of negotiation commences, however, qualifiers and contingencies in the form of "I will if . . .", etc., emerge. Still worse is the case of the people involved presenting desires that are mutually incompatible. For example, couples facing stressors frequently describe problems that arise because one person copes through interrupting when the other wants to talk, or a family has a child who wants to date but a parent is strongly against it, and both have compelling arguments. The question for the clinician changes from, "How can this be negotiated or bartered?" to, "How does this family or couple make decisions when the desires of the members are essentially incompatible?" The difficulty arises when the clinician asks this question and most families and couples talk about the specific desires, not the process of decision making. In response to this situation, I have successfully used the following analogy or metaphor.

The first step is to stop the couple or family by indicating that they need to back up for a moment and allow a change in the subject. This serves to signal the end of a discussion about their particular issues. I indicate that I will be describing a hypothetical scenario and I want to know what they would do if this were to happen to them. Then, I describe a family or couple on a limited budget who is on a trip to the grocery store. Shopping is almost complete and with the last three dollars, dessert is being decided upon. One person wants pie, another wants ice cream, and there simply is not enough money for both. I then ask, "What do you do? Who gets their way?" Invariably, people talk about taking turns and I ask how it gets decided who gets the first turn. I also ask how they decide to take turns and whose decision that is. We then talk about the option of no dessert, or of having cake when both agree they dislike cake but when it represents an option of dessert. One of the nice things about this analogy is that it places a new perspective on the problem so that capitulation is not viewed as a major loss of principle, position, power, or privilege. I remind them that this is an issue about dessert, not the main meal. The dessert aspect of the content diffuses the affective charge inherent in long standing disputes. Generally, it opens the way for working on the process rather than content of decision making. In addition, it is diagnostic in nature and allows the clinician to evaluate the quality of the problem solving/decision making.

REFERENCES

Davis, E.C., Hovestadt, A.J., Piercy, F.P., & Cochran, S.W. (1982). Effects of weekend and weekly marriage enrichment program formats. *Family Relations, 31*, 85-90.

Guerney, B.J. (1977). *Relationship enhancement: Skills-training programs for therapy, problem prevention, and enrichment.* San Francisco: Jossey-Bass.

Gottman, J., Notarius, C., Donso, J., & Markman, H. (1976). *A couples' guide to communication.* Champaign, IL: Research Press.

Haley, J. (1971). *Changing families: A family therapy reader.* New York: Grune and Stratton.

Jacobson, N.S., & Margolin, G. (1979). *Marital therapy: Strategies based on social learning and exchange theory principles.* New York: Brunner/Mazel.

L'Abate, L. (1981). Skill training programs for couples and families. In A.S. Gurman & D.P. Kniskern (Eds.), *Handbook of family therapy.* New York: Brunner/Mazel.

Madanes, C, (1981). *Strategic family therapy.* San Francisco: Jossey-Bass.

26

Charting the Transactional Map

Don D. Rosenberg

BASIC TECHNIQUE

A powerful intervention is to chart family transactions as a kind of map. Maps describe the sequence of in-session behavior of all family members at five crucial levels: (1) observed behaviors; (2) feelings occurring in the interactional context; (3) interpretations of others' behavior (especially projections); (4) self-image and self-esteem beliefs emerging within the interaction; and (5) repetitions of family-of-origin patterns. Charts are also circular; the end point of a pattern is usually the relief of the feeling or need that started it. Charting is invaluable whenever acting-out, complaining, repetitive patterns, arguing, getting lost in emotion, or narcissistic vulnerability dominate sessions.

Charts are created in-session as a shared family experience. Beginning with any event or complaint, ask for the family's view of the usual starting point of their repetitions. Keep inquiring about each successive step. Most important, each step in the map must include affect, interpretative, and self-esteem reactions, and family-of-origin recollections, not merely the external behaviors. The therapist controls discussion, labels statements in psychological language, uses quotes, and records the map or directs the family to record it.·

Charts can be written on a blackboard, marker board, or large paper, so each member can see the chart unfold and contribute to it. The completed chart can be transferred to the case file and a copy given to the family. Most charts have 10-15 steps. When the family is totally controlled by non-cognitive patterns, such as repeated hurt feelings, destructive acting-out, constant arguing (with the same dance to the same tune every time), take a whole session for charting. This short-circuits the usual pattern of telling the therapist the latest bad news, complaints, and failings.

The therapist should have at least several sessions in order to be familiar with the family. Once the chart is written, refer to it with the family in subsequent sessions, augment it with new data, have them suggest alternative behaviors and beliefs, reinforce changes from the pattern, delete steps that become obsolete, and, especially, refer to the map in order to understand and control regressions and crises.

BACKGROUND ASSUMPTIONS

The power of charting is revealed in the doing, but some observations help focus the technique. During couple or family sessions, most transactions, symptoms, and complaints are parts of stereotypic, defensive family patterns. This applies even to transactions involving the therapist. These patterns protect against the anxiety or affect associated with underlying issues. Issues may include lingering hurts, unresolved losses, developmental transitions, unacceptable feelings, separation fears, loathed self-images, etc. It is the underlying issues that drive the observed inappropriate or dysfunctional coping patterns.

Most family therapists claim they try to alter the system, that is, the transactional pattern, directly by altering subsystem boundaries, practicing new behavior, highlighting positions in the system, etc. However, systems therapy is almost never that pure. In other words, interventions into family transactions are functional. Therapists bring in the underlying issues. They comment on the protective function of the system, the unresolved issues, the emotional threat posed by change, and other, "deeper," issues. Charting outlines the sequence of behavior at both the underlying and the defensive levels.

Less experienced therapists often become embroiled in the defensive patterns, attempting to negotiate changes, suggesting alternatives, taking sides, unintentionally colluding. Charting keeps them from ignoring underlying issues or from feeling helpless.

Most interventions are auditory; therapists tell their observations to clients. Some interventions are kinetic; therapists move people around, defining boundaries. Another advantage of charting is that, while many people do not respond to auditory material, they may respond to charting, which is visual and participatory.

Besides this, the charting process substitutes cognition for acting-out in the session, focuses on patterns rather than complaints, makes sure each member can bring in emotions and sense-of-self, and is itself a sample of controlled, cooperative, reflective behavior, thus directly interrupting patterns brought to the sessions. It provokes discussion at deeper levels of risk and exposure.

For all these reasons—getting to underlying issues, visual presentation, and cooperative, participatory behavior that interrupts affect-dominated behavior—charting has always been a focal point in consultations. The supervisor or consultant can summarize the case material in the form of a transactional map. Consultees generally find this to be an integrative experience.

SAMPLES

Mr. and Mrs. Stone argued so vehemently that protective services threatened to remove their three-year-old girl. Their first child died at age 18 months four years earlier. Both Mr. and Mrs. Stone felt rejected by their respective mothers. Mrs. Stone clung to her daughter, who was described as a temperamental child, whom Mrs. Stone could not control and who had difficulty sleeping. One complaint was that Mr. Stone worked long hours, failing to help Mrs. Stone sufficiently at home. In session seven, interrupting the beginning of one of their arguments, the therapist drew a line down the center of the blackboard. Each was given a side and chalk. They were instructed to write their sequence as the therapist helped them define it. The chart as they mapped it is shown in Figure 1.

As we discussed the pattern, we discovered their coping skills were for one to leave, for her to cling to her daughter, for her to use the daughter to connect to him, and for both to repeat archaic family-of-origin rejection patterns. Namely, he acted self-sufficient and she clung and raged. As an adult who had been abused and rejected as a child, she was terrified of closeness and of sexuality. She did

Figure 1: Transactional Map of Stone Family
. . . .

<u>Mr. Stone</u>   <u>Mrs. Stone</u>

1. Sexually interested   2. Not interested
    Approach her   Turned off (Scared)

3. Has a nasty attitude   4. Angry because he
    Keep my distance   ignored us. Feeling over-
    Puts things off   whelmed with housework
    (Turns on his "dangerous   & watching child. Need
    & ugly" self-image, which   help. (Blames. Avoids
    is part his & part HERS,   closeness issue.)
    but easier for her to handle
    by pushing him away.)

                                  5. Feels hate. Says
                                      something mean. Worked
                                      up. Then out-of-control
                                      (So, could fighting keep
                                      us from grief & sadness?
                                      And scary closeness too!)

6. Feels out-of-control too   7. Feels sick of him,
    Says, "Good, I don't care."   repulsed. Says, "You
    (Unwanted)   forgot; why didn't you do
                                      it?" (Unloved)

8. Feels rejecting, cold
    "Fine, you do it."   9. "Fine, I'll do it."
    (Just what he did with his   Feeling hated by him
    mother, self-sufficiency   I'm no good, worthless
    to mask hurt.)   He hates and blames me
                                      (Just like mother.)

10. Sick feeling. Hate self
    for doing this. Feel I can't
    do anything right. Reminds
    me of hating mother & how I
    ran away from her.

11. Antagonize her, get her,
    show my anger, "Screw you!"

                                  12. Grab at him, scratch

13. "Fine!" Vindicated. Goes
    downstairs to sleep

                                  14. "Monday, you move
                                      out." Rejects him back
                                      Like fights with mom

                                  15. Daughter upset, goes
                                      to comfort. Reject mean
                                      daddy. [Later when she
                                      acts up, I can't control
                                      her. Tell him to.]

16. Disciplines daughter   17. After one of us goes
                                      away mad, we calm down

18. Next day, apologize   19. Feels accepted again

Commitment: Change "I don't   Commitment: Not to grab
care" into "You know I care"   or hit. Discipline
                                  daughter myself

not believe he shared her grief and felt he blamed her for the loss (two distance-creating beliefs). For him, connecting with women posed the threat of narcissistic injury.

The effect of charting was unusually dramatic. In the next session, they grieved for the lost child together. After that, arguing stopped. Mrs. Stone enrolled her daughter in childcare and got a job. The daughter was brought under control and the child's sleeping problems cleared up. Mrs. Stone also reconnected with her mother. Mr. Stone began helping more at home. After 12 visits, they felt finished when their complaints ended, but they still had intimacy and sexual issues that they were not prepared to resolve at the time. The most immediate purpose of their pattern, to avoid depression by submitting blame, projective identifications, transfer of guilt, and distance (a protection against rejection fears) was less necessary.

SUMMARY

The sample illustrates how the therapist breaks down the pattern into steps. All the members are included in the map. In the sample, the Stones were asked at what point their daughter was involved in their argument. The therapist brought in affects such as "unwanted," "unloved," "scared." The therapist also brought in their interpretations such as "he ignored us," "he hates me." The therapist also brought in self-image issues such as "I'm no good." Finally, the therapist brought in parallels to family-of-origin experiences. Note that jargon was avoided. This case was unusually successful in that charting opened up for discussion the most crucial, warded-off, underlying issues, namely, conflict about grief for the lost child as it related to their respective early life experiences and their projective identifications. However, charting indeed often directs the therapist to meaningful underlying issues and difficulties in the family.

27

Problem Definition and Treatment Protocol for Multi-Problem Families

Scot Allgood

Multi-problem and dependent families often create a great deal of stress for the therapist as they frequently bring a new presenting problem to each session. With a new problem for each session, it is difficult to define treatment protocols and/or monitor changes that the clients may be making. One way of treating these types of families is to use a modified behavioral technique that seems to work well with a variety of theoretical approaches.

During the first therapy session it is important to reframe the problem for the family in order to set the expectation that things can change (Haley, 1976). However, many problems need to be solved in stages. This technique helps the therapist clarify the stages and behaviors that need to change to help the family meet their goals.

The technique is a modification of the Subjective Anxiety Scale (also known as Subjective Unit of Disturbance or SUD) (Wolpe, 1982). The SUD scale requires that clients report their anxiety on a 0-100 point scale. The treatment goal then centers around reducing the clients' anxiety.

The modification of this technique for family therapy is that the therapist helps the family identify its top three to five problems. Each problem is identified by specific behaviors. Once the problems are identified, the family is asked to detail what would be different when each problem is solved. Each problem may have two to four behaviors that would need to be changed if the family were to reach the ideal goal. The behaviorally identified problem and the ideal goal become the anchors for the scale. The family then fills in what behaviors would need to change to meet 25%, 50%, and 75% of that idealized goal. Feedback from each person in the family is solicited throughout the process of goal setting. The final step is to identify the point in each presenting problem where the family would be prepared to terminate therapy. Termination would occur when the ideal goal is met in many cases. However, some goals would take a significant amount of time to accomplish and the family may terminate when 25% of the goal is met. An example would be a family who plans a vacation to promote togetherness, but is not financially able to do so for several months.

During the goal setting process the therapist should be emphasizing solutions instead of dysfunction. A problem emphasis implies a limited range of behaviors while a solutions emphasis frees both the therapist and the family to use a broader range of responses (Molnar & de Shazer, 1987).

This technique was used with a multi-problem couple whose presenting problems included poor communication. The couple could not talk for more than 2-5 minutes about any topic without getting into an argument. They had previously only talked about sex or the children just before they went to bed. The ideal goal was to be able to discuss sexual or parenting matters without arguing. The first solution (25%) was to find the time of day that they would attempt to discuss these matters. The couple's 50% point of meeting their goal was to learn and become proficient using "I" messages and clearly identifying/communicating feelings. The couple chose being able to discuss recreational and job related topics as the 75% point in meeting their goal.

By clearly outlining solutions in stages, the couple was able to accomplish their goals in a timely manner. The style or type of problem assessment and interventions used to help the couple meet their goals at each stage can come from many of the theoretical perspectives used in family therapy. This intervention is very useful for beginning therapists as it forces them to clearly identify treatment goals.

An advantage for the family in using this intervention is that they can chart their own progress and begin to internalize the idea that they can continue to meet their identified goal. In addition, for multi-problem families, this intervention focuses the treatment on basic issues instead of new disturbances that arise each week.

REFERENCES

Haley, J. (1976). *Problem solving therapy*. San Francisco, CA: Jossey-Bass Publishers.

Molnar, A., & de Shazer, S. (1987). Solution focused therapy: Toward the identification of therapeutic tasks. *Journal of Marital and Family Therapy, 13*, 349-358.

Wolpe, J. (1982). *The practice of behavior therapy* (3rd ed.) Elmsford, NY: Pergamon Press.

28

Treating Dual Career Couples

Catheleen Jordan
Norman H. Cobb

Dual career couples, spouses who are each highly committed to his/her career, present unique problems in marital therapy. Their special issues include negotiating home and work responsibilities, competition with each other on the job if in the same field, taking care of child responsibilities, and having time for self. Decisions about who cooks dinner or cleans the house, or about whose job takes precedence when promotions require moving to a new location, are routinely required.

The intervention presented here focuses on the key issues for dual career couples. The elements of the intervention are values clarification, communication training, negotiating and contracting, time management, and stress management (Jordan, Cobb, & McCully, 1989; Jordan & Cobb, 1990).

VALUES CLARIFICATION

First, the therapist helps each spouse to identify his/her goals and values related to family, spouse, and self. Questions to ask include: level of satisfaction with his/her own and his/her spouse's role as father/mother, husband/wife; expectations of how his/her life together would be; discrepancies between expectations and reality; areas in which each spouse is feeling overwhelmed or overburdened; frustrations, disappointments. Issues particularly salient for the dual career couple include who does the housework; how home responsibilities are shared; different performance standards; who takes the responsibility for child care issues; if the spouses are in the same field of work, competition for jobs, promotions, etc.; how the couple makes decisions about whose job takes precedence when conflicts arise (for example, if the baby has to go to the doctor, who takes off work to go?); extended family members' and friends' support of the couple's dual career lifestyle; criticism for "abandoning" children or for "doing women's work" around the house; elderly family members for whom care must be given.

These are just a few of the issues that may be relevant to dual career couples. The therapist can assist by helping the couple list areas of concern and then to share these with the spouse for discussion. Mutual and individual goals may then be established and the long-range consequences discussed.

COMMUNICATION TRAINING

After couples identify and examine their values and develop goals, the next step is to teach them how to communicate these to each other in a productive fashion. Therapists can teach both verbal and nonverbal skills of effective communication to couples. Verbal communication training (Stuart, 1980) focuses on use of "I" statements to state needs, active listening, and timing of messages. Also, leveling techniques to encourage expression of feelings and editing techniques to delete unproductive information can be taught. Deschner (1984) identified anger control techniques for couples including recognition of escalating anger, taking a timeout, admitting one's own technical error that contributed to the fight, and discussion of alternative solutions.

Non-verbal communication techniques can be taught. These include appropriate facial expressions, posture, voice, and physical proximity to partner (Hepworth & Larsen, 1990). Also, Gambrill and Richey (1988) identified important voice qualities including level, tone, pace, clarity, balance, and length of time talking.

NEGOTIATING AND CONTRACTING

After couples learn to communicate more effectively, the next step is to teach them how to negotiate and contract to resolve areas of conflict. Problem-solving training can help couples evaluate alternative solutions (Sheafor, Horejsi, & Horejsi, 1988). Steps are to describe the problem, identify each partner's stake in the problem, brainstorm all possible solutions, throw out any solutions unacceptable to either partner, and rate the remaining solutions. After a solution is chosen, it is tested and modified if necessary.

Contracts (Stuart, 1980) may be either informally negotiated or written in a formal fashion. Responsibilities of each spouse are specifically identified. Rewards and consequences are specified. Contracting helps couples to define which responsibilities should be shared versus those that are autonomous (Smith & Reid, 1986). Some couples maintain their autonomy by performing such tasks as banking or laundry separate from the spouse.

TIME MANAGEMENT

Time management involves establishing goals, setting priorities, and scheduling tasks (Curtis & Detert, 1981; Girdano & Everly, 1979). Hiring outside help may be a way to cut down on the demands of dual career living. Therapists may point out obstacles to effective time management (Curtis & Detert, 1981) such as procrastination, worry, perfectionism, fear of failure, avoidance, and overwhelming tasks.

STRESS MANAGEMENT

Therapists can help couples to analyze the stressors in their lives. Are these due to lack of organization or to overwhelming responsibilities? Programs for stress management (Friedman & Dermit, 1988) include four components: self-monitoring, daily relaxation exercises, cognitive restructuring, and environmental alteration. Irrational beliefs or unrealistic expectations that contribute to marital problems may be challenged (Granvold, 1988).

EXAMPLE

Tom and Julie were a dual career couple with promising careers in banking and merchandising. Both were equally committed to their work, to their 18-month-old child, and to each other. They were characteristically overwhelmed with their responsibilities, with their differing opinions about child management, and with their lack of time for each other.

Values clarification helped them identify similar and dissimilar values about work, child care, mutual intimacy, and friendships at work. The communication skills gave them tools to facilitate the negotiation of their differences and the planning of time for each other. For instance, they decided on a time sharing arrangement to cover child care needs when their daughter was ill or the day care center was closed. They also agreed to set aside money to hire a housekeeper for two days each month. The couple combined stress management and their need for quality time with each other by setting aside specific times for tennis and a Saturday night dinner date.

USES

This intervention is indicated when dual career couples present the listed issues in the assessment. Couples experiencing values conflicts report difficulty solving relationship problems. They report repeated arguments over the same unresolvable issues, such as disagreements about who is responsible for maintaining the home, or fights about whether the husband should take a job in another city and uproot the wife from her job. Additionally, couples may lack the skills to communicate their differences in a positive way, contributing to escalating, angry disputes over the same issues. These disputes remain unresolved because the couple lacks the skills to negotiate and contract to resolve their differences. Added to this for the dual career couple are the lack of time and stress management skills to help ease the pace of their hectic lifestyle.

OUTCOME

The skills training approach is a strongly researched area with a long history of successful utilization with couples, families, and children (Gambrill & Richey, 1988; Jacobson, 1977; Stuart, 1980; Weiss, Hops, & Patterson, 1973). Skills training coupled with clarification of couples' special issues, values, and beliefs, can help dual career couples attain the same excitement and fulfillment in their family life as they have found in their careers.

REFERENCES

Curtis, J.D., & Detert, R.A. (1981). *How to relax: A holistic approach to stress management.* Palo Alto: Mayfield.

Deschner, J. (1984). *The hitting habit.* New York: The Free Press.

Friedman, R., & Dermit, S. (1988). Popular stress management: A selected review. *Behavioral Medicine, 14,* 186-189.

Gambrill, E., & Richey, C. (1988). *Taking charge of your social life.* Belmont, CA: Behavioral Options.

Girdano, D., & Everly, G.S. (1979). *Controlling stress and tension: A holistic approach.* Englewood Cliffs: Prentice-Hall.

Granvold, D. (1988). Treating marital couples in conflict and transition. In J. McNeil & S. Weinstein (Eds.), *Innovations in health care practice.* Papers from the Health/Mental Health Conference, New Orleans: National Association of Social Workers.

Hepworth, D., & Larsen, J. (1990). *Direct Social Work Practice.* Chicago: Dorsey.

Jacobson, N.S. (1977). Problem solving and contingency contracting in the treatment of marital discord. *Journal of Consulting and Clinical Psychology, 45,* 92-100.

Jordan, C., Cobb, N., & McCully, R. (1989). Clinical issues of the dual career couple. *Social Work,* January, 29-32.

Jordan, C., & Cobb, N. (1990). Competency-based treatment for persons with marital discord. In *Structuring change.* Chicago, IL: Lyceum.

Sheafor, B., Horejsi, C., & Horejsi, G. (1988). *Techniques and guidelines for social work practice.* Boston: Allyn and Bacon.

Smith, A., & Reid, W. (1986). *Role-sharing marriage.* New York: Columbia Press.

Stuart, R. (1980). *Helping couples change: A social learning approach to marital therapy.* New York: Guilford.

Weiss, R., Hops, H., & Patterson, G. (1973). A framework for conceptualizing marital conflict, a technology for altering it, some data for evaluating it. In L.S. Hamerlynck, L.C. Handy, & E.J. Mash (Eds.), *Behavior change: Methodology, concepts, and practice.* Champaign, IL: Research Press.

29

What Is My Part?

Judith Rae

THEORETICAL BASE

In 1954 at the National Institute of Mental Health in Bethesda, Maryland, psychiatrist Murray Bowen began research on families. Bowen added what he learned from this research project to theory he had developed at the Menninger Clinic from 1946-1954, and in 1957 came up with a family systems approach to therapy that viewed the entire family as an emotional unit.

One of Bowen's basic concepts is "differentiation of self." One of the ways to achieve a more highly differentiated self is to "focus on self" rather than focus on others and/or blame others. Bowen (1978) advocates staying calm and observing accurately "to see the part that self plays" (p. 480).

Family Evaluation (Kerr & Bowen, 1988) explains how Bowen applied focusing on self to his work environment at the Georgetown University Medical Center where he was Director of the Department of Psychiatry's Family Center from 1959 until 1990:

> *The theory knew everything there was to know.* It might be modified or extended by factual data from the emotional system or from the differentiation of self, but never by 'spur of the moment' feelings from the therapist or theoretician. With an impersonal theory, it simply meant the focus was always on self instead of the other. This was used constantly in all administrative systems. Where there was conflict or disharmony in the work system at Georgetown, it simply meant that self had played a part, and if self modified his part, the others

would automatically change their part. The model has worked well through the years. (p. 373)

DESCRIPTION OF INTERVENTION

The intervention is simple. When conflict is demonstrated during a therapy session or talked about from previous times, the therapist explains that in her experience each person involved has a role in any conflict. Next, the therapist asks each family member to think about what his/her part in the conflict presented might be.

CASE STUDY

The Hamilton family consists of Mr. Hamilton, age 40; Mrs. Hamilton, age 38; Jennifer, age 17; and Matthew, age 16. Mrs. Hamilton made the initial phone call to request therapy for Matthew, who had been getting in trouble at school for misbehaving and low grades and in trouble at home for "talking back," using "dirty words," not doing his homework, and being uncooperative. I suggested all four family members attend the intake session, which they did.

All four family members clearly viewed Matthew as the identified patient. Matthew was constantly getting into trouble. To his sister, he was not only a pest, but a concern. Jennifer excelled in school and got along well with her parents. She wanted the same for Matthew. From the time they got up in the morning until they went to sleep, Matthew's misbehaving presence was evident. At work, Mr. and Mrs. Hamilton got phone calls from irate teachers and the principal of Matthew's school. The parents struggled daily with the problem of Matthew's behavior. He was the topic of most conversations.

Matthew himself knew too well what a disaster he was. (He called himself a "jerk.") He was always causing trouble and being yelled at. He thought himself worthless. But, they couldn't convince me. I insisted the *family* – not just Matthew – had a problem.

INTERVENTION

Without quoting Bowen, I merely suggested that whenever there is conflict, each person involved in the conflict plays a part. Going around the room, I asked each family member to speculate on what his/her part might be in the conflict with Matthew.

Mr. Hamilton suggested perhaps he pushes Matthew to do things Matthew doesn't want to do—such as 4-H. When Matthew was then asked if he *wanted* to be in 4-H, he said he didn't know. During the seven years he had been in 4-H, he had never thought about it. (Throughout the session Matthew had been fidgeting, making faces, making noises, and interrupting the others. After the question about 4-H, Matthew sat quietly and listened intently.)

Mrs. Hamilton decided she expects Matthew to do things her way and only her way. She laughed and said, "As if there's one and only way to take out the garbage or wash the dishes . . ."

It took longer for Jennifer to own up to her part. After some clarification with the therapist, Jennifer concluded that if she would get out of the middle of triangles—Mom, Jennifer, and Matthew; Dad, Jennifer, and Matthew; Grandpa, Jennifer, and Matthew; Grandma, Jennifer, and Matthew—then Matthew could learn to deal maturely with life on his own.

After some discussion with the therapist, Matthew verbalized his part. He said he annoyed classmates, teachers, and family members in order to get a response from them, and this made him feel alive. Other than when he was causing trouble, the only time he felt alive was when he was skating on his skate board. Living dangerously— whether through skating in the street or causing trouble—made Matthew feel alive.

KINDS OF FAMILIES

Any family is ripe for this intervention. Whether a child or adult is the identified patient; or the conflict centers between the parents; or one or more family members is physically sick, addictive, or has some other dysfunction, each family member plays a role in the conflict. And most adults and children can see their part pretty quickly if the suggestion is made in a non-blaming way.

One beneficial aspect of this intervention is that the family members can figure out their part in any conflict on their own — wherever they are. No therapist is required. No other person needs to cooperate. After the initial intervention, family members can take with them everywhere this question: What is my part?

REFERENCES

Bowen, M. (1978). *Family therapy in clinical practice.* New York: Jason Aronson.

Kerr, M., & Bowen, M. (1988). *Family evaluation: An approach based on Bowen theory.* New York: W.W. Norton.

30

The Comrade Stance

Thomas W. Roberts

THEORETICAL ORIENTATION OF INTERVENTION

One of my favorite interventions, although not used very often, is what I call the "comrade stance," i.e., the therapist relates to the client as an equal. This intervention is paradoxical and influenced by strategic therapy, but owes more to the work of Carl Whitaker. More than a technique to be tried and discarded, this intervention suggests that the therapist takes a particular stance toward the client and maintains it over time. Congruent with Whitaker's notion of absurdity, the therapist discards the traditional role of therapist, namely that of helper and client as helpee, and spontaneously interacts with the client as if he/she is a best friend.

BRIEF DESCRIPTION OF THE INTERVENTION

The therapist jokes, clowns around, abjures, advises, teases, becomes indignant with, discusses the weather, baseball, the Dallas Cheerleaders, and anything else that is unrehearsed and spontaneous. At times the therapist may alternate with an ancillary stance called "out-client the client," namely, the therapist may display symptomatic behavior similar to the client. The therapist allows him/herself to experience his/her own "craziness" in the therapeutic relationship. The therapist is uninterested in setting goals for treatment or discussing issues that should be worked on in therapy. The rationale for this stance is based on the "game of therapy" that some clients have fully mastered, which is consequently used to defeat the therapist. It is very difficult to defeat the therapist when he/she is a "comrade" and not the "therapist." In addition, when therapy is viewed as a relationship between two persons, the therapist is a real person within the client's system.

EXAMPLE OF INFORMATION NEEDED TO DETERMINE THAT THE INTERVENTION IS INDICATED

This comrade stance should not be used indiscriminately because many clients need more direction from the therapist and benefit from a more traditional role or style of therapy. This intervention seems more appropriate for the chronic client who has made a "career" out of mental illness. The client's system is impervious to intervention and he/she is expert at defeating traditional therapy, namely when the therapist is in the role of helper. This comrade stance should be avoided with paranoids and those with delusional systems because the therapist may become involved in an irrational belief system where there is no exit. I have found it most useful, however, for chronic clients who have trouble leaving home and have used mental health professionals as "surrogate family members."

BRIEF EXAMPLE OF APPLICATION OF THE INTERVENTION

This style of therapy was used with a 28-year-old male client named Bob, who had been dysfunctional since the age of 18 when he was hospitalized for bizarre behavior at his senior prom. In the next ten years Bob had been hospitalized on the average of once a year for 3-6 months each time. Family stress or tension was usually related to the exacerbation of symptoms that generally declined during the hospital stay. Throughout this ten-year period he lived with his mother, who had been divorced since Bob was a small boy, although attempts were made to move him into more independent living. These efforts at more independent living were generally met with increased tension and conflict with his mother, who voiced a desire for him to be on his own, but also sabotaged his efforts. Working with mother and son took two different therapeutic stances. With mother I operated as a traditional therapist in setting goals and working toward them. Knowing that she held the power in the family system, I asked for her help frequently by telephoning her to discuss Bob's case, having private meetings with her, and not making any plans without her involvement. With Bob, whom I saw in individual sessions, I used the "comrade stance" and began each session with small talk and never moved toward therapeutic issues, such as becoming more independent. When he raised an issue I generally would challenge him and suggest he not attempt something he probably would not be successful at. As time progressed his mother seemed less interested in his treatment and not as available to discuss his case. Bob began pushing me to help him become more independent from his mother, which I passively resisted. I continued to involve him in nontherapy issues, such as discussing television programs, going for walks, and playing billiards. Eventually he did get an apartment accompanied by much complaining, teasing, joking, and doomsday prophecy from me.

OUTCOME OF FAMILY'S RESPONSE TO THE INTERVENTION

This therapy case was quite successful and exceeded my expectations. During the five years of therapy with Bob, he had one hospitalization of about two weeks. He maintained independent living and his mother became more appropriately related to him and helpful in his progress. I continued my comrade stance with Bob but found that he was steadily making peer relationships that were replacing me in his system. He has terminated treatment and though not totally self-sufficient, he has not been rehospitalized and has a part-time job.

31

The Giving of Gifts — A Therapeutic Ritual

Evan Imber-Black

My favorite interventions all come under the broad category of rituals. Rituals differ from tasks whose intent is to address the behavioral level in the family, and address, rather, the behavioral, cognitive, and affective levels. Co-created by therapist and family, rituals rely less on concrete instructions and a specific direction for therapy and more on symbols and symbolic actions that invite a multiplicity of meanings and directions in the therapeutic system (Imber-Black, 1988; Imber-Black, Roberts, & Whiting, 1988). Rituals begin with ideas and actions that "fit" the family system as currently constituted, and carry the family and the therapist "to the new, the strange, the 'unfit,' which has the power to radically transform our previous notions of fitness" (Grainger, 1974, p. 11).

In my collaborative work on rituals with Janine Roberts and Dick Whiting (Imber-Black et al., 1988), we have found that while all rituals need to be tailored to fit a given family's circumstances, there is a ritual, which we have named "the giving of gifts," that can be used effectively either with families who are struggling with difficult or precipitous leaving-home transitions, such as divorced families in which a child is leaving one parent to go to live with the other parent, children who are leaving temporarily for an outside-the-home placement, families whose young adult mentally handicapped children are leaving to live in a group home, or with fam-

---

Author Note: I wish to express my ongoing appreciation to Janine Roberts, EdD, and Richard Whiting, EdD, for their collaboration with me on our work with rituals, and particularly for working with me to shape the ideas in the ritual "the giving of gifts."

ilies who are undergoing a normative leaving home process and who wish to mark this in a special way.

CASE EXAMPLE – THE GIVING OF GIFTS

A family consisting of two parents, Mr. and Ms. Berry, and two children, Karen, a mentally handicapped young woman, 22, and Andrew, a college student, 20, entered therapy, due to the mother feeling "depressed and overwhelmed." In an initial session with the parents, they related to me that Karen had been diagnosed as "severely mentally retarded" shortly after birth. At that time, Ms. Berry quit her job in order to care for her daughter. Karen went to special schools and the family did well until her adolescence. At that time, the parents, fearing that Karen could be exploited in the outside world, particularly sexually, began to be increasingly protective of her, while Karen's school was pushing the family to let her be more independent and to prepare her to live in a group home, an option that had not existed at Karen's birth. Andrew was expected to use his free time to take his sister to events and he grew resentful and withdrawn as he saw his own plans to go away to college evaporate. As the family and the school struggled over what was best for Karen, she became increasingly rebellious. By the time the family arrived at therapy after two years of struggling with the school over Karen's future, the parents felt confused and that they were "failures."

My work with the family initially explored the unanticipated life cycle change of Karen's eventually leaving home, and the effects of this on all of the members. I richly credited the parents for their contributions to Karen's development. As the parents felt more confident, I coached them to ask for and receive information from the group home regarding Karen's future there. Karen's leaving home was normalized and Andrew began to make plans to move away to college. As the family was facing many changes, however, fierce fights began to erupt between Karen and her parents. In a session alone with the parents, they cried and told me they feared for her future, using a phrase they had used frequently, that they believed they "had not given her enough" to equip her for life in the outside world.

Since the fighting had emerged just at the critical juncture of Karen's actual leaving in a family that had made much progress towards this transition, I felt that a ritual was needed to both facilitate and mark this important life cycle change. I wanted to offer the family a ritual that would simultaneously confirm Karen's adult status, promote a sense of confidence in all members and enable ongoing connectedness among the members.

I asked the parents and Andrew to each choose a gift for Karen to take to her new home that would enable her to stay connected to them and ease her passage to her new setting. I then asked Karen to choose a gift for each member that would remind them of her in a special way. I told them that these gifts were not to be bought in a store, but were to be either made or chosen from one of their belongings. Finally, I asked them not to tell each other about the gifts and to bring them to the next session for a special ceremony we would have together.

When the family came to the next session, they seemed excited and pleased in a new way. When they entered, Karen was carrying a large bag containing all of their secretly wrapped gifts. In the two weeks since the last session, there had been no fights, Karen had gone for several visits to the group home, and the family had chosen a date for her move, which they had been unable to do before the preparation for the ritual.

I suggested that the gifts be exchanged by each member giving a brief explanation of their gift, the recipient saying "thank you," and discussion held until after the gifts were given. This suggestion was intended to confirm the family as a group and enable equal participation, as Karen usually became silent during discussions.

Mr. Berry started the ceremony by giving Karen an oddly shaped package. It was his favorite frying pan, which he used for Sunday breakfasts and which he had previously kept from Karen, fearing she would scratch it. He said this was for her to use in her new home, and Karen smiled brightly and said, "Thank you."

Ms. Berry handed Karen a small package containing a half-full bottle of perfume and a pair of earrings. She explained that Karen frequently tried to use her perfume and she had refused. She also had often told Karen that she was too young for earrings. She took Karen's hand and said, "I think you're grown up enough for these — they belonged to my mother and she gave them to me and now I'm giving them to you." Both mother and daughter had tears in their eyes as Karen said, "Thank you."

The mood shifted dramatically as Andrew gave Karen a package of bird seed, saying he could not bring his whole gift to the session, but that Karen would understand. Going away to college meant that Andrew needed a new home for his parakeet. Over the life of the family, he had been allowed pets, while Karen had not. He called the group home and secured permission for Karen to bring the parakeet, and said he would teach her to care for it. As Karen thanked him, Ms. Berry expressed relief that the bird would leave home too!

Karen then gave her gifts. She gave her favorite stuffed bear to her mother, saying "I can't sleep with this in my new home — please keep it." She gave her father a new photograph taken at the group home, showing her sitting with several young men and women, saying, "These are my new friends." She gave Andrew her clock radio, an earlier prized Christmas gift, saying, "Don't be late for school."

Shortly following this moving ceremony, Karen moved uneventfully to the group home, Andrew left for college and the family ended therapy. When I called them one year later, Ms. Berry said both children were doing well and were due home soon for the holidays, and that she had returned to the university to prepare for work outside the home (Imber-Black, 1988).

DISCUSSION OF THE RITUAL

"The giving of gifts" ritual functions in a number of ways for families who are struggling with leaving home issues. The ritual both confirms and facilitates a process that is already in motion in the family. Through the symbolic actions of giving and receiving, the ritual affirms and makes simultaneous the contradictions of separation and continuing connectedness involved in this transition. Family members giving gifts are both able to give permission for separation and the assumption of adult life and to affirm ongoing, albeit, changing relationships. The usual complementarity of parents giving and children receiving shifts through this ritual to a symmetrical pattern where all are both givers and receivers, opening the family to the ongoing symmetry of parents and adult children. The ritual confirms individual boundaries as each person is responsible for choosing his/her gifts separately and privately. Dyadic relationships are confirmed between each person and the member leaving home. Finally, the whole family unit is celebrated in the actual ceremony.

Through trial and error, we have found that this ritual is best done in the therapist's office. This allows the therapist to serve as witness, similar to the position of a witness in normative life cycle rituals. This ritual often facilitates very strong emotion, whose expression is made safe in the therapeutic context. Many families are extremely angry when a member is leaving, particularly if the leaving is to a temporary placement or for a custody change. Conducting the ritual in the therapist's office allows for the transformation of such anger and the emergence of more vulnerable and tender feelings. Finally, if the family has experienced much criticism from outside systems, as in the case example, the therapist may symbolically represent an outside system in a celebratory and affirming stance with the family.

A variation on this ritual involves the giving and receiving of gifts between therapist and family at the end of therapy. Such a ceremony enables both family and therapist to capture the meaning of the therapy in symbolic form, allows for the expression of mutual appreciation, which therapist and clients often feel but may not express openly, and both enables and marks the transformation from the complementarity of therapist and client to the symmetry often experienced silently at the end of therapy.

This ritual makes excellent use of the family's own resources and creativity. Beginning with the simple instructions from the therapist regarding the giving of gifts that are not bought, but are made or chosen from belongings, family members are free to enter a thoughtful and creative selection process that allows them to reflect on meanings in their own life, in the life of the gift recipient and in the relationship. As a therapist who has used this ritual with many families, I have been privileged to enter and witness some of the most deeply moving moments among family members, while simultaneously being allowed to facilitate effective change.

REFERENCES

Grainger, R. (1974). *The language of the rite*. London: Dacton, Longmann, & Todd.

Imber-Black, E. (1988). Idiosyncratic life cycle transitions and therapeutic rituals. In B. Carter & M. McGoldrick (Eds.), *The changing family life cycle: A framework for family therapy*. New York: Gardner Press.

Imber-Black, E., Roberts, J. & Whiting, R. (1988). *Rituals in families and family therapy*. New York: Norton.

32

Use of Self and Space

Marilyn Belleghem

THEORETICAL ORIENTATION: GESTALT

My therapy room has no dominant chair specifically appointed "for the therapist." It is arranged with a loveseat, two cane-backed armchairs on each side and two upholstered tub chairs, on wheels, facing. The loveseat provides an opportunity for two people to sit side by side. Since it seats two, choosing it involves physical closeness and the opportunity for easy touching. The armchairs are light and are easily moved. The room is large enough for the armchairs to be moved back about three feet. The waiting room chairs are similar and can be brought in when needed. All the seats are the same height. The only significant difference is the cane-backed chairs have firmer support for the back.

When new clients enter the counseling room, they are invited to choose a seat. As the therapist, I then sit facing them. Often clients are uncomfortable with this choice as they are accustomed to other professionals who tell them where to sit. This initially gives them permission to make choices and sets up a non-judgmental atmosphere. As an initial assessment vehicle, I am able to determine the client's use of space.

Some individuals have grown up where the most powerful person in the home, traditionally the father, has a set place to sit. The reaction I perceive in these clients is often a powerful and significant point at which to start therapy.

Since it is my intention to empower individuals to be the best they can be, and to be self accepting in an adult/adult relationship, the atmosphere is set up at the beginning of my contact.

When clients return on a regular basis, most tend to gravitate to the same chair initially chosen. I then have options. I can move closer to them, request they move, or sometimes I rearrange the furniture. I use this to break the habitual behavior and help them become comfortable with new choices.

Some clients change chairs during the first session and some choose a different chair for returning sessions. How an individual uses space becomes useful information in the therapeutic process.

The flexibility to move seats allows for boundaries to be built. I have found this to be particularly applicable in therapy where the initial seating may be Mom and the kids versus Dad, or in a blended family, Mom and her children on one side and Dad and his children on the other. By positioning the parents on the loveseat and the children on the chairs opposite them, new sub-systems can be built. I can move in one of the chairs on wheels to support either group. I will also ask one group to leave the room while I support the other.

The freedom the individual has within the counseling room enables one to pace, stand at the window, sit in the corner, leave the room for a coffee refill or a washroom visit. Some expect me to chastise them, and I remind them they are the ones paying for my time and space. This opens up considerable new areas for them to look at how they make choices and how they use their resources.

This technique is advisable in all situations where the therapist works in the here and now, and is confident to give up the role position.

33

Unconscious Fears

Jerome Adams
Matthew Eastwood

Mr. and Mrs. R, both in their mid-thirties, were referred for therapy because of marital conflict. The family has a history of multiple problems including alcoholism, domestic violence (not current), hospitalization, unemployment, and stress related to the management of their four children. One child is physically handicapped, another is on juvenile probation.

Mr. R is a recovering alcoholic with five years of sobriety and regularly attends A.A. Mrs. R's physician has prescribed Xanex for her anxiety attacks. These attacks began two years ago, following her husband's near-fatal automobile accident. Her husband believes she is abusing the drug. Following the car accident, Mr. R underwent extensive physical rehabilitation and had to give up his job as a construction worker. Mr. R is undergoing vocational rehabilitation by pursuing a college degree. Mrs. R is completing her nursing degree.

It became apparent in the course of treatment that this couple was struggling to restructure their relationship in a number of ways. They were negotiating more egalitarian roles as parents, providers, and partners to each other. The anger and arguments centered around issues of power, control, and individual responsibility.

The couple made excellent progress until the tenth session when Mr. R left what his wife and the police believed to be a suicide note on the evening of Mrs. R's graduation party. Mr. R was angry about the letter being misunderstood and humiliated that the police had needlessly committed him to a hospital for the weekend. During the session, Mr. R assailed his wife for her "addiction" to drugs, her irresponsibility as a parent, and stated she made all of the decisions in the marriage. Mrs. R voiced her resentment regarding her husband's lack of trust, his refusal to believe her statements regarding her drug dosage, and hinted at separation if things did not change.

INTERVENTION

The following strategic reframe was given to the couple at the end of the session in the form of a team opinion.

> We were puzzled about why there was so much tension between the two of you and thought there was more going on than meets the eye. We see the intensity as predictable and a sign the two of you are succeeding with each other. Our impression is there is a tremendous amount of fear and hurt feelings on both sides. The fear is the two of you will lose each other and this occurs when you are succeeding in different ways.
>
> Mr. R, we think you are afraid in a number of ways. First, you are afraid of losing your wife to drugs. You are willing to be supportive but are unwilling to 'enable' her drug use. The fact that she appears to be taking more pills than she is saying worries you. You know how hard it will be for her and are afraid the drugs will get the better of her. Second, we think you are worried about where you will fit into this relationship as things get better. Your wife is graduating, and even though you may not be fully conscious of this, your worry is that you may not have a special place with her any more. This is not an uncommon worry. You are a long way from graduating. Your wife has succeeded. It is natural, although no less frightening, to wonder, "What will she think of me?" or, "Am I special to her?" Third, the alcohol expert on the team startled me with this thought, but it is one that makes sense to me. Again you may not be fully conscious of this, but one special thing, and something you are rightfully proud of, is your sobriety. When she succeeds in getting sober from drugs, in some peculiar

way you might worry you will lose this special something you bring to the marriage and to your wife. These are natural worries that create tension. You are left wondering: "Am I needed?" What is the next step?

For your part, Mrs. R, we think you are worried about success as well. You are worried he won't remember how special he is to you as you succeed (e.g., your graduation, getting off Xanex). You worry he will not be able to keep in mind how important he is to you and feel left out. He may even run from the thought and check out first. Your marriage might come unraveled even though that is the last thing in the world you want. He was sick to the point of death on your anniversary. He still does not believe it was your pain too, to think of losing him. We also think if you enjoy your success (e.g., let people throw you a party, or congratulate yourself for beating Xanex), he would see that as 'false pride' rather than a celebration of something you feel good about. You worry he will say "that's it" and dismiss you. We are not surprised at how much fear and tension exists between the two of you. To us, this is a sign of progress. But you are worried to death about what is going to happen to the two of you and this comes out as misunderstandings and anger. It is easier to be angry than afraid of where you stand.

COMMENTARY

This intervention addresses the dynamics of the therapeutic system in a number of ways.

First, it is not uncommon for strategic therapists to anticipate negative consequences of growth or change. This intervention *reframes* an angry, escalating, and potentially toxic interaction as fear of success. It *normalizes* this fear as an integral part of the change process, and implies that the couple continues to improve.

Second, the intervention serves as a *process interruption* maneuver. The goal is to stop the in-session hostility and reduce the likelihood of hostile exchanges following the session. By punctuating a break in the session to confer with the team, the therapist interrupts the cycle of escalation. Second, the content of the intervention blocks the hostile exchange not by confrontation or further exploration of their anger, but by an appeal to the more benevolent intentions that motivate the exchange, namely, the couple's fear of losing each other.

Third, the language of the intervention is carefully chosen. By labeling fears as "unconscious fears" the team implies they are difficult to manage or control. It *joins* with or fits the couple's reality by underscoring their acceptance of the A.A. belief in the unmanageability and lack of control over life's events. Punctuating control as illusory enables the couple to better accept the fears that accompany change, and provides a frame that legitimizes relinquishing control of these fears.

OUTCOME

In the subsequent session the couple reported a more pleasant atmosphere at home, no arguments, and they were once again cooperating with each other as they had before the crisis erupted. Moreover, they had managed to handle their son's unanticipated return home from his group home placement without incident. Mr. R's joking comment that "some things you just can't control" indicated to the team that the intervention had indeed registered.

34

Satir's Parts Party with Couples

James R. Bitter

Virginia Satir (1978) began to explore the parts of individuals as a means of acknowledging, integrating, and harmonizing multiple aspects — both positive and negative — of human beings. She noted that all too often people denied, distorted, or projected parts that fit uncomfortably as an adolescent or adult even though those same parts had once served the child's need for survival. She also knew that people often exaggerated parts that were used to shield or offset perceived weaknesses. Satir's Parts Party is a group approach that allows individuals to see their strengths and weaknesses in a psychodramatic scene. Within the Parts Party, the individual can explore parts that are useful, parts that are liked and disliked, and new resources, some of which are "transformed" parts that started out as negatives. Throughout the experience, a focus on the relationships between parts and a striving for harmony inform the process and provide a vehicle for personal integration (Satir & Baldwin, 1983). Satir often used a variation of the Parts Party with couples as a means of helping each person experience the richness of the other while noting the many ways in which two intimate individuals' parts can interact.

A Parts Party with a couple starts in much the same way that one is enacted with an individual. One person is chosen as the "Star," as the center of focus for the first drama. The Star's partner is asked

Author Note: I would like to thank Virginia Satir for the best decade of training I ever had.

to watch and even to act supportively for the Star, but it is unwise for a partner to play one of the parts at the Star's party.

Preparation for the experience begins when the facilitator, called the Guide, asks the Star to list between six and ten names of people or characters who are well-known, probably from public life. The only requirement is that the persons or characters chosen must strongly attract or strongly repel the Star and be "interesting enough to invite to a party" (Satir & Baldwin, 1983, p. 259). Politicians, movie stars, sports figures, and characters from novels often head the list. The names of the people chosen as parts are listed together with descriptive adjectives for the person. The Star's adjective for each personality defines the role to be played and indicates the Star's reaction or experience of that part. The Guide asks the Star to indicate whether s/he sees the adjective as strongly positive (+) or strongly negative (−) and this information is also listed. Preparation is complete when the Star selects people from a group to play each part. The Guide facilitates a discussion between the Star and each person playing a part to make sure that the actors are approaching the party in a way that fits for the Star. When costumes are available, the role can take on a wonderful familiarity for the Star, players, and observers. Even a simple name sign for each player with the role and adjective listed helps to ground the part.

Physical space is arranged to approximate a place to which the Star might invite guests to a party. The "parts" players are asked to leave the space, organize themselves for an entrance, and come to the party in any order they choose. The Star acts as an observer-host but is not expected to act within the party. Generally, the party progresses in four phases: (1) the entrances and first meetings of the parts; (2) interaction of the parts; (3) the transformation of the parts; and (4) the integration of the parts.

ENTRANCES AND FIRST MEETINGS

Parts players often enter the party in much the way that the Star initially presents different aspects of self. Watching the order and the style of entrance is often meaningful to the host. The parts invariably find ways to make contact with each other, forming dyads, triads, and small clusters in an effort to meet. The Guide freezes the action when these first meetings are in progress and simply notes which character is with whom. As the party progresses, the Guide may freeze the action several times to highlight the shifts in the connections that are being made at the party. Each "freezing of the parts" is an opportunity for the Star to hear how the parts are feeling and thinking. The parts players are asked to exaggerate their roles.

INTERACTION OF THE PARTS

Parts will naturally develop alliances and conflicts with other parts that are often familiar to the Star. The dialogue between parts may be representative of an internal dialogue the Star has had many times. When the Guide freezes the action, the parts will now be asked what is going on and how the player feels about the experience. When the Star has had a chance to hear this set of reactions, the Guide directs each player to dominate the party, "asking them to take obvious action and not just talk" (Satir & Baldwin, 1983, p. 260-261). Through action and movement, each part reveals a plan of action that is often competitive and creates chaotic interaction.

TRANSFORMATION OF THE PARTS

As the parts move through their plans to dominate the party, the Guide freezes the action and asks how people are feeling. The discomfort that is reported is the motivation for transformation. The Guide simply asks, "What would you like to do or become? What would help to make this party go better for you?" Some parts will actually choose to move or act in an opposite manner from their previous approaches. Some will make more subtle changes. New connections and cooperation are the key to helping transformation take place. For example, aggression, connected to intelligence and kindness, becomes leadership. Stubbornness cooperating with wisdom may become persistence. Even "evil" can transform into humanness when coupled with love or forgiveness. The possibilities are endless.

Sometimes, the Guide or Star will note that one or more parts are having difficulty transforming. Often a part is missing, a part that is present in the person but perhaps seldom activated. Maybe the part is wisdom, peacefulness, clarity, organization, or lightness of being. The addition of this part to the party makes it possible for a final harmony to be achieved.

INTEGRATION OF THE PARTS

Satir created a ceremony to facilitate the integration of parts. The Guide asks the player of each part to present the adjectives (the original ones and the transformed ones) to the Star as a gift, asking at the end, "Will you accept me?" As the Star accepts or finds a place for the parts, the parts players stand in a close circle around the Star. The Guide asks each of the players to place a hand gently on the shoulders of the Star. With the Star's eyes closed, the players move gently in a circle, allowing the Star to feel their hands and experience a symbolic harmony of the parts. As the hands and the parts move away, the Star is asked to assess and articulate the feelings present at that moment. The Parts Party ends with the Star listening to the parts players' personal experiences in the process as well as a de-roling for all.

At the end of the first Parts Party, the Star's partner is asked by the Guide to share what he or she learned from watching the experience. "What appreciations for the Star were generated by the experience?" "Is there a difference in how the Star's behaviors or motivations are understood?" "What new meaning is now possible for the relationship?" A second Parts Party is then conducted for the other partner, who invites a new set of guests to a new party experience.

At the end of the second Parts Party, the Guide asks for a large curtain (or some other barricade) to be placed between the couples' two sets of parts. The parts players for each person in the couple are asked to assemble on opposite sides of the curtain and to arrange themselves in any order. Front row seats are provided for the couple and the Guide. On command, two parts, one from each side of the curtain, present themselves and address the part they encounter from the other person's side. The process is repeated until all parts of the couple have encountered each other in random dyads.

The effect is often humorous. There are all-too-human mismatches that help the couple to see what happens when one person's part runs into an incompatible part in the other. For example, when one person's sexual part runs into another person's grumpy and complaining part, the result is predictable. In the context of a Parts Party, however, it is clear that each person has access to other parts, and that different choices can be made when the normally difficult encounters of life occur. Two rotations of random parts-dyads is usually more than enough to underline the possibilities.

The couple's Parts Party ends with the couple sharing with each other what they have learned. When children of the couple are present, it is extremely important for the children to share what the experience was like for them and what they learned. Small children will often make meanings that need to be heard and sometimes clarified. Older children and adolescents may experience their parents as peers, often for the first time; they see that Mom and Dad are whole people who struggle just like they do with strengths and weaknesses, change and growth. The facilitation of the Guide is essential at this point to help keep the focus on the shared experience of the couple.

A Parts Party with a couple requires a group of at least fifteen. The group members may be other couples involved in a group experience or in group therapy for couples or families. They may be friends or associates of the couple who agree to participate in the Parts Party. The purpose of the experience is to build personal integration and relational connectedness. It is important that each person in the couple is open to and capable of both. A Parts Party is a wonderful process for supporting or helping couples who are anticipating marriage or who are about to live together.

REFERENCES

Satir, V. (1978). *Your many faces*. Millbrae, CA: Celestial Arts.
Satir, V., & Baldwin, M. (1983). *Satir: Step by step*. Palo Alto, CA: Science and Behavior Books.

35

The Family as Consultant to the Therapist: A Technique for Facilitating Termination with Reluctant Families

Joseph L. Wetchler

Most family therapists eventually encounter the situation of having a family that has solved its presenting problem, has no other treatment issues, yet is reluctant to terminate therapy. While this may be seen by some as a lucrative windfall, most clinicians are usually disturbed by their treatment family's high degree of dependence on them. The technique of using "the family as a consultant to the therapist" is designed to facilitate this impasse and enable families to terminate therapy. It is based on concepts derived from structural (Minuchin, 1974) and strategic (Haley, 1987; Watzlawick, Weakland, & Fisch, 1974) family therapies; however, it looks at the family/therapist interactional system as its point of focus.

When a family is reluctant to terminate therapy, the therapist often looks for other issues that the family wants to discuss but has not previously mentioned or that have recently arisen. If no other issues appear to be significant, yet the family is hesitant to end treatment, the therapist may decide to schedule sessions at longer intervals to gradually "wean" the family from therapy. If neither of these work, and the family still seems dependent, the therapist may need to look at the therapist/client interactional system.

Whatever the initial reasons may be, families can become dependent on their therapist, a situation that interferes with termination. If the therapist is perceived as someone who helped them solve their problem (whether or not the therapist intended this), a hierarchical imbalance may develop in which the family sees itself as being one down to the therapist. This view is maintained by an interactional pattern in which the family communicates to the therapist about problems and the therapist communicates about solutions. Even the therapist's suggestions about termination can be viewed as proof of greater knowledge of the family's needs, reinforcing the family members' feelings of dependency.

Some authors have suggested that therapists can facilitate termination by crediting the family with the change (Stanton, 1981), being confused about what caused the change (Haley, 1987), or telling family members that they can have only one more session to use when they see fit (Watzlawick, Weakland, & Fisch, 1974). While these may facilitate termination, they do not get at the possible hierarchy issue between family and therapist and may leave families disempowered.

The technique of using "the family as a consultant to the therapist" addresses the issue of a potential power imbalance. The therapist discusses a problem with the family that exists in his/her own life, or that he/she often faces with clients, that is related to the problem that they solved in treatment. As the family is an expert on this problem, the members are asked to make suggestions about how the therapist could address this issue. In doing this, the hierarchy and flow of communication is reversed, with the therapist assuming a one-down position by asking the family members to share their expertise. Also, this enables them to further clarify what they did to solve their problem.

THE L FAMILY

The L Family entered treatment for help with behavioral management of their four-year-old daughter. After diagnosing a cross-generational coalition between the father and daughter against the mother, the parents were assigned the task of jointly negotiating rules and consequences for their daughter's behavior. This resulted in an improvement in the daughter's behavior and led to several sessions of marital therapy which also proved quite positive. After several discussions about termination, the couple stated that while they were happy with their daughter's behavior and their marital gains, they were reluctant to terminate therapy even though they were meeting only once per month. This prompted the therapist to use "the family as consultant technique." The couple was told that the therapist's daughter (who was of similar age to the identified patient) had started to show some behavior problems similar to their own child's. As they recently had been so successful in solving this problem with their own daughter, could they give a few suggestions? After showing some initial shock, the couple gave several ideas that they had found helpful in solving their problem. During the next session the family wholeheartedly agreed to the therapist's suggestion that they consider termination, provided the therapist remembered to follow their suggestions with his own daughter.

MRS. Q

Mrs. Q entered treatment following her divorce to "rebuild her world." Through her work in therapy, she had obtained a job, developed a support group of several other divorced women, learned how to manage the family finances, and had begun to date other men. Even though she stated that she had solved her problems and did not wish to work on them any more, she felt hesitant to terminate therapy. As she had been so successful at getting her life back in order, the therapist asked if she could give him some suggestions that he could use in working with other women who were in situations similar to her own. She literally swelled with pride as she listed several of the strategies she had used in solving her problems. At the end of the session the therapist thanked her for her help and asked her to again think about whether she really needed to continue with treatment. She proudly returned to the next session to announce her decision to terminate therapy.

DISCUSSION

These cases exemplify the potential use of using "the client as consultant to the therapist" to facilitate termination. In each example the clients were placed in the role of expert and enabled to see how they had resolved their problems. Further, by helping the therapist with a similar problem, they saw themselves as equals, which enhanced their feeling of personal power and facilitated their decision to end therapy.

REFERENCES

Haley, J. (1987). *Problem-solving therapy* (2nd ed.). San Francisco: Jossey-Bass.
Minuchin, S. (1974). *Families and family therapy*. Cambridge, MA: Harvard University Press.
Stanton, M.D. (1981). Who should get credit for change which occurs in therapy? In A.S. Gurman (Ed.), *Questions and answers in the practice of family therapy* (pp. 519-522). New York: Brunner/Mazel.
Watzlawick, P., Weakland, J.H., & Fisch, R. (1974). *Change*. New York: Norton.

36

The Struggler

Amith BenDavid

Reframing is usually associated with strategic therapy, originally with the MRI group (Watzlawick, Weakland, & Fisch, 1974). In this model, reframing is seen as part of the communication process. It is designed to change the conceptual and/or emotional setting or viewpoint in relation to which a situation is experienced and to place it in another frame that fits the "facts" of the same concrete situation equally well, or even better, and thereby change its entire meaning. The change does not come from the confirmation of the client's reality but from creating a new one. The target in strategic family therapy is the system, the whole family, or the marital relationship. The way to do it is by disrupting the rules in organization around the "problem." For example, labeling a jealous husband as "loving" and "caring" may allow the wife to view his jealous behavior differently and thus respond to it differently.

Barton and Alexander (1981), describing Functional Family Therapy, state that "the most active and powerful vehicle for reattribution and change for the Functional Family therapist is that of relabeling. Relabeling is a form of message that both 'revalences' behavior and describes functions to family members" (p. 422). The therapist's task, in order to revalence behavior, is to consider dialectic or antonym properties of a given phenomenon, such as relabeling the distance of an authoritarian father as active leadership or the distance of a teenager as a struggle for individuality. The goal is always to find positive antonyms so that "this revalencing of roles, behaviors, emotions, or other dimensions of family life reduces defensiveness in family members while helping create an alternative value or affect associated with the phenomenon" (p. 423). For example, a distancing wife, who wants to keep her individuality, can be reframed as wanting to help her husband have the time he needs to do his work and have a good time with his friends.

Working with learning disabilities that involve a minimal brain dysfunction is a common occurrence in family therapy. These children are often labeled as having an "attitude" problem by the school system that has a hard time dealing with the multiple problems these children present. The families, however, are usually left to deal with their problems alone, torn between their loyalty to their children and the conflicting messages of responsibility and blame sent by the school system.

The S family had been living for generations in a rural area of Indiana and were farmers by profession. Their oldest son (of four children), who was 12 years old, presented at our clinic with complaints from the school system that he, F, was lazy and undisciplined. In short, F had an "attitude" problem. The boy had been thoroughly tested in school, but the results were only of marginal learning disability, and the school was lacking the resources to give him remedial learning.

The family "bought" the school's labeling, and organized itself around this lazy boy with an attitude problem. Mother sat for hours on end to make the boy write the homework he had a hard time understanding; his brothers and sisters made fun of him, since they were doing better at school than he was; father was angry and disappointed and distanced himself in order to avoid the hurt and frustration that the boy was arousing in all family members.

The goal of the intervention was to co-create a new reality that would free the family to relate to the boy in a new, creative manner. Labeling the behavior of the boy as "struggling" disrupted the pattern of behavior of the whole family around the child. The boy was relabeled as struggling to understand what was required of him, struggling to be a good son to his parents, and struggling in school to make sense of school material. The relabeling (reframing) was done in front of the whole family and each of the children was asked how he/she thought that F was struggling in school and in the family. The parents were introduced to the idea and asked to give their thoughts. Finally, F himself was asked, and he recounted in a very dramatic way how hard it was for him to sit in front of these pages of written material when it took such an immense amount of time and effort to make sense of what was said there and what he was expected to do.

It took about three sessions to change the valence of the behaviors of each one of the family members. As a consequence, mother started a crusade against the school system and its labeling of the boy as lazy, secured special education classes for the child in a nearby county, and was able to allow him and herself more freedom to grow.

REFERENCES

Barton, C., & Alexander, J.F. (1981). Functional family therapy. In A. Gurman & D. Kniskern (Eds.), *Handbook of family therapy*. New York: Brunner/Mazel.

Watzlawick, P., Weakland, J.H., & Fisch, R. (1974). *Change*. New York: W.W. Norton & Company.

37

Motorcycle Madness:
A Structural Intervention
with a Life-Threatening Disorder

James L. Hawkins

This paper describes a dramatic intervention in a family with a suicidal, behavior-disordered adolescent. The enactment selected to bring about needed structural change is deliberately vague in order to access the power of apparently spontaneous second order change.

An emphasis of this paper is the need for careful preparation by detailed yet focused information gathering, and patient, perhaps even elaborate, reframing. Family history information in some detail is useful in selecting an intervention with a high probability of success. Careful reframing motivates a family to behave in ways that might otherwise seem odd to them. This paper also illustrates how several conceptual schemes may sometimes be useful in defining the problem, selecting the intervention, and negotiating a cognitive framework with the family.

It is probably the case that the structural approach is most useful with families holding traditional hierarchical power expectations. In the following family example, it is interesting to note that the parents had a traditional parenting paradigm, but a rather egalitarian view of marriage. In practice, they achieved neither.

The parents brought their nineteen-year-old son to me after he was nearly arrested for drunk driving. He had then revealed to the

---

Author Note: I would like to thank Elinor M. Adams for critical comments on the original draft of this intervention.

parents that he had recently received two reckless driving tickets on his motorcycle, admitted to driving the cycle as well as the car while drunk, and bragged about driving the cycle down the wrong side of freeways at high speed "to see what would happen."

Mark, let us call him, had been a "wild kid" since he was very young. He had been burned in a kitchen accident at age two. Mother blamed herself for the accident. She now believed that her guilt prevented her from setting limits on Mark. She felt that her husband also blamed her and had withdrawn from her at that time. Throughout Mark's life, Dad would play with Mark but he also seldom disciplined him. Dad's work kept him away from home most evenings and weekends casting the burden of parenting onto Mother, also professionally employed. She said that she felt that after the kitchen accident, Dad had "disappeared." Both parents regretfully concurred with this view.

Because Mark's life was again in jeopardy, both parents reported that they felt as if they were in a time warp having been returned to Mark's age two. Mother once again felt disabled by her guilt. The father volunteered that this time he did not want to withdraw, but felt helpless to know what to do.

Mark, though attentive, said that all he was trying to do was get a little excitement into his life. In his charmingly manipulative way he said that he knew that his mother loved him, but that he could talk her into anything. His father was always fun in contrast with Mother, who, while manipulable, was too serious.

The parents asked me to see Mark privately to try to persuade him to enter therapy. I agreed to try one session if Mark would agree also. I would be able to confirm my diagnosis and also strengthen the case that some family action was the best, perhaps the only avenue of help. Or perhaps the parents were right: Mark might listen to my advice.

Mark maintained a defiantly friendly attitude throughout the meeting, and, as expected, denied any problems whatsoever. He said that he was coming only to please his parents. I said that I was too. He said that he would not continue this for long as this "therapy stuff is stupid." He explicitly rejected my suggestion that he enter chemical dependency treatment.

In the third meeting, I explained to the family that I believed

Mark to be sub-intentionally suicidal. We talked at length about his developmental history and how the parents had failed Mark in the crucial three-year-old phase, for perhaps understandable reasons. The parents agreed that failure to set limits then and subsequently was tantamount to emotional neglect. I sympathized with the pain that had been unspoken for all of these years.

Mark had successfully sidestepped their feeble control efforts throughout his life as well as more competent recent efforts by the father. Simply urging the parents to take an even stronger stand would have produced only more failure. Somehow they had to "take charge" benevolently. With Mother's encouragement, I scheduled Dad and Mark for a session the next week. Mark agreed to avoid life-threatening activities until then.

After a few minutes of settling in, I put on the table the enactment I had planned. I told Dad that he had to somehow convince his son that both he and his mother loved him so dearly that Mark would have some reason to live. A long silence followed my admonition to the father. I resisted offering any more explicit suggestions despite several pleas from Father. At last, Dad said, "I can think of only one way. Mark, come sit on my lap."

For 30 minutes, Mark sat on Father's lap talking softly, absent his charming surliness, listening to his dad recall fifteen years of worry and concern. Dad apologized for only being able to play, leaving the hard stuff to Mom. He was passionate in expressing his wish that Mark not inadvertently kill himself, that he find some excitement that did not risk his life stupidly. Once the dad had spontaneously initiated the change, I felt free to offer direction whenever I thought he was running out of steam. Finally, I told Dad to bring this to a close in any way he wanted. They stood, embraced, wept.

This kind of vague inducement should only be utilized in difficult circumstances where the possible benefit clearly outweighs the risks. The ground must be prepared so well that the therapist can resolutely stand by despite entreaties from family members to "help." In this regard, the intervention is similar to those sometimes recommended in treatment of life-threatening psychosomatic illnesses. In this instance, however, the goal was to have the family become more "enmeshed" rather than less.

Supporting the selection of the intervention were several additional considerations: Mark was on the verge of not cooperating further in the sessions; the reframing was extensive and detailed even to the parent's own apperception that this was just like when Mark was age two; the father had volunteered with the mother's blessing to "try."

I scheduled a session for Mother and Father for the next week. In this session I arranged for Dad to continue monitoring his son's behavior while conferring regularly with the mother: "Mom knows Mark better than you do."

Thus, Mother was restored to a powerful, yet complementary, parenting role consistent with the family's values. I instructed the parents that they should spend at least one evening a month together where the subject of Mark was off limits. They were to call me only if things got out of control again.

Incidental contact with the family one year later revealed that Mark had stopped drinking altogether although he was still using marijuana, had sold his motorcycle, was on the Dean's list, had moved out to an apartment with a girlfriend, and was talking to a recruiter about possibly joining the Marines as a helicopter pilot! Apparently the only drawback to the Marines was that Mark wasn't sure he could handle the regimentation. The father had taken a job with evenings and weekends free.

38

Desperately Seeking French Fries

Eleanor Adaskin
Maria Gomori

This article outlines sculpting as an intervention with the family of a catatonic young woman. Sometimes in our work, we laughingly say that helping enmeshed families to individuate is like trying to make French fries out of mashed potatoes. This family illustrates the difficulty of becoming and remaining a French fry in a mashed potato environment.

We chose to illustrate family sculpting because of the frequency with which we find it useful in helping families. Sculpture can be used in therapy, training, or consultation with individuals, groups, and families. We use sculpting for developing the diagnosis and intervention and to help the family see, hear, and feel their own and each others' perceptions of how the family functions. Families can also portray their desired outcome for the hopes and wishes they have for the family in the future, once certain goals are achieved.

Family sculpture has been developed over the last twenty years by therapists such as Satir (1988), Duhl, Kantor, and Duhl (1973), and Papp, Silverstein, and Carter (1973). Family sculpting is a powerful visual and kinesthetic tool, providing an action-oriented intervention. It uses body postures and spacing as a demonstration of the family's patterns of communication, power, closeness or distance, and relationship to the outside world. Sculpting makes the covert family patterns more visible, and the abstract dynamics more concrete (Satir, Banmen, Gerber, & Gomori, 1991). Our use of sculpture in practice and teaching has been based largely on the work of Satir.

We will focus our sculpting example on a young, recently married woman, Beth, 26, who was admitted in a catatonic state during a psychotic episode. When we called to arrange for the family to come in, Father spoke to us on the phone and agreed readily, but stated that mother was in a wheelchair severely disabled with arthritis, and the session would need to be held at home. He cautioned us that his wife should be protected from any stressful discussion.

Beth's husband, Tom, 26, and her older sister, Barbara, 28, also agreed readily to a family session conducted in the home. Everything there was organized for the comfort of the disabled mother. All family members showed extremely loving and protective behavior towards the mother and gracious hospitality towards us.

All members were most anxious to be helpful in "taking care of Bethie." For generations, taking care of the old and sick was regarded as a central family obligation and value.

Our observation of Beth's interaction in the family at this point led us to see her as a "good little girl" desperately fearing something. Even with much kind prompting, Beth had great difficulty saying anything. She continued shaking her head soundlessly, eyes staring in fear, and whispering, "I don't know." Tom stated that her withdrawn behavior started when they moved to another part of the country where he was stationed.

Mother was a competent 60-year-old woman, long-suffering and badly crippled. Within the limitations of her disability, however, she was subtly in charge of the family. Father gave priority to looking after his wife. An unspoken rule became apparent in the family: Family comes first, especially the sick member.

After becoming more comfortable with the family, establishing an atmosphere of safety and trust and obtaining sufficient information, we said, "We'd like to show you our picture of how we think everybody feels in this family and then we will ask you how this fits your picture. Would you be willing to try this with us?"

PHASE I INTERVENTION: PORTRAYING THE PRESENT STATE

Using Satir's communication stances to demonstrate the family's communication and the feelings behind it (Satir, 1988; Schwab,

Baldwin, Gerber, Gomori, & Satir, 1989), we had all the members arrange themselves around Mother's chair. Because Mother was unable to kneel in the position of the placating stance, she was asked to wear a worried expression as she gazed at Beth. We asked her to hold out her two hands as a way to express both her desire to help and her need for help.

In front of Mother, we placed Beth on her knees in a placating stance which represented self-blame and discounting of herself. We asked her to put out her two hands toward Mother to ask for her help and forgiveness. We placed Father standing behind Mother, supporting her on the shoulder with the touch of one hand, while placating her and the family with his other hand extended toward each in turn. His back was positioned slightly bent forward, representing his servitude to the family's needs. He was portrayed as standing on his feet to demonstrate his strength in coping and providing as the head of the family. We asked him to look at Beth in a sad and imploring manner.

To show Barbara's independent living situation and her role throughout life as co-parent, helping Dad to look after Mom and Beth, we placed her standing slightly farther apart from the family and closer to Father. To demonstrate Barbara's worry about the current situation, we asked her to reach out her hands toward Father and Beth, expressing her concern that they take care of Mother, while at the same time Barbara was gazing with concern at Mother. We placed Tom standing behind Beth with his hands on her shoulders, looking towards us for help.

During the process of arranging the members of the family, we did not tell them what interpretation we were assigning to these positions. We simply asked them to take on the positions reflecting their picture, and let the experience of being there and seeing the others in their positions have its own non-verbal impact. We then asked them each in turn how they felt in the positions and invited them to rearrange their positions to more accurately represent their feelings and relationships together.

Mother looked tearful at the sight of Beth on her knees before her. All members instinctively moved closer toward Mother. Beth began to tremble and cry, then broke through her long silence. She haltingly shared with us her guilt that, because she had moved away from the city, she had broken a promise to always be there to take care of Mother. Mother began to cry, and stretched out her hands toward Beth, saying, "Oh Bethie, I never knew that you thought you had to stay here. I've always wanted you to put your marriage first. Of course your place is with Tom." Father was tearful, too, and said, "I never realized you felt so responsible for staying near us. We missed you terribly, but we want your happiness even above our own."

When we asked Barbara how she felt, she wiped her eyes and said, "I understand how Bethie feels. I feel very responsible, too, maybe even more so since Bethie's been gone. I often feel I should have done more for Mom and Daddy, and I realized it more when I was standing apart over here."

Turning back to Beth, we asked how she felt about what everyone was saying. She began to talk more freely, saying, "I feel so badly that I let Mommy and Daddy down." We asked what she had expected of herself. She said she had always tried to be a good girl and to help her parents. She described herself as bad, evil, and selfish for getting married and moving away.

Beth was convinced that her parents blamed her for leaving them and felt disappointed that she was not able to carry out their care in the way that they had done for their parents in their early marriage and as the generation before them had done for ill members. Beth said that she believed children should always put their parents first. With the source of this problem brought out into words and postures, she became more available for therapeutic contact.

At this point, we thought that it would be helpful to dramatize the price of illness that Beth was paying, choosing this way of punishing herself. We said, "Beth, would you allow us to show you our picture of what you are telling us?" She agreed, and we asked her to lie flat on the floor. Once in this position, her crying increased. We asked, "What's happening for you right now, Beth?" She said, "I don't deserve their love."

Mother began to reach toward her from her chair. Tom said, "I'm beginning to understand how hard it has been for Beth. I thought she was just lonely in the new place, but I had no idea how she was suffering, and I guess I was pretty busy being away with my new job." Dad reflected, "We've always relied heavily on the girls to keep the household going. They've been such good daughters, but maybe we didn't realize how hard it would be for them to leave home.''

Barbara, too, looked thoughtful. She added, ''I have often felt guilty about having my apartment and living my own life. I know Mom and Dad aren't too happy about my living with my boyfriend, but I've just had to make decisions for myself to establish a separate life. It's been a pull for me too.''

PHASE II INTERVENTION: PORTRAYING THE DESIRED STATE

Next, we asked the family to show us their picture of how they would like this family to be. Tom stretched out a hand to help Beth to get to her feet. They stood close together, a little apart but not distant from the other members. Tom suggested that the parents really did need help, aside from what the daughters could offer. He volunteered to help explore what services were available. He placed Barbara at a comfortable distance on her own, though still connected through gaze and an outstretched hand. Dad continued to be placed behind Mom's chair with a helping hand on her shoulder, indicating his primary commitment to his wife. Tom's picture clearly illustrated the need for clear boundaries in the family.

We asked each member in turn how they felt about seeing and experiencing this picture. All agreed verbally that it represented a goal that would be desirable to them. However, we knew that the process would require long-term follow-up to assist each member in making the necessary changes to achieve it.

PHASE III INTERVENTION: STEPS TO ARRIVE AT THE DESIRED STATE

To assist the members in making the bridge between the two sculptures of present state and desired state, we asked them to return to the original positions of how they are under their current stress, then asked them how they would like to change it. Beth said, ''I want to get up off the floor but I can't do it myself.'' The members all participated in suggesting how each would take part in the family changes in a way that would enable more freedom without loss of their connection. Tom's help enabled Beth to get to her feet; other concrete plans were established for each member and the family as a whole.

COMMENTARY

This first dramatic sculpture opened the process of work between the family members and ourselves. It was a breakthrough that opened the door for the family to share more open communication than they had before. The use of sculpting cut through the polite, friendly chit-chat and Beth's silence, and facilitated members having a direct experience with their own struggle between family altruism and individuation. It has provided reliable themes and insights for the family's change process over the ten-year period during which the family has occasionally kept in touch to cope with various crises.

Although we had hoped to be able to facilitate the emergence of a family-size plateful of French fries, we were humbled by the power of mashed potatoes. Nevertheless, we remain convinced that family sculpture can provide a powerful tool for helping at least several members to become and stay French fries. Beth has never had to be readmitted to the hospital, and has survived two severe postpartum depressions to emerge as an independent, happy person, wife, and mother of three.

REFERENCES

Duhl, F., Kantor, D., & Duhl, B. (1973). Learning, space, and action in family therapy: A primer of family sculpture. In D. Bloch (Ed.), *Techniques of family psychotherapy: A primer* (pp. 47-63). New York: Grune & Stratton.

Papp, P., Silverstein, O., & Carter, B. (1973). Family sculpting in preventive work with well families. *Family Process, 12*, 197-212.

Satir, V. (1988). *The new peoplemaking*. Palo Alto: Science and Behavior Books.

Satir, V., Banmen, J., Gerber, J., Gomori, M. (1991). *The Satir model: Family therapy and beyond*. Pato Alto, CA: Science and Behavior Books.

Schwab, J., Baldwin, M., Gerber, J., Gomori, M., & Satir, V. (1989). *The Satir approach to communication*. Palo Alto: Science and Behavior Books.

39

Termination Rituals

Eric E. McCollum

Ending family therapy can be an anxious time for a family. While they may have made good progress, family members often worry that the presenting problem will recur when therapy ends or that the changes made are not as durable as they appear. The family therapist must not ignore this worry by focusing exclusively on the positive and admiring the good work done in therapy. I have found that a task or ritual that specifically addresses the anxiety about relapse can be quite effective as part of the termination process. I have used this technique when working with families in outpatient treatment and with families who have a child in residential treatment.

Termination rituals derive theoretically from the strategic (Haley, 1976) school of family therapy and from Viktor Frankl's (1967) paradoxical intention. Frankl's idea is that attempts to suppress a fear only serve to give it more power. In termination rituals, then, families are asked to embrace the fear that they will have a relapse. Doing so shows the family the depth of the change they have made and lets each person know the control they have over whether the family returns to its old, problematic ways. It also helps the family members to see that *they* have made the changes, not the therapist, allowing the therapist to more completely disengage from the system. This idea can be operationalized in several ways.

At the most straightforward level, the therapist can simply acknowledge the fear and ask the family to specify what early warning signs of relapse they might look for. Some families will take great relief in open discussion of their fear. Noting warning signs of difficulty helps the family see that the return of problems would be part of a process occurring over time. They would not simply awaken one morning to find themselves again immersed in difficulty.

Besides discussing the fear, each family member can be asked to list what specific things he or she would have to do to take the family back to where they were when therapy began. This serves to establish that each family member has some measure of control over what happens in the family and also reminds them of the changes they have made during therapy. In a marital therapy process, for example, the husband might say that he would have to keep his feelings to himself and devote extra time to work in order to create problems again. His wife might say that she would need to try very hard to read her husband's mind and to pry his feelings out of him at all costs. Consideration of these actions will lead the couple to decide that the likelihood of either thing happening again is remote.

When the preceding interventions don't reassure the family, they can be asked to actually try, in a limited way, to recreate the problems they were having when they initiated therapy. They can be instructed to do this either in a therapy session or as a homework assignment. Components of the earlier interventions are incorporated in this, of course, since the family members would have to think what their part was in the problems in order to recreate them. Reenacting a relapse is illustrated in the clinical example.

Having families list warning signs of relapse and think about how each member might contribute to a relapse can be done with any family ending therapy. It is a useful exercise when the therapist feels there is little danger of relapse and the family is being overly anxious or when the therapist feels the family is ignoring the possibility of a return of problems. Encouraging families to enact a relapse, however, should only be attempted with families who are overly anxious about problems returning and who are not calmed by listing warning signs and thinking of each member's contribution.

CASE EXAMPLE

Doug was a fifteen-year-old boy who had been in a residential facility for eighteen months. Among the reasons for his admission were the recurrent and verbally abusive fights he had with his mother. These fights had resulted in neighbors' calling the police on two or three occasions. During the course of his inpatient treatment, Doug and his mother had worked hard on this issue. They had not had any fights for a long time, even on passes home. However, when it came time for Doug to leave the hospital, both he and his mother began to worry that they would start fighting again. Each feared not having the support of family therapy, which I couldn't continue for administrative reasons.

Talking about their worries didn't decrease them, nor did trying to make up a list of "early warning signs." Ironically, Doug and his mother worked together cooperatively and with great concern as they discussed this issue. In the past, such an intense issue would have provoked a fight. Finally, I said I thought they needed an answer to whether they would fight again and I suggested they do a "scientific experiment." On their next pass, Doug and his mother were to go to a restaurant. They were to order a meal and then they were to spend the next hour acting as they used to act before Doug came to the hospital. This was to include having at least one fight. Their most intense fights had been in public places, thus my recommendation that they try the experiment at a restaurant. They both left looking worried but swore that they would try the experiment. We planned a meeting the next day to evaluate the outcome.

When Doug and his mother returned, I asked how it had gone. They looked sheepish.

"We didn't do it," Doug said. I looked at his mother who nodded. "We tried," she said, "but we couldn't keep it up."

Doug and his mother had taken my suggestion seriously. They had gone to a restaurant, ordered a meal and began to try to fight. Doug's mother complained about Doug's clothes. Doug called her a bitch and told her to mind her own business. She pretended to cry but broke into laughter instead. As soon as she did, Doug begun to laugh, too. They spent the rest of their time talking about how bad things had been between them and how much they enjoyed the changes they had made.

Doug and his mother didn't report any conscious insight occurring as a result of the prescription. They didn't say that they now knew that they had control over whether they fought or not. However, they did turn their attention to other issues in therapy sessions, didn't mention their fights again, and began to report looking forward to Doug's coming home.

REFERENCES

Frankl, V.E. (1967). Paradoxical intention: A logotherapeutic technique. In H. Greenwald (Ed.), *Active psychotherapy* (pp. 337-352). New York: Atherton.
Haley, J. (1976). *Problem solving therapy*. San Francisco: Jossey-Bass.

40

Self-Esteem: Everyone's Favorite

Norman H. Cobb
Catheleen Jordan

Nearly all family members believe that self-esteem is important. However, very few parents and even fewer children have any idea how to define or improve the self-esteem of family members. Self-esteem is a particularly important issue for the family, because the family is the primary setting in which the complex web of realistic and unrealistic expectations and standards are usually learned and maintained. Clinical interventions with individuals' self-esteem requires changes in the family system of beliefs and expectations. Families may benefit from being guided through an exercise in examining expectations and setting the stage to restructure members' self-esteem.

Self-esteem results from a comparison of the self-concept and the ideal self (Pope, McHale, & Craighead, 1988). People are fairly objective when they describe role components of their self-concept, such as "parent," "employee," "tennis player," "student," or "friend." People also have cognitive images or schema in which they picture the ideal parent, employee, tennis player, or some other type of idealized person, such as the morally perfect person. For example, children are taught critically important information about what they should be like. Likewise, parents take on culturally defined roles and continue to evolve their self-esteem in light of their own concepts and self-evaluations. Self-esteem evolves from a comparison of the objective self and the ideal self: a comparison between what people know about themselves and what they believe they should be like. These critical judgments are highly affected by the environment, particularly the family setting. Interventions, therefore, have a better chance of success when they are used in the family context.

INTERVENTION PROCESS

Step 1

The intervention is largely an educational and experiential process. Family members are asked to make lists of their own objective descriptors: swimmer, student, father, and so on. Beside each descriptor, they write down what they would like to be doing if they were the kind of swimmer, student, father, etc., they would like to be.

The clinician may wish to specify that the family members focus on the following five categories: social, academic, family, body image, and global (Pope, McHale, & Craighead, 1988). The social world refers to relationships with others and feelings or beliefs that others like him or her. The school setting is an area where children and adolescents quickly learn that they are being judged by peers and teachers. The family setting involves feelings of being liked, safe, and respected. Body image includes personal looks and physical performance. The global category encompasses other broad judgments that family members make about themselves.

An important lesson for family members is to understand that individual members will not share the same values, perceptions, and beliefs. In the particular case of self-esteem, family members' idiosyncratic values, beliefs, etc., indicate what is important to them. The subsequent efforts to improve self-esteem will depend on family members' ability to enable positive comparisons between individuals' personal evaluations of their self-concepts and their idealized, prized pictures of themselves, rather than changing values, perceptions, etc., to "fit" some hypothesized family norm.

Step 2

Each family member shares his or her list and everyone votes to determine if the idealized satisfaction level is sufficiently within the grasp of the family member. If the family members do not challenge unrealistic expectations, the clinician must intervene. For example, the following are some typical examples of unrealistic expectations: In the academic area, children with a long history of B grades cannot be expected to suddenly or even gradually start making A's. Socially, adolescents are sometimes expected to date more persons or date a "nicer" type of person. Parents are sometimes expected to earn more money to buy a new house, new car, or more clothes for the resident teenager. Other expectations may include being better parents by requiring fathers or mothers to spend more time at home, cook more meals, or schedule vacations to Disneyland. The unrealistic goals must be changed unless the family has a new, acceptable plan or strategy to accomplish them. One final word: Clinicians should keep their expectations focused on individuals or the family; family therapy may not be the best place for partners to voice expectations pertaining to marital issues.

Parents should be instructed that when expectations are too high they provide serious blocks to the development of children's self-esteem. Parents can be made aware of this fact by asking them a question such as: "What would happen to your self-esteem if you believed that your worth was dependent on becoming a National League football player?" Unfortunately, many expectations communicated to children as well as to parents are equally exaggerated and unreachable.

Step 3

Family members are asked to rate the degree to which each person, including him or herself, has reached the acceptable goal or goals. The following is suggested as a usable scale:

Individual and Family Expectation Rating Chart

Level 1. (125%) Exceeded expectations. Perhaps goal was too small given your abilities or the expectation received too much emphasis. Relax, pat yourself on the back.

Level 2. (100%) Congratulations! Expectations are met. You have completed the goal.

Level 3. (90%) With very little additional effort, expectation will be met.

Level 4. (75%) Already completed three-fourths of expectation; on track and will meet expectation in the near future.

Level 5. (50%) Already met half of the expectation and, with new efforts and support from the family, expectation will be met.

Level 6. (25%) Just getting started but expectation can be met given enough time and support from family and others.

Level 7. (0%) The expectation is new and requires everyone's attention and support.

Step 4

If and when the family member accepts the goal recommended or negotiated by the family and clinician, everyone in the family secretly writes down how close the described person is to reaching his or her goal and gives the ratings to the person. Finally, that person compares his or her own rating with every members' rating and reports the results to the family group.

Step 5

As a final stage, family members may plan steps or ways to help the person effectively meet the expectations. The clinician may choose to teach problem-solving skills or contracting to help members plan for change.

USES

The intervention is indicated when family members exhibit low self-esteem or when members describe conflicting or unclear expectations and standards. The plan is largely preventive in nature.

The plan outlined above takes on different forms as families vary in degree of dysfunction. For example, families who have the capacity to communicate and support their members will need less support and direction than will families that are overly critical and confrontive. Dysfunctional families that are uncooperative, punishing in their interactions, or primarily crisis oriented cannot be expected to give family members sufficient support or feedback to evolve positive self-esteem judgments.

OUTCOME

Family members report understanding the idea of self-esteem and experiencing changes in their own evaluation. Important by-products of this approach are the feelings of support and mutual caring exchanged by family members.

REFERENCE

Pope, A.W., McHale, S.M., & Craighead, W.E. (1988). *Self-esteem enhancement with children and adolescents.* New York: Pergamon Press.

41

A Cross-Cultural Double Date

Martha Gonzalez Marquez

Working with immigrant families can be a challenge for therapists. Stressors that these families must endure are often not apparent in therapy and can cause misunderstandings on the part of the therapist. It is important that therapists become aware of the possible difficulties immigrant families may be experiencing. One of the key areas that may be causing an immigrant family stress is that of acculturation. Sluzki (1979) describes five stages of acculturation: (1) preparatory stage; (2) migration; (3) period of overcompensation; (4) period of crisis decompensation; and (5) transgenerational phenomena. Each stage is uniquely different and mandates different interventions. However, some family members experience acculturation and/or assimilation at different rates. Indeed, some therapists believe this factor to be a basic assumption when working with immigrant families (Montalvo & Gutierrez, 1990).

While remaining sensitive to cultural norms as well as to different acculturation rates, a ritual was developed to assist couples who were experiencing tension due to uneven rates of acculturation. Following a form of the Milan Systemic model, a couple was told to schedule one night a week for a "date." To plan for this date, the couple was to decide those aspects of the date that should be from their culture of origin and those that should be typically "American." This "double date" assignment was given with no other stipulations. The aspects could include food, apparel, type of activity, or any other characteristic of a date. Since it is frequently inconsistent with some cultural norms for the parents to leave the children while they are "out on a date," the stipulation that the children not accompany the parents was not emphasized.

This ritual can be understood from varying standpoints. It can be considered paradoxical in that it is inevitable for the family to have both cultures involved in their date since they bring with them their culture of origin (often through their choice of language) and the date will occur somewhere within the host culture. Also, prescribing for the couple exactly what their source of confusion is may give them a more controlled sense of the situation.

It is often the fear of not having input into the partner's changes that causes great stress. This ritual also emphasizes the idea that a combination of the cultures, not an exclusion of one, can produce a positive and fulfilling experience for the family. The ritual gives the family permission to live their lives in a multicultural fashion. Systemically, the family is given a prescription not to change what they are currently experiencing.

Used with appropriate couples, this ritual can have positive outcomes. It is of utmost importance that the therapist be aware of the cultural norms the family wishes to maintain. Often there are several basic cultural rules that neither partner is willing to alter. Individuals who are at a stage of rigid rejection of either their culture of origin or the host culture may not benefit from this type of ritual. Respect for each individual's stage of acculturation is crucial.

The couple mentioned earlier responded to the ritual with relish. The date was a positive experience and both partners claimed they felt a release of tension. They expressed surprise at how unique the experience had actually been for them. The couple also claimed they would continue the "double dating" after therapy ended.

REFERENCES

Montalvo, B., & Gutierrez, M.J. (1990). Nine assumptions for work with ethnic minority families. In G.W. Saba, B.M. Karrer, & K.N. Hardy (Eds.), *Minorities and family therapy* (pp. 35-37). New York: The Haworth Press.
Sluzki, C. (1979). Migration and family conflict. *Family Process, 18*, 379-390.

42

Healing of the Memories

Au-Deane Cowley

INTRODUCTION

There is much in the literature about the harmful and sometimes irreparable damage done by "narcissistic wounding" in childhood. Little attention, however, has been given to the wounding and betrayals that leave scarring marks on the adult lives they impact. It has been written that pain is morbid only when it goes unexpressed, for unhealed grief cripples or inhibits adult functioning. It matters little whether the wounding comes from external sources or is a product of self-sabotage — the aftermath is the same: the sense of "not-okayness," the hopelessness and self-pity, all of the negativity that occurs when dreams are lost and one's heart feels as if it has been broken.

Healing the wounded heart is a process of filling what Bradshaw (1988) calls "the hole in the soul." Since one of the basic goals of good mental health and of therapy in all of its various wrappings is to help the person to love the self, healing work is of the utmost importance. Miller (1981) has written about the necessity for de-repressing childhood pain, and letting go of circumstances that keep psychic energy recycling in old conundrums. If we are to help clients free up life-force energy for loving and creating in the here and now, we must take seriously the job of healing the past. As Branden (1972) has observed: "No pain is so destructive as the pain one refuses to face, and no suffering is as enduring as the suffering one refuses to acknowledge."

In her book, *Creative Visualization*, Gawain (1982) developed some specific "clearing exercises" to facilitate the forgiveness of self and other. Doing the work of grieving and forgiving not only releases bound-up energy but also empowers the person with a sense of copefulness. When despair work is not done, one retains a sense of powerlessness, psychic numbing, fragmentation, and alienation—a narrowed sense of awareness.

Houston (1988) has written a thoughtful article about the function of "wounding" entitled, "The Sacred Wound," wherein she postulates that "soul-making begins with the wounding of the psyche (soul) by the larger story." This wounding of the soul can either become a "sacred" wound that opens us up to new deeps (illumines us) or a "sickening" wound that keeps us stuck in the same old story, blaming and seeking revenge or using energy to deny or ignore our pain ("maddens" us) (Houston, 1988). When we are able to help self/others move out of the pain and into the meaning and purpose to be found in "the larger story," no matter whether we choose to call it de-repressing, clearing exercises, or healing of the memories, we are engaging in the healing art of Therapeia.

THEORETICAL ORIENTATION

Theoretically, healing techniques or exercises have come mainly from the experiential or transpersonal therapies. Insight and "working through" as utilized by psychodynamically-oriented therapies can provide some cognitive relief and behavioral techniques can help us shape new responses to pain; however, to get a different "felt sense" (Genlin, 1978) of our experience of life requires an involvement of the affective as well as the cognitive dimension. Redecision work, as done by the Gouldings (1979), emphasizes the importance of getting in touch with harmful life scenarios on an emotional, as well as a cognitive level. This reliving or imagined restructuring must occur in a safe environment with a trusted guide.

DESCRIPTION OF THE INTERVENTION

Healing interventions can be utilized across a broad spectrum: physical woundings such as illness, accidents, birth, or genetic defects; acts of violation upon one's person such as rape, incest, child abuse, torture, robbery; or the *Necessary Losses* (Viorst, 1986) and unnecessary ones as well, such as the loss of a deep relationship, the loss of a job, loss of status, the loss of financial security; even the larger woundings that affect whole cultures and nations, or the planet itself (Houston, 1988). For some, pain is personal — for others, planetary. The art of the intervention is to co-create a uniquely different application of the intervention for each client system. A general guideline for implementing the intervention follows.

1. The first step in healing of the memories is to de-repress denied emotions of the false self and get in touch with the true Self's authentic feelings;
2. relive the traumatic moment in all of its original emotional intensity;
3. accept the betrayal or loss as one of the unalterable facts of your life;
4. do the grief work of mourning the loss, wound, or pain;
5. make a re-decision about the event from a position of adult consciousness if dealing with a childhood event or from a place of centered clarity if it is more recent;
6. when it feels authentic, do a clearing exercise to forgive everyone involved in the wounding incident;
7. if it feels right, one may want to repeat an I AM affirmation at this point, for instance, "I am choosing right now to release all past pain and to forgive myself and everyone in my life. All barriers to our full expression and enjoyment of life are dissolved now that we are *all* forgiven and forgiving."

APPLICATION OF THE INTERVENTION

The example I want to share comes from a marital and family therapy case and the not-too-uncommon "wound or betrayal" of infidelity. It represents a variation on the above guidelines to fit the unique situation. The client had suffered a betrayal by the two people he loved most in the world — his wife and his brother. Intellectually, he realized that to keep obsessing about the images he created inside his head of his wife and his brother together was not going to do anyone any good, but emotionally he was reduced to tears so often that it was impairing his capacity to work and to be present as a father to his children. He compared his inability to quit obsessing to trying to stop a "runaway horse" that was out of control.

I utilized the example of the out-of-control runaway horse to elicit from him any times in his own life when he had felt his life was out of his control, asking particularly for those times when he had done something that he would have given anything if he had not done. He related well to this and as we talked, he gave intellectual assent to the fact that this must have been how it was for his wife and brother—out of control and not being able to turn back.

To anchor this emotionally, I utilized a variation of the healing of the memories by asking the client to get into a relaxed state and then to imagine himself out for a peaceful horseback ride, just relaxing and enjoying the steady, comfortable rhythm of the horse as it walked along a path. Then, I asked him to imagine that suddenly, to his horror, the horse was getting out of control. I described to him his struggle to control the horse, knowing full well that he would never want to hurt someone he loved, but realizing that the horse is totally out of his control and the damage is done before he can do anything to prevent it.

The damage to the loved one was not "serious"; it did not even show. However, we all knew that it was there. I talked of the pain he felt at having been the intentional agent of pain to someone he loves, of his feelings of remorse, of the loss of trust that occurs when you wound a loved one, of the pain of having a loved one hurt you.

After a pause, I compared the runaway horse incident to what might have occurred with his brother and his wife. I invited him to picture them together just sharing and talking about their problems—perhaps even consoling each other—with no intention of it being anything more. I then asked him to imagine the horror and terror that developed in both of them as they realized their feelings had gotten out of control and they had gravely wounded someone they both loved dearly. I asked if he could feel their remorse and the helplessness of knowing that it was too late for them to prevent that hurt. I wondered aloud if he was able to tune into the shame and sorrow that was experienced by each of them as they had to confront and experience his pain.

The client's nonverbal reaction during the guided imagery helped me to keep in touch with his process. He cried and shook his head as if he was able to experience some of the same distressful feelings his brother and wife might have experienced. He recounted times when he, too, had set in motion forces that hurt someone he loved and the way he realized he couldn't undo the damage he had inadvertently caused.

To close the imagery, I suggested there was a universality of that kind of experience in every life. All of us could relate to having hurt someone we loved in ways that had not been our original intention. We have all thoughtlessly erred when in retrospect we desperately would have liked not to have erred. I expressed my belief about the inevitability of human frailty and of the humanness of "mistakes" and how we all have hoped for understanding and forgiveness at such times. I could see that the client had relaxed and that the intensity and grief seemed replaced by a calming effect. After a pause, I gently invited him to return to the room and share his response to the imagery experience.

The client verbalized that the imagery had helped him to gain a new sense of resolution and "relative peace" about the whole situation. It had helped him integrate at a new level of awareness the pain his wife and brother had suffered. He knew that they both loved him and he believed them and his own insides that they would never risk hurting him again. He also got in touch with the times that he had unintentionally hurt his wife and the mutual causation that had been part of her vulnerability. He was able to see his brother as the insecure, inexperienced person he was and to have compassion about his betrayal. He talked about his decision to focus on the years of love between them all, rather than on the one negative incident, and we worked out some images and affirmations he could utilize to accomplish that. We also anticipated ways he could reactivate his sense of commitment to forget/forgive the past and to go forward when, and if, he had any recurrence of negative or obsessive feelings.

OUTCOME

The client and his brother were able to begin rebuilding their once very close relationship. The wife and client were able to begin rebuilding their love and trust and to correct relationship problems that had built up between them over the years. The children and grandparents were very relieved to see an easing of the tension and conflict within the family system. The therapist resolved to trust her intuition more often and vowed to utilize imagery more confidently, when indicated, to help heal the memories that rob us all of peace of mind.

REFERENCES

Bradshaw, J. (1988). *Bradshaw on: The family*. Deerfield Beach, FL: Health Communications, Inc.

Branden, N. (1972). *Breaking free*. New York: Bantam Books.

Gawain, S. (1982). *Creative visualization*. New York: Bantam Books.

Genlin, E.T. (1978). *Focusing*. New York: Bantam Books.

Goulding, M.M., & Goulding, R.L. (1979). *Changing lives through redecision therapy*. New York: Brunner/Mazel.

Houston, J. (1988). Sacred psychology: An introduction to the nature of the quest. *New Realities*, March/April, 41-46.

Miller, A. (1981). *The drama of the gifted child*. New York: Basic Books.

Viorst, J. (1986). *Necessary losses*. New York: Simon and Schuster.

Burning the Affair:
A Ritual for Starting Over
and Recommitting

Robert A. Urlacher

THEORETICAL ORIENTATION

This intervention is most closely associated with the Milan systemic orientation of therapy (Selvini Palazzoli, Boscolo, Cecchin, & Prata, 1978; Tomm, 1984). The Milan systemic orientation believes that:

1. the mind is social: that is, problems are viewed as problems in interactions between people not within them;
2. a circular epistemology is most effective: the therapist should look for circular, rather than linear patterns. Linear (blaming) hypotheses are viewed as one piece of the whole circle; and
3. understanding and knowledge lies in the differences between things: for example, in therapy a Milan therapist would be interested in how a problem is different than it was five years ago or how it might be five years in the future. Two interventions often used by the Milan group are systemic reframing, where problem behaviors are given new meanings, and rituals, where the therapist asks the family members to perform certain behaviors that will hopefully create more clarity about the problem situation.

DESCRIPTION OF THE INTERVENTION

Couples who are brought into therapy after one member has had a sexual affair outside of the marriage are dealing with many questions about their relationship. Typical questions include, "Why did the affair occur?" "Is our marriage savable after something like this?" and "How can I forgive my spouse when he/she has hurt me so badly?" These questions need to be addressed, but at some point, the couple needs to make a choice about the future of their relationship and "put the affair behind them." Although this may sound like a natural outgrowth of discussing and dealing with questions such as the ones listed above, couples at times have a hard time "feeling different" about their spouses even though they have cognitively decided to "start over." This is where the "Burning the Affair" ritual has been helpful. In this ritual, both spouses are asked to think back on the affair.

Specifically, the couple is asked to write down three things on a piece of paper: (1) all the ways in which the affair was painful; (2) the ways in which the affair hurt the marriage; and (3) the things about the affair for which they are sorry. On another piece of paper they write down what they learned from the affair occurring in their marriage. The couple is then asked if they want to get rid of the painful aspects of the affair and start over with a renewed commitment to the marriage. They are also asked if they now have ways of learning what they learned from the affair in other, less harmful ways. If both agree, they make a statement to each other that they "are putting the affair behind them and are ready to start over." They then put their pieces of paper together and burn them over a waste basket, symbolizing the end of the control of the affair over their marriage.

INFORMATION NEEDED TO DETERMINE THAT THE INTERVENTION IS INDICATED

This intervention is indicated when the couple overtly state that they want to put the affair behind them but one of the spouses (usually the spouse who did not have the affair) is having a hard time not thinking about the affair or is allowing the affair to dictate his/her behavior (e.g., spying, suspicion). The ritual helps to punctuate the recommitment to the marriage for both partners in a symbolic manner. This allows both spouses to experience the ending of the affair in a new and different way than just saying that they want to forget about it. If one or both spouses indicate overtly or covertly that they still harbor intense anger and/or resentment, this is not a good time for this ritual. The therapist needs to assess and make a judgment as to whether a spouse's inability to "stop thinking about the affair" is a sign of unresolved anger that needs to be addressed or if it is an interactional pattern that is keeping the couple stuck in a dysfunctional pattern created by the pain of the affair.

EXAMPLE OF APPLICATION OF THE RITUAL

This intervention was used with a young couple where the wife had a brief affair and the husband brought them into therapy wondering whether the marriage had any hope of surviving. Both spouses wanted the marriage to continue, but the husband wanted a "Professional's opinion" about whether the marriage could last after something like this happening. After spending ten sessions discussing possible reasons for the affair, and helping both spouses to see their parts in the occurrence of the affair, they were asked to think about whether they were ready to put the affair behind them and start over. In the eleventh session, the couple said they were ready to try to put the affair in the past. They were each given a piece of paper and asked to reflect very deeply about the four questions listed above. After they answered all four questions, they were asked again to examine their lists and to "be sure" that they were ready to put these pains in the past. After receiving confirmation that this was the case, they made a statement to the other that they were going to start over and put the affair behind them. They then jointly burned their lists.

COUPLE'S RESPONSE TO THE INTERVENTION

This intervention occurred just before I had to leave town for two weeks. After returning, the couple canceled the next two scheduled sessions. After the second cancellation, I discussed over the phone the meaning of the cancellations and the couple said they felt they did not need to come anymore and that they felt they were doing fine on their own. Termination was completed over the phone.

REFERENCES

Selvini Palazzoli, M., Boscolo, L., Cecchin, G., & Prata, G. (1978). *Paradox and Counter paradox.* New York: Jason Arónson.

Tomm, K. (1984). One perspective on the Milan systemic approach: Part II. Description of session format, interviewing style, and interventions. *Journal of Marital and Family Therapy, 10,* 253-271.

44

A Strange Thought

Richard L. Graves

Dear Dr. Nelson:

I have had trouble deciding upon a "favorite" intervention for your book partly because I don't think so much in terms of interventions as simply responses to whatever family situation presents itself to me in my office on a particular day, at a particular hour.

After some thought, I have realized I tend to use a certain response, or preference, that has been both useful to families and freeing to me. I use this at an appropriate moment, which could be any time during a session, but there is a rhythm that one must be in "sync" with and so it is difficult to define the "appropriate moment." I think a therapeutic rhythm develops between therapist and family in much the same way as a canoeist develops a rhythm with white water in a river or a stand-up comic develops one with an audience or an artist develops one with a painting.

How I begin in my response is something like, "I have a strange thought" or, "This weird idea just popped into my head," followed by, "I could be wrong" or, "I'll just say this and then you can dismiss it if it's out in left field." Then I proceed to say whatever I think about the situation: about one person's feelings or about the interaction between two people in the family or about the family as a whole.

Author Note: I would like to acknowledge my indebtedness to both Carl Whitaker and Donald Williamson for their influence on this way of working in therapy.

There is no inherent theory for this type of intervention,* except that it makes conscious or overt what I think is unconscious or covert, without taking any kind of out-on-a-limb position. A family is free to disregard the statement if they think it is not helpful or if they are not ready to hear what was said. I am always amazed at what clients take away from a therapy session, so I think one can say whatever and hopefully some of it will be useful to them. Also, the remarkable part of this for me is the freedom to say what I think, which keeps me from being stuck with their garbage without any recourse but to swallow it. Again the issue of timing is very important and one has to be ready to accept the family's rejection of what was said and go on to something else.

One comment about the statement following my "preface." It's usually not heavy or terribly interpretive, but generally what strikes me at the moment. It can be in simple words or in more metaphorical language, depending again on the flow of the family/therapist unity. For example, I once said to an angry husband, "I've got this strange thought. This could be really way off, but I think there's a monster in you." And to his wife, I said, "And that's the reason you married him."

The one drawback to this technique occurred with a family I had seen for some time. After a while, whenever I started to say something, one of the kids would say, "We know. You could be wrong, but . . ." The good part of this was they started talking this way to each other, which gave everyone the freedom to speak his or her mind without fear of disapproval, a major theme in this family.

I hope this is useful to your book. It's been fun writing.

Sincerely,

Richard L. Graves

---

*Actually, this type of intervention is very much in the mode of the symbolic-experientialists, such as Carl Whitaker. — Eds.

45

Family Meetings:
A Tool for Developing Roles and Rules

Emily B. Visher
John S. Visher

In first marriage or nuclear families the patterns of the family develop slowly over an extended period of time—father may rake the leaves and mow the lawn, mother may take charge of the marketing and cooking, and the children set the table and wash the dishes. Everyone in the family knows what is expected and the consequences of not performing these routine chores are predictable. Other activities may also be routinely scheduled: Father drives the children to school in the morning and they ride the school bus home in the afternoon; weekends are devoted to Little League baseball or an occasional picnic at the beach or other outing.

Stepfamilies are different. When a stepfamily is born, the individuals come together with no shared history. Both adults may have been in charge of the marketing and cooking in their separate households, the children may have had no chores because they have been coming and going between their divorced parents' households, and weekends may have been devoted to awkward visits between children and adults who are trying to maintain parent/child ties and form new potential steprelationships. When the remarriage takes place, the individual members of the new stepfamily are now under one roof, often without a clear idea of who is going to take which responsibilities or how decisions will be made. There is little or no family loyalty or sense of belonging to the new family unit.

Frequently, stepfamilies are seen in therapy shortly after a remarriage when household patterns have not been established. At other times they are seen when the roles and rules are still amorphous and troublesome. We have found that in these situations, Dreikurs' concept of a "family council" or family meeting is an effective way of clarifying and establishing patterns of doing things in the household so as to bring the greatest satisfaction to family members (Dreikurs & Soltz, 1964). For individuals who do not have a long history together, it can be helpful to experience a family meeting in the presence of a therapist. The therapist can teach and model how it is done so that the family can experience working together to reach important decisions about the day to day tasks of living together, and secondarily how to begin working towards satisfactory family integration.

When it becomes appropriate, the therapist can introduce the family council idea in the following manner:

> I think it might be helpful for you to figure out what things are necessary to keep your household running and then decide who's going to do what. I wonder if one of the children would be willing to write down the list of things all of you think of?

Have paper and pencil ready to give to a volunteer. If no child volunteers ask a specific young person if he/she would be willing to write the list. It has been our experience that one child usually volunteers or will accept the task if asked by the therapist. If this does not happen, one of the adults can do it. If a child is not willing to be the recorder, we would be matter-of-fact and not introduce a discussion of what the non-participation of the children might mean. The reason for attempting to have a child write the list is to create a more even balance of power in the unit; giving a child this important task can help augment the power of the young people and make for more equality between the adults and the child or children.

When the group is satisfied with the list, the next step is for the therapist to ask them how they want to figure out who will take responsibility for each task. Frequently the adults volunteer to do certain tasks, especially those that might be too complicated for young children to perform. Then children follow the adult lead, often more readily than the adults expect. In one family, a 16-year-old said he would do all the marketing for the family. When asked why, he confessed that he would enjoy driving the car since he had just received his driver's license and, in addition, he liked knowing that he would be able to go to the refrigerator and find some drinks and food that he enjoyed. His family accepted his offer with a smile. If they had not, perhaps a discussion between the adults and the young man would have been necessary before proceeding. If some tasks are not chosen by anyone, there are ways to make them more desirable. For example, jobs can be traded every week or so, small sums can be paid for special work, or several persons in the family can work together to make the tasks go more easily.

Next comes the question of what the consequences would be if the assigned tasks are not completed in a satisfactory manner. Often the adults are surprised that the children suggest more stringent consequences than the adults would have suggested. At future family sessions, the group can discuss how things are going and make modifications as necessary.

The Bennett family illustrates the value of this intervention. Marsha and Keith had been married for eight months. Each had children from a previous marriage. Clara, 12, and Donald, 10, were Marsha's children, and Ellis, 15, was Keith's son. The children were with Marsha and Keith except for three weekends each month. The couple came for help because the tensions in the house were increasing rather than subsiding. The couple were first seen alone by the therapist and their description of the household suggested that chaos was the order of the day. Marsha and Keith appeared to have similar perceptions and to be working together as a team, but to have little sense of how to help their children or ease the tension in the household.

The children and adults came together for the next appointment. After drawing and discussing the genogram of the family, attention was focused on the resentments and unhappiness in the household. In the safe environment of the therapist's office, the group talked together about what changes were needed to improve their household functioning. With Clara recording the list, they outlined the necessary household chores. Marsha volunteered to do the shopping and cooking. Keith then agreed to vacuum the house each Saturday. The adults were amazed when 15-year-old Ellis said, "I think Dad and Marsha are doing too many dishes. I think we kids ought to do them." By the end of the session most items had been settled and during the next meeting it was decided that less desirable tasks were to be rotated on a two-week basis. When a chore was not done, the "guilty party" could not watch TV until the job was completed. At this point Ellis said, "This means Dad and Marsha, too," to which all agreed, the children with particular emphasis!

Over the next weeks, the tensions in the household diminished; the family began to have meetings of their own at home to resolve their difficulties. The couple reported that the family sessions were relatively smooth although the children did not always respond enthusiastically when one was scheduled. Eventually, although the meetings remained effective, when the adults called for a "family council," the children would take action to correct the problem so that the meeting would not have to be held. With clear expectations and ways to alleviate tension, the household functioning improved dramatically. The fact that the process was one involving everyone resulted in the family gaining more sense of connectedness and belonging to the family unit.

Group membership and a sense of belonging comes in large measure from shared positive experiences and memories and the security of knowing what to expect. By illustrating the value of family meetings within a therapy setting, stepfamilies can utilize the model at home. A direct result can be the clarification of roles and rules and the establishment of family patterns. An indirect result can be the connectedness and integration that comes from the process of working together and finding solutions to mutual difficulties.

REFERENCE

Dreikurs, R., & Soltz, V. (1964). *Children: The challenge*. New York: Hawthorn Books, Inc.

A Family Intervention:
Introducing Sex as a Subject

Barbara J. Lynch

Frequently the therapist is faced with a difficult situation when there are behavioral signs that a serious condition exists and at the same time there is a strong prohibition against speaking about it. The presence of an unspoken family secret casts a menacing shadow over the process of treatment. The family is pleading with the therapist to help them break the vow of silence while threatening with retaliation if the breach is actualized. Therefore, the goal of the intervention is to encourage the family to speak in ways that respect their anxieties and support their resistances. Nowhere is this more true than with sexual issues.

A technique that forces a family to talk about the secret in an acceptable manner has been highly effective. First, however, the therapist must break the silence by actually mentioning aloud that which has heretofore only been hinted. An example would be, "I've been trying to come up with some possible reasons why your daughter (son) has been behaving in the ways you describe. I have several possibilities, but I need your help to determine what exactly is going on. Once we know, we can make significant progress." Some family member usually asks the therapist to continue, which the therapist does by enumerating several options briefly: "There is evidence here that there could be some form of psychiatric problem or perhaps there is a genetic defect. Then the difficulty might be the result of some sexual trauma, or even an extreme behavioral problem. So I guess the list would be psychiatric, genetic, sexual, or behavioral." At this point, the therapist has the greatest likelihood of getting the family to begin to speak about sex by asking, "Which of those do you think it's least likely to be?" or better yet, because the question carries a powerfully subtle message, "Which could be eliminated?" Most families reply, "sex."

The therapist looks for agreement among family members and continues to model the idea that it is acceptable to talk about sex in the sessions. "Mr. X, what would you eliminate?" If he does not mention sex, the therapist should respond with, "So you don't agree with your wife that sex can be (should be, could be) eliminated. What evidence do you have that makes *you* think there might be a sexual root to this problem, or for that matter a genetic cause?" (or whatever else was stricken from the list).

Each age appropriate family member should be approached with the same question, which begins with summing up what the other members have said and, each time, mentioning sex, e.g., "Your parents (don't) agree that sex can be eliminated as the cause of the problem. What do you think?"

The typical child response, "I don't know" should be restated within the frame of the goal: "So you don't know whether sex can be left out as the possible reason for your family's problems." Particular attention should be awarded to the IP's reply and the nuances inherent in the response.

If the first family member to reply decides to leave sex on the list as a potential 'cause' of their difficulty, the therapist must introduce sex as a topic. Some possible responses are: "I'm curious, most people mention sex first. How did you happen to leave sex on the list of possibilities?" or "That leaves genetics, sex, and behavior as maybes. What can you eliminate next?"

An entire session devoted to making the talk about sex in the family an acceptable topic is valid in and of itself. The family is left with the thought that sex is associated with the problem and they may continue with a disclosure process at home and then at a subsequent session. However, some families are so anxious that this alone will not be sufficient to break through the denial. In that case the therapist must continue to forge ahead. "I was going over what we accomplished in our last session. We were looking for reasons why the problem exists. You all wanted to eliminate sex. But the more I look at this family, the less likely I am to see you as a family with genetic (psychiatric) disturbances. And there are some signs that some therapists might associate with sex. I'm not sure they're significant but I don't want to be too hasty right at this point."

If the family gets defensive and wants "proof," the therapist should be prepared with data and respond, "Well, there's promiscuity (isolation, etc.) which, when taken with (other behavioral signs), could lead some people to think there was a sexual trauma as a cause. I'm not sure that's so, I think we need to eliminate it completely before we go on. Then we can all be comfortable."

When someone hedges, e.g., "Aren't there other possibilities?" the therapist should respond, "Once we've eliminated these, we'll have to find others. These are only major reasons, there are others." The therapist can also comment on the process: "These are difficult issues to look at. I'm sure that most families would rather not think that these could be reasons for their problems."

There are several ways to use a team to heighten the intensity of this intervention. "The team thinks I was too hasty in arguing (agreeing) with you that sex could be eliminated." "The team totally disagrees with us, they think we're overlooking sex as a possibility." "The team is divided on the idea of how much sex plays a part in this family's problem." "The team believes that if sex were a possibility in this problem that there would be other symptoms that you haven't mentioned."

The intervention has as its goal making the covert overt; putting the problem into the realm of present reality; breaking the bonds of shame. The intervention falls into the broad category of heightening the intensity and reframing. As such it could be considered 'structural' (Minuchin & Fishman, 1974) in origin, although there are distinct overtones coming from both the strategic and the communication models of Haley (1976), Watzlawick, Weakland, & Fish (1974), and Madanes (1981).

REFERENCES

Minuchin, S., & Fishman, C. (1974). *Families and family therapy*. Cambridge, MA: Harvard University Press.
Haley, J. (1976). *Problem solving therapy*. New York: Harper.
Watzlawick, P., Weakland, J., & Fisch, R. (1974). *Change: Problem formation and problem resolution*. New York: W.W. Norton.
Madanes, C. (1981). *Strategic family therapy*. San Francisco: Jossey-Bass.

−47−

The Tell-It-Again Intervention

D. Ray Bardill

The husband of a marital pair I had been working with for about six months came for his therapy session in an extremely upset condition. His opening statements were, "I am going to divorce my wife. She is wrong in how she treats me. I can't live with her anymore. I am leaving her. The marriage is finished." When I asked him to tell me what had happened to make him decide to divorce his wife, he gave the following story:

I came home night before last on the verge of one of the greatest legislative successes of my career. I told my wife about a bill that was sure to pass in the state legislature the next day. It was a bill I had worked on for several years. It was sure to pass. Her response upset me. She seemed mildly interested in my success.

The next morning she announced that she was not going to work. She wanted me to take our daughter to nursery school on my way to the legislature. That was not too bad, but she did not once mention my bill. Can you believe that!

That morning, the bill was passed almost immediately. I was so excited. I called my wife to see if she could join me at the club for lunch. She said she had already made plans to meet a girlfriend for lunch. She was so insensitive to my feelings! She does not care for me! She is so wrong in her actions!

Early that afternoon, another one of my bills passed. I couldn't believe it! I again called my wife to ask her to join me and some friends for a celebration at a local pub. Can you believe it? She refused again. She had already picked up our daughter from nursery school. She said she had no one to take care of our daughter. She is not acting right in our relationship. That is not all! I asked her to go to a party with me that evening. She agreed to do so.

That evening when we stopped to drop our daughter at the sitter's, the sitter was sick. We could not leave our daughter with the sitter. I had to force my wife to go to the party anyway. She sat in a corner with our daughter all night. She did not show any enthusiasm about my success. I can't take it any longer! My wife is uncaring. She has no feelings for me. I am leaving.

When he concluded the story, I asked him to do something for me. I asked him to tell me again the just-described events of yesterday. I instructed him to tell me the story without making his wife wrong. He said nothing for a period of time. I again asked him to tell me what happened but without making his wife wrong. Finally, he said, in a very matter of fact delivery, "I got up, went to work, and came home yesterday." I smiled and in an "aw, shucks" delivery said to him that I had a little more in mind than that. It took him several times and most of the session to be able to tell me about the events of the previous day without making his wife wrong. When he finally told the story without making his wife wrong, tears came into his eyes and he said, "I came here today ready to divorce my wife; now I can't wait to get home and give my wife a big hug." It was one of those rare times when as a therapist you feel goose pimples. Why did the intervention work?

First, the tell-it-again intervention is a technique that enables the patient to verbalize a sequence of events from a perspective that differs from the one previously used to make meaning out of the event. In effect, it demonstrates that an event may be viewed from other perspectives. The possibility of an alternative way of exploring meaningful events is brought into awareness.

Second, in the case example, the right/wrong dynamic in marital situations had been given attention during previous therapy sessions. The patient had experienced me as a therapist who refused to deal in relationship rightness and wrongness. When the critical therapeutic moment came, the stage had been set to deal with one of their major relationship dynamics.

Third, in over 30 years as a therapist, I have never seen a marital case where the right/wrong dynamic was not a major factor. Human beings simply have a dreaded fear of being wrong, not being right. Basic to this therapy process is the therapist's ability to model an intention to deal with the right/wrong dynamic in a way that does not establish relationship rightness or wrongness. This means neither spouse is allowed to win or lose or be right or wrong in *relationship* issues.

Fourth, the tell-it-again intervention is useful in any situation where blame and right/wrong are major dynamics. The intervention is both simple and complicated. The patients are simply instructed to describe the situation without making anyone bad or wrong. The intervention is complex because the patients will have difficulty "telling-it-again" without blaming. Gentle persistence and non-blaming on the part of the therapist when the patients have difficulty following instructions is necessary.

The human inclination to find fault with, or blame, others is a powerful dynamic. In our society, we are taught from infancy that the rewards in life come from being right. For instance, when infants walk and talk at the "right time," we praise them. When our children bring home the "right" grades (As, of course), we as parents are pleased. On the other hand, being wrong is a matter of deficiency or shame. We punish people for being wrong. Being wrong becomes a threat to acceptable self-esteem. It is no wonder that we fear being wrong.

The tell-it-again intervention is directed to the relationship dynamics between and among people. Communications theorists long ago alerted clinicians to the difference between the relationship and content levels of a spoken message. Relationship considerations about right/wrong differ from the considerations that apply to the content level. For instance, content disagreements may be resolved by appeals to written sources such as encyclopedias and dictionaries. Relationship disagreements are more complex because they are founded in different perspectives or points of view. The resolution of relationship disagreements must take into account the human being's fear of being wrong.

Tell-it-again provides a gentle but forced frame of reference which posits the possibility of a point of view not based in content right/wrong dynamics. The domain of relationships is brought into focus. To put it another way, it has become clear that a spouse cannot constantly win or make the other spouse wrong on the content level without ultimately losing on the relationship level. The relationship will suffer. To put it still another way, human beings are not likely to become more loving and caring after being proven wrong. To win in marital relationship issues, one must empower one's spouse. Being right in content issues may well mean losing in relationship matters. Tell-it-again is a powerful intervention because it addresses one of the most fundamental dynamics at work in the domain of human relationships.

Family Therapy and Psychoeducation

Don Dinkmeyer, Jr.
Don Dinkmeyer, Sr.

Family therapists have not considered the psychoeducational process an important element in family therapy. However, most of the literature related to family therapy indicates that effective therapy is an educational process. Family change is based upon insight, information, and skills.

There is a long history of educational approaches through family therapy. Alfred Adler (1911) believed that most of the problems of parents and children were due to poor relationships. He believed the challenge was to teach the parents more effective ways of working with their children. As early as 1922, Adler organized the first child guidance center in Vienna. The center was received enthusiastically and expanded to 31 such centers across Vienna. Centers were primarily located in public schools and the emphasis was clearly educational. There was a large number of people in the audience when Adler worked with the family. The audience became part of the educational experience insofar as they learned from the ideas presented.

Rudolf Dreikurs (Dreikurs & Soltz, 1964), a student of Adler's, immigrated to Chicago. In 1939, he began a Family Education Unit at the Abraham Lincoln Center in Chicago. Dreikurs worked with the parents of the most difficult children in special afternoon sessions. These sessions were counseling sessions, open to the public.

Family Education Centers have continued to thrive in the Chicago area and across North America. A wide variety of books, booklets, and audio and video tapes have been developed to serve this population. Public demonstrations with an educational emphasis are a cornerstone of the Adlerian commitment to families.

RATIONALE FOR PSYCHOEDUCATION

Many parent-child relationships and family problems have a common thread. Parents often have no alternatives to their present behaviors. Education plays an effective part in the treatment of family problems. It creates ideas and alternatives for the families and builds more skilled behavior in the parents. As a result of this approach, problem solving in family situations is increased, and thereby, change is produced.

EDUCATION AND THERAPY

Therapists often think that education is very different from therapy. Educators work directly and didactically with parents and children, presenting information. Therapists, from their point of view, are involved in a different process and level of skill.

Therapy is not always clearly differentiated from education. Adlerians have considered therapy to be an educational process. They believe change occurs because the client has learned something about himself or herself and relationships and is choosing a different belief and behavior.

The therapist initiating work with a family must identify whether the need is primarily for education, therapy, or both. Often there are problems in the beliefs held by both parents and the children that indicate a need for therapy. For example, beliefs may include, "I am entitled to get my way"; "I am right"; or, "I have rights." At other times, the family may lack information on how to motivate, discipline, encourage, or enlist cooperation. Lack of information indicates a need for education. Therapy and education may not be mutually exclusive.

The therapist assesses skills the parents have for communicating effectively, using logical consequences, encouragement, holding family meetings, and other areas. When the therapist assesses the skill level of the parents, the appropriate role for psychoeducation is clarified. Supplying the family with a book or booklet that describes

the practices and relationships we recommend for parents acceler-
ates the family's progress.

PSYCHOEDUCATION WITHIN THE FORMAT OF FAMILY THERAPY

Psychoeducational materials can be used in family therapy. We
focus primarily upon the books and materials that we use, although
other materials and conceptual frameworks can apply. In our first
session with the family, a basic assessment of the family's communication skills, the family values, and other skill areas are essential.
We are particularly interested in determining such things as the ability of the parents to learn to:

1. identify the goals of the misbehavior;
2. encourage;
3. communicate through reflective listening;
4. communicate through "I" messages;
5. discipline effectively through logical consequences;
6. recognize discipline situations which require a variety of approaches; and
7. work within family meetings.

If psychoeducation is indicated, we then provide the family age-
appropriate educational materials. The approximate divisions are:
early childhood, child, and adolescent. We ask them to begin by
reading the first chapter between this session and the next week. In
the following sessions, we often spend about 10 to 12 minutes asking questions about the concepts and clarifying how some of the
ideas might be applied to the family. This is usually done with only
the parents present. We then begin to give very specific homework
that applies the concepts to their family. For example:

1. identify a goal of misbehavior in your children before the next
   session;
2. consider some ways to respond to that goal more actively and
   constructively; or
3. identify specific ways to encourage your child and do this in
   the ensuing weeks.

SUMMARY

Family therapy with an educational component provides an opportunity to expand the family therapy process. In contrast to dealing with the family only in the session, families have concrete "work" and concrete information beyond the therapist's office. Educational materials such as books and pamphlets and the discussion arising from the concepts in these materials stimulates rapid growth, the development of skills, and change.

We have found that awareness of the ideas and new methods often bring changes to the family within a few sessions. Parents' attitudes change in the process of reading and discussing; they begin to learn that they are part of the problem and stop blaming the child.

Most importantly, we have been able to reduce some of the stress and aggravation that is experienced by parents by teaching them ways to deal with dysfunctional behavior and misbehavior. We have helped parents to learn how to encourage and apply more logical consequences in discipline. Psychoeducation has considerable potential for family therapists. While it is often not part of the therapist's original training, it can supplement it, expand skills, and provide an additional tool for successful family therapy.

REFERENCES

Adler, A. (1911). *Understanding human nature*. London, England: George Allen & Unwin, Ltd.
Dreikurs, R. & Soltz, V. (1964). *Children: The challenge*. New York: Hawthorn.

49

Revisiting the Generations

Maxine Walton

I was trained by Ackerman Institute faculty. Consequently, my orientation is systemic and eclectic. This intervention reflects strategic, Bowen, and Satir family therapy models, among others. Family systems' theoretical base supports assisting individuals in assuming responsibility for themselves relative to their behavior, feelings, and interaction within the system. Inasmuch as family of origin generational patterns and messages impact upon what is going on within the nuclear system and determines family rules, roles, and interactions, exploration of the latter is required with many troubled families. I use whatever interaction is indicated in helping families resolve their issues.

I work with some black families who are in the Juvenile Court System. Their children have been removed or are at risk of being removed because of neglect and/or abuse. They become angry and frightened and view all larger systems as powerful, threatening, and hostile. Therefore, they become obstinate and oppositional in their interaction with representatives of the system. It may be their only way of establishing a position of control over their lives.

It is imperative to remove these families from a powerless position by helping them revisit their black family generational survival shells, coaching them to use the larger system positively, thereby insuring realistic control of their life. Structural/strategic methods of intervention were used in the case of a 38-year-old black man, Mr. M, who had been reared in a dysfunctional system. He had made gains toward living the "good life." His daughter had been born out of wedlock, although he had assumed responsibility for her since birth. When her mother did not want her, Mr. M became her primary parent. She was placed in foster care because of physical abuse when Mr. M struck her with a broom handle, which was reported by the school. Mr. M and his daughter were seen conjointly and with her mother and Mr. M's sister who acted as a surrogate mother in family therapy sessions.

Mr. M was validated for his commitment and love for his daughter. Parenting shells were reinforced as we revisited his family of origin and explored alternatives to the physical abuse he had experienced as a child. Modeling of voice intonations used in relating to people he had loved and freeing his daughter to talk about needing to be hugged and wanting to spend quality time with him impacted positively on their relationship.

However, when it was necessary for Mr. M to follow through on a court-ordered procedure, he became oppositional and refused to do so. The court worker appealed to me to help him move from his stuck position. I confronted Mr. M with the consequences of his behavior and we revisited the black generation legacy of using the system even when pride was sacrificed in order to accomplish goals of survival and progress. We explored the alternatives of being self-defeating and losing custody of his daughter or cooperating with the system and accomplishing his goal of the return of his daughter. Mr. M left the session saying he would "think about it."

The court worker reported that Mr. M's attitude toward the system was pleasant and cooperative. At time of closure, Mr. M and his daughter were reunited.

50

The Family Regulator of Change Reframe

David Lawson

In changing a family's frame of a problem or reframing its presenting concern, the perceptual, emotional, and conceptual scheme for the problem is given a different meaning (Watzlawick, Weakland, & Fisch, 1974). The cognitive frame that gives meaning to a particular sequence of organized family behaviors is altered, making possible a different interpretation of the problem and, in turn, often precipitating new solution perceptions and behaviors (de Shazer, 1982).

Based largely on Fisch et al.'s (1982) general intervention of "going slow" and Bateson's (1979) concept of multiple communication, I have found "the family regulator of change" is a useful reframe for so-called oppositional and uncooperative family members. Applying this reframe to a family member's problem behavior places the behavior in a more benevolent frame of reference for the family. The family's interpretation of the member's uncooperative behavior can be expanded to include the possibility that his or her behavior also acts to protect the integrity of the family change process by helping the family maintain a slow, gradual, but lasting change rate. Consequently, if the family accepts this frame, the typical urgency with which they present their problem is lessened and a concomitant reduction in the intensity of their problem-maintaining efforts can occur.

The family's usual linear view, which often leads to blaming a particular member for the problem, is implicitly challenged. An alternative frame which includes the possibility of noble intentions (Stanton, Todd, & Associates, 1982) of the member's behavior can provide the family with a sense of mutuality as opposed to opposition. Additionally, the therapist presents simultaneous messages of change and no change to match the family's double view of change (Bateson, 1979). With the problem family member being viewed as functioning as the regulator of family change and thus a protector of family stability, that family member can be appreciated for his or her sensitivity to and regulation of the optimal change rate for the family.

I have found that the regulator reframe generally seems most effective with family problems in which one party moves slowly if at all toward change while another party moves or desires to move more rapidly and persistently toward change. I have had less success with this reframe when all parties are moving at the same or a similar change rate.

CASE EXAMPLE

In the following case example, the family was initially seen in therapy because the 15-year-old daughter (Theresa) had run away from home after her parents denied her request to attend a social event as a result of a single occurrence of excessive drinking with her friends. After addressing the drinking behavior and running away, it became apparent that the parents were most concerned about Theresa's uncooperative behavior and her often defiant refusal to comply with their stated demands. Theresa agreed with her parents' report saying that she "just didn't want to cooperate" and was not planning on cooperating "in the near future." The parents stated that this had been Theresa's characteristic manner of responding for about two years. In the second session, which included Theresa and her parents, the "family regulator of change" reframe was presented as follows:

> You've shared with me all the different things you have done to get things moving and especially for you, Mr. and Mrs. Johns, in your frustration in getting Theresa to cooperate with you. It's particularly noteworthy how persistent Theresa seems to be in maintaining her position of slow or little change in situations where Mom and Dad have a definite idea as to what Theresa needs to do. (The parents agree that their daughter is indeed persistent and seems to dig her heels in when asked to do something.) Mr. and Mrs. Johns, perhaps Theresa

is attempting to communicate something or do something for the family, maybe at another level of awareness which she's not in touch with just yet. (The parents again agree that Theresa may be trying to say something to them but they're not sure what it is.) I have seen patterns like this before and I'm not sure if it fits this family, but if I may I'd like to share a hunch with you. (The parents want to hear my hunch.) It may sound a little strange to you, but through my years of working with families, I've found that someone in the family seems to volunteer to watch, Theresa, and make sure that the family doesn't change too fast. Sometimes, when the family is moving and changing faster than what a family member or members can adjust to, this member will do something to slow that change down some, you know like your (to Theresa) cautiousness in responding too quickly to the requests of your parents. A lot of this is an unconscious thing we're not even aware of. It seems to be a natural, almost automatic thing that families do. I could be wrong, Theresa, but it seems that you may be functioning as kind of regulator of family change (Theresa appears uninterested but her parents listen attentively.) Each family seems to have their own unique rate of change and when that rate speeds up too much, the family has a hard time comfortably maintaining the change for any length of time. (Mother and father verbally and nonverbally agreed and stated this had been their experience in several situations.) People often need time to slow way down (pause) and even stop (pause), in order to consolidate their gains before they change any more. (Mother and father again agreed, stating that going slow and steady seemed to make sense.) I'll count on you (to Theresa) to continue helping the family maintain a slow, gradual, and firm change like you've been doing. You might need to regulate a little firmer sometimes more than other times, maybe even stop changing altogether, but you'll know when and how.

After presenting the regulator reframe, it was suggested that the family think about what was discussed in the session and not to make any changes in their behavior toward one another, i.e., Theresa's uncooperativeness with her parents and the parents' maintaining their current rule structure. Theresa appeared unaffected by the reframe or the assignment. A session was then scheduled for two weeks later. In the next session the parents reported that Theresa was still uncooperative and oppositional, but the duration and frequency of her behavior had decreased significantly. I expressed cautious optimism and suggested that they attend to the ebb and flow of any change, large or small, during the following week. The parents were asked to consistently stick with the rules they had established for Theresa and to request rather than demand her cooperation. For the next three sessions, assignments revolved around requests that Theresa vary the rate of change in the family by changing the duration and frequency of her oppositional behavior and to observe the effects on the family. Emphasis was placed on the necessity for Theresa to maintain her position as the regulator of family change. Regardless of my requests to either increase or decrease her strategies for regulating the family's rate of change, her oppositional behavior steadily decreased from session to session. The family members cooperated with my requests and continued in therapy for five more sessions (for a total of ten sessions) over the next three months. At the end of therapy, the family reported more cooperative behaviors by all family members with occasional relapses of progressively shorter durations. With the regulator reframe presented early in the therapy process, I was able to return to it periodically when the inevitable disagreements arose between Theresa and her parents and when progress had been made and a restraining tack was deemed appropriate.

REFERENCES

Bateson, G. (1979). *Mind in nature: A necessary unity.* New York: E.P. Dutton.

de Shazer, S. (1982). *Patterns of brief family therapy: An ecosystemic approach.* New York: Guilford Press.

Fisch, R., Weakland, J., & Segal, L. (1982). *The tactics of change.* San Francisco: Jossey-Bass.

Stanton, D., Todd, M., & Associates. (1982). *The family therapy of drug abuse.* New York: Guilford Press.

Watzlawick, P., Weakland, J., & Fisch, R. (1974). *Change: Principles of problem formation and problem resolution.* New York: Norton.

— 51 —

A Story

Amith BenDavid

Storytelling is a very powerful technique that transcends specific therapy schools. Its power comes in part because of the special place we all give and remember of storytelling in our own childhood. It can be seen as a reframe and thus be thought of as effecting an indirect change, thus pertaining to a strategic framework. It can be seen as having a profound effect and helping clients to "experience" through identification something different, thus pertaining to a symbolic-experiential theoretical framework.

Storytelling is most suitable for clients who are able to use imagination and language in an inventive way. There is no case I can think of that storytelling would be contraindicated, although the content of the story chosen has to be very carefully thought out. When the goal of the intervention is to reframe the behavior in a different framework and with a new meaning, the therapist has to be careful to create a story that would be close enough so that the meaning does not fall into a different logical category. When the goal of the intervention is to facilitate change through experiencing a deep insight emotion, the content has to be rich, powerful, and emotionally touching. The reading of the story, the intonation, and the emotions depicted by the therapist contribute to the final effect of the intervention as well.

The following story is designed to help a person who has been through divorce to let go of the past and the persons of the past. This intervention is suitable for any situation when there is a termination of a love relationship because of separation, death, divorce, etc. The important part of this intervention is to convey the sense that the client saw him/herself in a dyadic situation previously, with somebody else, but now she/he is alone. The important message is how much energy, strength, and enthusiasm can result from such a development in the client's life. The story goes like this:

> Once upon a time, deep in the heart of a quiet, dark forest, stood a tree. And in one of its uppermost branches there hung a curious object. It resembled a little brown silken pouch, and it hung on the underside of a high branch deep in the quiet, dark forest. No, wait, it isn't clear whether there were one or two pouches. Wait, yes there were two pouches that hung there through a long, long winter. All through the winter, the creatures inside the pouches kept growing, and come the spring, one of the pouches disappeared. The body in the other pouch, though sad and lonely, kept growing and growing until one spring day, it had grown so big that the pouch gently began to tear.
>
> The little creature stirred and felt its new space, and then gradually pushed its head outside the pouch, and it suddenly saw that the other pouch was not there. The little creature was torn between the wish to return to the pouch and wait for the other creature to return, and a bright shape it saw just ahead. Lured by the shining, beautiful color, the little creature cautiously crept forward inch by inch. At last it moved right into the golden shape. As the warmth spread over its body, it felt energy beginning to surge. Steadily it began to feel its strength and it stood up ever straighter, lifting its head. Its heart began to swell with a feeling almost like love, almost like power, almost like strength, almost like joy.
>
> As it grew warmer and warmer in the golden shape that surrounded it, it began to unfold from its body a wonderful, wonderful pair of translucent wings that kept spreading wider and wider. As the wings became more powerful, they began to beat the air until, with a surging leap into space, the creature flew higher and higher . . . free, beautiful, searching its way into the world.

52

Beginner's Luck:
A First Fortunate Family Encounter

Julia Halevy

Attempting to choose a favorite intervention among the range from, "I wish I hadn't done THAT" to, "Oh my, it really does work" is a rather complex task. While I believe we all tend to learn much more from our failures, my very first, extremely serendipitous case represents the loveliest of my memories as a therapist and sealed my commitment to the family therapy field.

My first intervention took place in a rather strange setting: in 1979 I was participating in a family therapy training program while working as a roving, hit (and miss) psychologist in a series of middle schools in the Province of Pistoia, Italy. My job, essentially, was to make a place for myself in these schools. I was, like most new practitioners, excited, cocky, scared, and foolish. But I put up a good front and acted as if I knew what I was doing, which turned out to be a good idea in that particular context.

I had constructed my role through the political networks of teachers by establishing myself in the faculty lounges and talking to teachers on their breaks about what I could offer them. If they found themselves experiencing difficulties with a class or with a specific student, I asked them to invite me into the classroom, introduce me as a colleague, and allow me to sit in the back of the room and observe. Following my observation, I met with the teacher again to discuss what I had seen and to go over possible alternative interventions. If it appeared that I might intervene directly with a child, I called the parents, met with them, discussed my observations, and asked permission to see the child. While psychotherapy was not yet generally popular in Italy, I found teachers and parents were delighted to utilize my resources, such as they were.

During one of my visits to the teacher's lounge in a school in Montecatini (home of the famous spas), an Italian teacher came to talk to me about a problem she felt was quite unusual. She had a student in the seventh grade who was not a behavioral problem, except that he never talked and he could neither read nor write with any semblance of clarity. In Italy, in order to be admitted to the middle school, children pass a State examination at the end of the fifth grade; therefore, there was quite a bit of mystery surrounding the process by which Marco had managed to get this far in school with so few skills. When I observed Marco's behavior in class, I noted a silent, morose, average-sized (if such a person exists) seventh-grader who stared incessantly at the ground, elbow on thigh, chin and mouth in hand, rather like Rodin's "Thinker." He seemed quite sad and isolated.

When Marco's mother arrived to talk to me, she seemed quite pleased that the school had taken an interest in him. She informed me that Marco's father was extremely critical of him, and that the father thought the world of Marco's younger sister, a bright, popular, attractive fifth-grader. Because Debora, who was a child-care worker at a spa, focused so much of her presentation on Marco's father, it occurred to me the problem was most likely systemic. I asked her if she thought it would be useful for me to see the whole family and if she thought her husband would come to therapy. She felt positive that this would be the best course for her family and promptly arranged it.

The family, Debora, in her mid-thirties, Alberto, in his early forties, Marco, 12, and Suzanna, 10, arrived at my office in Pistoia the following week. I saw this family for four two-hour sessions and I have practiced longer family sessions ever since. I also discovered that families are wonderful teachers and this family was the ideal training ground in a systems perspective. It converted me hook, line, and sinker.

Carefully, during the first session, I talked with each of the family members, finding ways to join with them individually, to establish their boundaries within the session. Debora was the most animated; she seemed to enjoy my position of power, despite the obvious handicap of my gender. Debora was quite involved with Marco. She looked through his papers when he came home from school, cleaned up his room for him, and generally cared for him as if he were quite a bit younger than twelve. I alluded to my experience of parenting my own three children and was able, over the sessions, to suggest some different ways of dealing with specific issues. She appeared to feel supported and strengthened.

The second lesson that I learned quickly through this case had to do with issues of gender and power. Because my supervisor had warned me to be careful not to lose the father and that positive outcome was unlikely without him (at the time I was too inexperienced to understand that this was a sexist view), I felt wary of Alberto. He presented himself as an unquestioned and unquestionable dictator, doling out praise to his daughter and shoveling out criticism toward his wife and son. I found myself bristling at his lack of consideration for these two and wondered what was keeping him locked into his rigid stance. Feeling daring and finding that Alberto seemed to enjoy talking during the sessions, I did some probing sorts of confrontation about his treatment of others in the family. While he did not change his position, he didn't seem to mind my pushing, and I hypothesized that his commitment to the family was really quite strong. I learned that it was not only unnecessary, but actually insulting to assume that the male member of the family should need coddling to stay in therapy. Later in therapy with this family, I also learned that supporting Debora in expressing her own needs and in establishing limits was vital to the positive outcome, and that confronting Alberto as clearly as I had confronted Debora established a rule of parity that the couple could carry on outside of the sessions.

My training at the time was principally structural, with some strategic thrown in for Italian flair. In an attempt to experiment with changing the rigid structure (father-daughter coalition against mother-son), my first intervention was to prescribe that the mother and daughter find some enjoyable activity to share and that the father and son do the same. We discussed the specifics of the tasks and times for these to be accomplished during the last part of the session and scheduled a second session for the following week.

The next week, during the car ride on the Autostrada from Florence to Montecatini, I listened to the previous session, which I had taped. There are enormous advantages to walking into a session having just heard the discussion of the week before. I was already immersed in the family's issues and could map out some directions to explore.

The family, of course, had not followed my prescription. The parents were too busy; the children really were not interested. It just didn't fit. Debora complained a little more forcefully about the way Alberto treated her. Alberto was willing to talk a bit about his work and the pressure he felt in supporting the family. Debora continued to protect Marco and Alberto continued to hold Suzanna up as an example of perfection. His eyes glowed with joy when he spoke of her. Suzanna turned out to be a truly lovely child; she did not appear to use her advantage as the one who is best loved by the most powerful member of the family to make Marco feel worse. There seemed to be a distance between the two children, but I did not see hostility.

Having failed with the first prescription, I decided to take structural change in small steps. I asked the parents to leave the room and instructed the two children to carry out an assignment for me. My purpose was to establish better boundaries between the sibling and parental subsystems and to provide space for an alliance between brother and sister with the hope of then continuing with some couple's work with the parents alone. The prescription did have a paradoxical twist to it, and I had quite a good time delivering the task to the children.

I asked Marco to write three complete sentences, each containing just one error. Each sentence had to be different from the others and each mistake had to be a new one. I said that because I thought this would be very difficult for him, Marco should ask Suzanna to help him. I instructed the pair to close the door during their work on this task and not to tell their parents what the task was. While they were

certainly surprised by this, the children appeared thoroughly delighted. When I called the parents in, I told them I had given the
children some work to do and had instructed them not to disclose
the task. I asked the parents not to push the children to tell them
what they were doing and that we would see the results at the next
session.

The following week, the children arrived full of energy. After I
explained the children's assignment to the parents, Suzanna and
Marco showed me a piece of paper with three complete sentences,
each containing one mistake. They talked about how much fun it
was to do such a "silly" assignment and seemed to have enjoyed
keeping the secret from their parents. Marco had needed little actual
help from Suzanna; she had merely checked his work and she was
very proud of him. The children sat next to each other for the first
time since we had begun to see each other.

The new alliance between Marco and Suzanna must have created
some systemic discomfort because, quite quickly, the parents began
to fill the session with some mutual recriminations and Marco slunk
back into a passive stance. He took a piece of paper out of a notebook and began to fold it. I continued to listen to the parents and to
ask them questions while I watched Marco out of the corner of my
eye. He was creating intricate figures, animals and birds, one after
another—quickly, intently, as if he were a master.

Alberto was sitting on one side of Marco. I could see he was
getting impatient with the session; he regarded the children's assignment as useless and was tired of arguing with Debora. Marco
was holding a piece of paper thoughtfully when Alberto waved his
hand in front of him shouting, "You see? He's good for nothing.
All he does is fold paper into these stupid objects!" I continued to
talk to the parents as if nothing had happened, having secretly
wanted to become an Origami master in my own school days, but I
was shocked that Alberto did not see the wonder of what Marco was
doing. So while we continued to talk, I tore a piece of paper out of
my notebook and graciously made a square out of it. I handed the
paper to Alberto and suggested he try to make something too, and
nonchalantly continued our conversation which, by now, was simply background music to me. Debora filled in Alberto's silence as

he struggled with the paper. He folded and turned and unfolded and turned and crumpled and uncrumpled and became quite red in the face. After several minutes, Alberto shoved the piece of paper at Marco and said, "See? Your father is good for nothing. I can't even fold a piece of paper!"

Alberto was close to tears; he began to talk about his fear of failure, his fear that his son would be a failure, his feelings of having failed his parents. I could see Debora warming to this side of him; she began to comfort him, to tell him how much she appreciated his efforts, how much she respected him. He reciprocated by expressing his appreciation for her hard work both at the spa and within the family.

A few days later, Marco's teacher came up to me in the lounge and told me all the teachers wanted to know how I had taught Marco to read and write in such a short amount of time. He had been completing assignments quite competently, as if he had been doing so for years. I told her I really hadn't taught him anything about writing at all, but that I hoped things would be better for him and his family.

At the final session, Marco's family was quite relaxed and full of plans for everyone. The parents were spending more time with each other and less with the children. Marco was feeling more confident about school; he and Suzanna were enjoying each other's company and support. A month or two later, I received a thank-you card and some embroidered placemats from the parents. I called to thank them and learned that Marco was still doing well in school and the parents were still feeling good about each other.

Before I left Italy in 1981, I called the family's home. Marco reported that his father had high hopes for Marco's future and was planning private school for him. He said the whole family was fine. I sent my regards to the rest of the family.

While I have managed to work well with other families over the years, I have never experienced such joy (and quite a bit of pride) as I did following this intervention. This case was crucial to my development as a professional because I began to believe that I could actually become an effective therapist despite the list of my own shortcomings that I carried around with me. I learned that miracles do happen and that systems miracles are possible. I learned that men did not need humoring and cajoling to be involved and caring husbands and parents. I learned that it was possible to relieve the symptom rapidly by calling the family together and by not seeing the child alone. I learned to take risks, to follow my instincts and to say what I believed. I learned that I would need to invent therapy as I went along and to attempt to be my creative best at all times, no matter how much I think I to know. I learned not to be afraid to confront, and I learned to accept myself as a role model for women who seek to come into therapy with me. I am grateful to Marco and his family; I often wonder about them and I wish them the very best. I hope I will never forget my experience with them or the sense of wonder it left me with.

53

Defining Conflict as a Demonstration of the Family Problem

Don D. Rosenberg

For many reasons, the therapist needs to decide when to encourage and when to discourage open conflict and needs to control its process. When conflictual families show disagreement, they often end up feeling powerless. In some situations, as in spouse-battering, arguing may re-traumatize or frighten the family. Sometimes, uncontrolled conflict leads to members' leaving treatment. The therapist often feels ineffective. Further, permitting conflict to escalate in the session may tacitly condone or reinforce it. Lastly, it promotes a non-rational, non-observing mode of behavior that is not oriented towards change.

Consider the intent of clients who have a full-blown argument in front of their new therapist. While there are some few people who genuinely lose control, most clients do not. Each family member may mean to *show the therapist* his or her viewpoint, why he or she is right and the others are wrong, what it is really like. They do this in their systematic way. For them, that is an appropriate role to play in therapy. In part it is self-serving, in part thespian, in part a sample of the system.

It can also be positive. It is a help-seeking message to the therapist, saying, "See what I mean. Isn't it awful? Do something about this." If the client is taking the therapist into account and is trying to affect his or her observations, that becomes something positive to recognize and to shape. Realizing this gives the therapist a class of simple techniques.

POSTPONE DEMONSTRATION OF THE PROBLEM

While an enactment of the system is useful, for the reasons discussed above, out-and-out conflict probably is not. To block argumentative, unproductive interactions in the first session, the therapist can say, "I appreciate that you need to demonstrate your argument for me now. But I really need to get this background information so I can help you. I'd like you to save your demonstration for next session." This not only helps the therapist be in charge, it defines conflict as controlled while giving the family an opportunity to cooperate. Setting aside a time for a "demonstration" in effect mitigates the conflict.

BE GRATEFUL FOR DEMONSTRATIONS

A second variation is to thank the clients for "demonstrating" their pattern. For example, "Thanks for demonstrating that argument for me. Now I know what you are up against, so we can look at how you can change it." This redefines the argument as having a therapeutic purpose.

THANK THE CLIENT FOR SHARING

A third variation is useful for dealing with painful emotion. In this case the therapist accepts the client's deep feelings, saying "I'm glad you shared this with me. Now I know how deeply you feel, how deep is your reaction. I did not realize it before. I'm glad you have been able to lay this all out for us to understand and use to help you."

BE GRATEFUL FOR A VIEWPOINT

Clients who present their position strenuously and rigidly often seem provocative. It would be more helpful to accept this behavior rather than to fight it, saying, "I want to thank you for your demonstration of just where you stand. You have done well to show me YOUR way of understanding what's going on, your point-of-view, so I can see how important it is to you. So you'll probably understand why I need to get everyone else's unique way of understanding it too.''

SAMPLE

Sally was an angry, dramatic woman with a tendency to blame her husband, Phil, for all her dissatisfactions. She presented herself as a highly responsible woman, but Phil as a reckless, debt-ridden man. Phil was a recovering drug abuser. Phil presented himself as a reserved, thoughtful man. Both had good jobs, but Sally claimed her money ran the household and Phil's seemed unaccounted for. Their pattern was for Sally to criticize Phil and praise herself. Phil became defensive and explained himself or counterattacked. Sally became more animated, furious, even histrionic, in her criticism. Then Phil became more defensive. They threw out a variety of past hurts and argued about which one perceived events correctly. Without a means of resolution, their argument permitted limited possible solutions, namely, separations or long silent periods.

The first time through, they enacted their pattern, even beginning with a quarrel in the waiting room, until the therapist asked some historical questions. Later, when he sensed they were cuing one another to re-escalate, the therapist said, "Excuse me. I would like to get through this history and get to know you. So I'd like you to stop this demonstration of the argument now. Save the demonstration for the start of our next meeting so we can really take the time to understand it." They both agreed. The rest of the session, they stayed in an informative and more problem-solving mode.

The intense argument returned in the fourth session. Instead of experiencing this session as a setback, the therapist thanked them for demonstrating the pattern. "Now I know," he said, "just how intensely you both can feel about this. Now I want to take the time to understand how each of you feels in depth." This interrupted the argument and set the stage for teaching them to listen in a less judgmental, less defensive way while the therapist probed each spouse's feelings.

This class of interventions, a kind of relabel or paradox, has proven useful with most conflict situations. The first sample ("Postpone the demonstration") should be avoided when narcissistic vulnerability is very intense and the request to delay the demonstration may be seen as rejecting. The third sample ("Thank the client for sharing") is useful in borderline conditions and is a useful fallback, generic intervention. One additional note: certainly there are other families whose issues are kept below the surface and for them conflict needs to be made explicit. Their over-control needs to be interrupted. This can be done in a similar way, as in, "I'm glad you showed me how important it is to keep a lid on this. That shows us how careful we need to be to bring out and share your feelings."

54

Sculpting Progress and Change

Martha Gonzalez Marquez

Evaluating progress and change in family therapy is essential for the successful treatment of families. In some fashion, a therapist must be cognizant of a family's current status regarding the attainment of their desired outcome. It is often reinforced to therapists that a periodic "check-in" with clients regarding their goal attainment is necessary to confirm that the appropriate direction is being followed. Although paper and pencil techniques have been developed to measure goal attainment, they can be expensive as well as time consuming. Often this may require pre- and post-tests, which may not be economically or situationally feasible. Instant feedback in the form of dialogue may be insufficient and inaccurate, however. Nevertheless, monitoring progress and change is imperative for both the clients and the therapist.

An experiential sculpting exercise can be used to assess progress with few restrictions. Indeed, the process of change in therapy can be portrayed in a session through "spatial analogies" (Piercy, Sprenkle, & Associates, 1986). The therapist begins by showing the family an imaginary line that begins at the wall opposite the door to the therapy room. The therapist explains that the line continues towards the door and ends "somewhere outside" the door. Then the therapist stands at the beginning of the line and claims that this was where the family was at the beginning of therapy and walks along the line towards the door. As the therapist nears the door, s/he explains to the family that within this area is where the family would like to be by the end of therapy.

Each member of the family is asked to find a place on the line where they believe they are currently in therapy in terms of progress. In essence, the therapist is asking the family, "How much change do each of you feel has taken place?" The therapist can then ask where along the line each would like to be. A processing of the positions that members have taken on the line is vital. Individuals can be asked some of the following questions:

- Were you aware of others' perspectives on progress?
- How do you feel seeing where other members are?
- Where did you think others actually were?
- Where would you like to see each member?
- How long do you think it will take to get to your desired place?
- Where do you feel you are "stuck"?

The exercise, done in this fashion, assumes that no regression has occurred. The wall signifying the beginning of therapy cannot be moved backwards. It also gives each member of the family the opportunity to express their feelings of progress or stagnation to the other members. An exercise such as this one invites the concept of differences within the family system (Satir, 1983). It will be evident that change may occur for individuals within a family at different rates and at varying degrees. It may be illuminating for families as well as therapists to observe these differences.

This exercise also invites movement to take place. The symbolic representation of progress and change in an active sculpting exercise can stimulate the family's desire to move in their treatment. This exercise can also serve as a source of reference during the remainder of treatment. Finally, by vaguely indicating to the family that the end of the line is somewhere beyond the door, the therapist reinforces the concept that change can occur and progress can be made both outside of therapy and after therapy.

Since the purpose of this exercise is the assessment of progress and change, it can be used with a wide variety of presenting problems. Regardless of the presenting problem, it is important to process thoroughly the meaning and the affective component behind each family members' position on the line. This exercise, if done properly, is rich with information that can be used throughout the remainder of treatment.

A typical initial response to this sculpting exercise is laughter. Clients enjoy the opportunity to express themselves in a different manner. Some clients claim they appreciate the "creativity" aspect of the sculpt. The most common individual response encountered is surprise at where other members chose to stand on the line. Some comment that they were unaware of the proximity between members of the family. In general, families claim to have gained a new perspective concerning their progress with the use of this exercise.

REFERENCES

Piercy, F., Sprenkle, D., & Associates. (1986). *Family therapy sourcebook*. New York: The Guilford Press.

Satir, V. (1983). *Conjoint family therapy*. (3rd ed.). Palo Alto, CA: Science and Behavior Books, Inc.

55

The Turtle Who Was Afraid He Could

Tammy Mitten

DESCRIPTION OF THEORY

The following intervention is a right brain approach designed as a means of communicating with the symbolic world of couples who are experiencing an emotional impasse in their relationship. The intervention has been used within the framework of symbolic-experiential therapy (Whitaker & Keith, 1981). Symbols are embedded in memory during childhood and are formed as a result of one's experiences within his/her family of origin. Although symbols may be resistant to change, healthy families are open to new experiences and information that often results in symbols being altered. In comparison, an unhealthy family is not open to new experiences and information; thus, symbols frequently become fixed and rigid, inhibiting growth. The primary goal of symbolic-experiential therapy is to integrate the world of symbol and the world of experience (Connell, Garfield, & Whitaker, 1990).

The following story may be effective with couples who are experiencing an emotional impasse in their relationship, in which the distancer-pursuer pattern is identified. The story may be particularly useful with couples who are resistant to treatment or with couples who tend to intellectualize as a primary defense. Stories cannot be analyzed by the left brain. This makes it possible for the therapist to communicate with the right hemisphere of the couple, thus bypassing resistance.

CONTRAINDICATIONS

The intervention may not be effective with couples in which one or both are cognitively limited. Clients who have extreme difficulty tolerating ambiguity and are panicked by spontaneous feelings may also not respond well to the intervention. Prior to telling stories in therapy, it is important for the therapist to establish a good relationship with clients so that he/she is not perceived to be using stories as a means of manipulation. Therefore, it may not be a good idea to · use such an intervention during the first or second interview.

CASE EXAMPLE

This story was told to a couple during the fourth session of treatment, with the goal of providing an implicit message regarding how the couple might make necessary changes in the relationship. The couple requested services in order to deal with marital problems. Sandy complained that Greg was not meeting her emotional needs. Greg complained that Sandy was "too demanding." Greg believed that he was not capable of "loving someone." Greg's father divorced his mother when Greg was 13 years old. After the divorce, Greg had no further contact with his father. Greg described his father as a "very distant man."

Greg's mother remarried shortly after the divorce. She married a man 15 years older than she was. Greg got along well with his stepfather; they had many common interests. However, Greg was somewhat uncomfortable with the relationship because he felt that his stepfather spent more time with Greg than he did with his wife. Greg has one older brother. Greg described himself as being extremely rebellious during adolescence. He had a history of alcoholism and drank heavily when he first met Sandy. Greg's biological father also had a history of alcoholism.

The dynamics in Sandy's family of origin were quite different. Sandy had one younger sister. She described her parents as being quite rigid. They were very strict and always expected her to be "perfect." She was attracted to Greg's rebelliousness. However, she was concerned about his alcohol problem and encouraged him to quit. He had not drunk in over two years. Since then, the relationship deteriorated somewhat. Greg thought this was because he was not able to tolerate intimacy and often pushed Sandy away. Sandy had difficulty tolerating distance in the relationship due to lack of boundaries within her own family. Greg and Sandy requested treatment in order to deal with these issues.

The story is broken into segments with symbols being identified as they relate to the dynamics of the couple for which the story was constructed. Therapists will need to change the story by replacing the symbols that pertain to the couple described in the case example. Some of the symbols in the story are universal symbols and these will not need to be replaced.

THE TURTLE WHO WAS AFRAID HE COULD

Once there was a turtle who came from a family of male turtles who only came out of their shells at nighttime.

Symbols:

Turtle: symbol for fear of intimacy.

Turtles' shells: represents husband's tendency to withdraw following periods in which he feels closer to his wife due to his fear of intimacy.

Afraid he could: reframes intimacy as something that turtle is very capable of experiencing. This is not a lack of skill, but rather fear related to what it would mean to allow himself to enjoy intimacy. He would be more vulnerable and this may be painful for him.

Nighttime: has multiple meanings: symbolic of destructive aspects of personality; relates to history of alcoholism and acting out; also represents history of alcoholism and acting out in family of origin; represents father's and stepfather's difficulty tolerating intimacy.

The little turtle had never really questioned this except that one evening when he was ready to go out for the night, he tapped on his father's shell, but his father said that he was never coming out again. He warned his son, "Remember, don't go out at night anymore."

Symbols:

> *When ready to go out:* represents period in which an adolescent needs to individuate from the family.
> *Tapped on father's shell:* adolescent needs support from parents at this time; his father was leaving him.
> *Father's warning:* represents loyalty issues. How can the son be intimate if he perceived his father as not being capable of tolerating intimacy?

Well, the little turtle continued to go out at night and one night, he found another turtle whom he became very close to, an older turtle. These two turtles were very similar so they got along very well.

Symbols:

> *Older turtle:* represents stepfather.

Most importantly, though, the older turtle only went out at night, too. Although the older turtle thought about what it would be like to go out in the daytime now and then, he believed that going out only at night was just the way it was supposed to be with men turtles. He said it had something to do with evolution. The little turtle did not understand but he grew to become very close to this turtle and before he knew it the older turtle was calling him "son." This made him very happy.

Symbols:

> *Older turtle only going out at night:* represents stepfather's difficulty tolerating intimacy as well.
> *Something to do with evolution:* represents the changing of traditional roles of men and women in society.
> *Turtle did not understand:* implies that story is a means of relating to the unconscious.

Once upon a time there was also a female turtle. Her family only came out in the daytime. These were the family traditions.

Symbols:

> *Daytime:* has multiple meanings: represents intimacy; represents wife's family of origin and the message implicitly re-

ceived from them that she "Always needed to be good"; highlights the differences between husband's and wife's family of origin.

One night, a very unusual thing happened. This female turtle didn't get in until after dark. It was that very night she happened to meet this male turtle whom she thought was quite attractive. He was interested in her, too, but said that if they were to get to know each other, she would have to go out at night.

Symbols:

Thought was quite attractive: individuals tend to be attracted to those with personality characteristics opposite from their own.

At first she was not quite sure what to do, but really wanted to get to know this turtle so she began sneaking out of her shell at night and returned before her parents noticed.

Symbols:

Not sure what to do: represents conflict related to family values.

Well, to make a long story short, the two turtles fell in love and one day the female turtle suggested that they try something different. She wanted the male turtle to stay out with her for one whole day, 24 hours. But this meant that the little turtle would have to be out in the daytime.

Symbols:

Wanted to stay out for one whole day: represents wife's positive influence on husband; represents wife's request that husband allow himself to be more intimate within relationship.

The male turtle kind of wanted to, but he started to think about the older turtle and about his father so he thought, "Well, maybe, but first I'm going to talk it over with my father." He meant the older turtle because by this time he had started to call him "Dad." This made the older turtle happy.

Symbols:

> *First have to talk with my father:* implies that problems with intimacy are connected to loyalty issues

When the little turtle returned home, the older turtle had a friend over. This friend was on the right side of the older turtle. Maybe that's not really important. But anyway, the little turtle sat to the left of the older turtle and began talking about the female he had met who wanted him to stay out for 24 hours. The older turtle shared that he had experienced similar feelings at times. But then, before you knew it, the older turtle was rambling on again about "evolution" and how male turtles were just supposed to go out at nighttime. The turtle to the right of the older turtle didn't say a word about all of this. It didn't seem like he totally agreed with the older turtle because earlier he had been talking about how he wouldn't mind marrying another turtle who could tell stories like he could. You see, he thought he was a good storyteller, and accurately so!

Symbols:

> *Friend on right side of the older turtle:* friend represents the right brain.
> *Turtle sat on the left side:* left side represents left brain and relates to husband's difficulty expressing emotions.
> *Friend thought he was a good storyteller:* suggests that right brain is being addressed by this story.

Anyway, he didn't mention as to whether or not this female turtle that he might marry ever asked him to stay out for 24 hours and the little turtle didn't ask. It might have been that this little turtle wanted to remain loyal to both of his fathers, or maybe that wasn't it, but anyway, he didn't know what to do.

Symbols:

> *Or maybe that wasn't it:* offering a suggestion to the right brain, but allowing it to be discarded, if it's not appropriate.

Then one night before falling asleep, he had a dream. This dream took him many years into the future. The whole thing felt really strange. There were millions of turtles of all sizes and, guess what? Well, they all stayed out all day and all night. It didn't seem like they ever went to sleep. The little turtle accidentally overheard one of the turtles telling another turtle (he wasn't sure if they were male or female because they looked so much alike) about how things were in the old days. The turtle was saying something about "evolution." The little turtle didn't really understand.

Symbols:

> *Stayed out all day and all night:* represents integration of both positive and negative aspects of personality.
> *They looked so much alike:* represents changing roles of men and women in society; suggests that in this generation, it may be acceptable for husband to enjoy intimacy.
> *Didn't understand:* again, implies that message is being communicated to the right brain.

But when he woke up in the morning, he could hardly wait to see the female turtle and guess what? They stayed out for 24 hours. Even longer, because they lost track of time and the nights turned into days and the days into nights. They experienced each other in many different and exciting ways.

Symbols:

> *Lost track of time:* represents that the right brain has no concept of time; represents that intimacy is experienced by the right brain.
> *Days turned into nights and nights turned into days:* makes suggestion to couple via right hemisphere, suggesting that they both integrate aspects of the other's personality.
> *Experienced each other in new ways:* suggests that if couple becomes more integrated, they can experience increasing levels of intimacy.

One night, when it was time for them to go to sleep, they were holding one another and one of the turtles (I'm not sure which one because they both looked a lot alike by now) was talking about how he/she felt relaxed and peaceful, only to realize that the other turtle was sound asleep and mumbled something about "transcendence." The little turtle didn't quite understand, but guessed it didn't matter. THE END!

Symbols:

> *Said something about "transcendence":* increasing levels of intimacy result in a sense of connectedness.
> *Didn't quite understand:* implies that this story may not be consciously understood.

RESPONSE TO THE INTERVENTION

Greg responded to the story by smiling and commenting, "Whatever." Sandy responded with, "I kind of liked it. I'm not sure what all of it meant, but I kind of liked it." The story itself became a therapy symbol. Therapy symbols consist of significant encounters experienced between the therapist and the family. The story became part of the culture shared between this couple and myself and referring to the turtle during the later stages of treatment was symbolic of the earlier experience. The story, perhaps, provided the couple with a visual image that simplified the more complex interactional patterns that inhibited their growth and offered them a suggestion regarding how they might disrupt these patterns. This may be one way of intervening in the symbolic world of our clients. This couple made significant changes over the course of therapy. Upon termination, they were given a copy of the story as a symbol of the therapy process, their hard work, and a reminder of how they might continue to make changes in their life.

REFERENCES

Connell, G., Garfield, R., & Whitaker, C. (1990). The process of in-therapy consultation: A symbolic-experiential perspective. *Journal of Strategic and Systemic Therapies, 9,* 1, 32-38.
Whitaker, C.A., & Keith, D.V. (1981). Symbolic-experiential family therapy. In A. Gurman & D. Kniskern (Eds.), *Handbook of family therapy* (187-225). New York: Brunner/Mazel.

−56−

Making Contact:
The First Intervention

Jane Gerber

The orientation for the context out of which this article comes is the Virginia Satir paradigm: a system generic to the entire field of family therapy and beyond. It is my belief that the very first intervention, the most basic one any of us makes regardless of our therapeutic orientation, is making contact with another person. It sets the tone for the process or fate of the relationship. It is also the beginning of translating strangeness into familiarity. Since life talks to life, within the context of making contact we free up energy and free ourselves to take risks. Because our energy is free, the risks become minimized, and more options are possible. It seems to me that most of our education has been done holding in energy, not releasing it!

The following describes the process of this first intervention. My beliefs about people run parallel to those underpinning the Satir paradigm, so when I initiate a meeting with a stranger, I first make a conscious inner preparation for contact with this person. The philosophy underlying this is:

- We are all born little.
- We are all manifestations of a life force.
- We are all energy sources.
- We are all unique and at the same time have many similarities.

Author Note: I am indebted to my teacher, my colleague, and my friend of more than thirty years, Virginia Satir.

I initially approach the essence of another person, not just what I see and hear or what I observe of their behavior. I make an inner preparation. Since this person is another manifestation of a life force I go towards them with a sense of celebration. I prepare my mind to meet someone who is unique. I center myself and clear my mind so that I am not preoccupied or distracted. I ready myself to being available and this leads me to being present. The difference between fully present and not fully present is related to how people respond to me. To be present is a first lesson in integrity!

Then there is outer preparation. I am conscious of energy boundaries — mine and the other's — and I act accordingly. Our "second skin" is about the length of a right angled arm, or roughly 18 inches. The area between that second skin and a person's body is sacred space. This space needs to be respected and not invaded unless invited. Our hands give messages of invitation. We give off neurological responses. It is through touch that we receive, not through the mouth. For example, someone whose major response to life is a placating stance may say "Yes" when they are really feeling "No."

I need to be creative about eye contact. One of the ways I can do this is by sitting face to face with the person. If I'm with a small child I can be on the floor with them, or a step or stool can bring us to eye level. Since I am fairly tall I know that a person shorter than I am, standing, has to look up at me and, over time, this can place a strain on their eyes, neck, and back muscles. I also know that to tower over someone may exacerbate concern in that person of being overpowered or dominated.

I know, too, that not only eye level but eye contact is important. For example, if I walk towards a person, extend my hand, address them and keep my eyes fixed either on the ground or off in space, chances are that person will not feel a sense of connection with me. It is important when I address that person that in that moment they become my foreground.

So, having given myself full permission to meet another, the literal meeting can take place.

Engaging the Difficult Adolescent from Behind the One-Way Mirror

Lynne Shook

Adolescents with problems pose a difficult challenge to parents and therapists alike. Help must be offered in a manner that responds to the adolescent's almost childlike need for nurturance as well as his or her developing sense of competence and independence. If such a balance is not achieved, parents and therapists can find themselves with a contrary adolescent – one who is sullen and withdrawn, challenging and disruptive, or both. The technique presented here uses the one-way mirror as a symbolic boundary between childhood and adulthood, and allows therapists and parents to help the adolescent move more easily between the two worlds.

A STRUCTURAL/STRATEGIC VIEW OF THE DIFFICULT ADOLESCENT IN FAMILY THERAPY

Adolescents who don't want to be in therapy with their parents will generally do one of two things to make their feelings known – refuse to speak or threaten to walk out of the session. A strategic lens might reframe this contrary behavior as a protective maneuver by the adolescent on behalf of his or her parents (Haley, 1980). By making it difficult for the therapist to conduct the business of therapy in the usual way, the parents (and the therapist) are spared the possibility of failure. From a structural point of view, the adolescent's behavior can be viewed as an attempt to regulate the boundary between family members and an outsider – in this case, the therapist (Minuchin, 1974).

Clinicians commonly respond to the difficult behavior of the adolescent in family therapy by seeing him or her alone in individual sessions, hoping to appeal to the adolescent's developing sense of autonomy. While this approach respects an important aspect of adolescent development, it doesn't challenge the adolescent's protectiveness directly, and maintains his or her role as gatekeeper to the family. The following technique provides the clinician with a way to engage the adolescent in conjoint family treatment that exaggerates contrary behavior, uses it as a force for change, and respects the adolescent's drive towards independence in the process.

THE TECHNIQUE

To use this technique, one must have access to a one-way mirror, a team behind the mirror, and phone communication between the observation and treatment rooms. The session is begun as usual and proceeds until the therapist feels that the adolescent's disengagement from the process will inhibit further progress. At this point, the therapist invites the adolescent to join the team behind the one-way mirror to watch the session proceed. (In my experience even the most recalcitrant adolescents have been too curious about what goes on behind the mirror to be able to resist this offer.) The adolescent is told that he or she does not have to speak to the team behind the mirror, but that if he or she does, the conversation cannot be held in confidence.

Once the adolescent joins the observation team, one member sits beside him or her, introduces the other team members, and points out aspects of the observation room technology. As the interview with the rest of the family proceeds, the team member begins to discuss with the adolescent the interview going on in front of them. Once the adolescent is sufficiently engaged in the treatment process from this one-step removed position, he or she is encouraged to share his or her observations with various family members by phone across the one-way mirror. When ready, the adolescent rejoins the session in progress. At the end of the session all family members meet the observing team, but only the adolescent has been given the opportunity to function as a team member. This technique is most effective when the therapist and the team member who "adopts" the adolescent have a close working relationship and share clinical orientations.

CASE EXAMPLE

Rob (16), James (14), Sam (11), and Sally (4) were brought to family treatment by their father John (40) and mother Susan (39). Both parents complained that family life was too chaotic. The two oldest boys were noisy at home and "too rough" with the youngest boy. The oldest boy was doing poorly in school. Sally seemed to be getting lost in all the commotion at home, and clung to her mother more than both parents felt was normal for her age. Past efforts by the therapist to help the parents set ground rules with the boys had been defeated by Rob's sullen lack of involvement in family meetings, and she decided to use the technique presented here.

The therapist began by asking the parents to talk with Rob and James about their concern for Sam's safety. Efforts on the father's part to explain that Sam was too young to be included in the oldest boys' so-called friendly brawls were met with stony silence on the part of Rob. The therapist turned to Rob and suggested that he join the team behind the mirror since he apparently didn't want to get involved in a discussion about the problem at this time. After Rob left the room, the therapist asked the two parents to continue talking with each other about suitable guidelines for safe rough-housing in the home.

Rob sat down with the consulting team, said little initially, but was obviously fascinated by being able to watch his family interact from behind the mirror. The team member designated to "adopt" Rob introduced herself and the rest of the team and carried on in a general way about the observation room's technology. As Rob's father suggested to James that he and Rob ought to use boxing gloves if they wanted to fight, Rob commented as an aside that he'd like to see his father take his own advice. The team member encouraged Rob to send that message to his father over the phone and Rob agreed. As the father explained to the therapist after the call that he was also sometimes drawn into these brawls, Rob commented to the team member that he felt that his father was having "some kind of identity crisis." When pressed, he explained that it made him uncomfortable to fight with his father, particularly since he felt that he was now strong enough to beat him. The team member encouraged Rob to phone this message in to the father. "Dad," he said over the phone, "even though I may be as strong as you are now, you will always be the head of the family." At this point Rob returned to the session and reiterated to his mother and the therapist what he had said over the phone. With this information, the therapist was able to help the father and oldest sons arrange to compete in a less physically dangerous way. Sam could be brought into their games in a more controlled fashion; Sally felt safer and was able to establish greater distance from her mother.

COMMENTS

This technique has been used with a number of adolescents and each time, the adolescent has confided in the team member behind the mirror in a way that he or she was unable to do in front of it. One way to explain this is that the adolescent's contrary behavior is exaggerated by inviting him or her to leave the session, brought under the therapists' control by bringing him or her behind the mirror, and redirected back to the session through the medium of the telephone.

Another way to explain the quasi-conspiratorial relationship that develops between the adolescent and the team member is that the technique recreates a relationship between grandparents and their adolescent grandchildren of another time. As an ally of the adolescent (and an implicit ally of the parents), grandparents have traditionally offered adolescents a haven from which they can see the world, complain about their parents, and return home with a greater degree of freedom and responsibility.

REFERENCES

Haley, J. (1980). *Leaving home.* New York, NY: McGraw-Hill Book Company.
Minuchin, S. (1974). *Family and family therapy.* Cambridge, MA: Harvard University Press.

–58–

The Use of Metaphor in Providing Feedback on Structured Assessment Procedures

Amy D. Frankel

RATIONALE

In recent years, there has been an upsurge in the development of family assessment measures (Carlson & Grotevant, 1988) designed to assist clinicians and researchers in operationalizing complex family processes. Family therapists seem somewhat reluctant to utilize these instruments in the context of their clinical practices. Family therapists may view the use of such instruments as an attempt to take the richness and fluidity of family process and to reduce it into scores, or they may believe that structured measurement procedures are linear expressions of a system's circular process (Floyd, Weinand, & Cimmarusti, 1989).

One way of bridging the gap between scores on family assessment measures and information that will have meaning for the family is the use of metaphor. A metaphor can be defined as a "means to carry from one place to another" (Friesen, 1985, p. 113) or as a method of linking the meaning of two ideas or modes (Duhl, 1983). It is this linking function of metaphor that makes it ideal to use in giving the family feedback on their test results. Metaphor is the ideal bridge between the modes of test data and of family process.

DESCRIPTION OF THE INTERVENTION

This technique can be tailored to fit a wide variety of instruments. As used here within the context of the feedback session, the family is first given the test information in a standard fashion. The family is given an explanation as to what their scores, or profiles, on the test were as well as a translation of what this information means to them and to their treatment process.

After the more traditional feedback is presented, the clinician gives the family a metaphor that feeds back the same information but in a manner more reflective of the family's idiosyncratic themes and personal realities. The metaphor should incorporate the underlying constructs of the measure utilized in the assessment and link these constructs to the family's own metaphors and themes.

GUIDELINES FOR USE

This technique can be utilized at any time in the treatment process where formal assessment procedures are appropriate. Structured family assessments done in the initial phase of treatment allow clinicians to generate specific preliminary hypotheses concerning the family's structure and interactional sequences surrounding the presenting concern (Floyd et al., 1989). Family assessment may be useful when a therapeutic impasse is reached and the therapy process seems "stuck." In this case, the instruments may yield data that has not been considered. This prompts new, more useful hypotheses. Structured assessment procedures may also be used when therapy is terminating to provide both clinician and clients with a concrete measure of change.

The metaphor developed for use in the feedback session must be reflective of the variables measured in the test as well as of the family's own reality. Glimpses into the family's personal reality can be gained by listening to metaphors that they use in describing their life or by listening for the emergence of recurring family themes.

EXAMPLE OF THE INTERVENTION

This intervention was designed for use with a family that consisted of a 34-year-old divorced mother, her 14-year-old son, 16-year-old daughter, and an estranged 18-year-old son. The family presented to a university family therapy clinic with a concern about the daughter's behavior. She had been recently hospitalized for acute anxiety attacks that followed on the heels of her divulging that the estranged brother had been sexually abusing her. Her fear of the brother was grounded in reality for he had previously beaten her to the point where she had required hospitalization and he was now threatening to kill her. There was a history of both physical and sexual abuse in the family that extended back at least three generations.

The Clinical Rating Scale (Olson, 1988) was used as an observational measure of family functioning. The Clinical Rating Scale (CRS) is based on the Circumplex Model of family systems (Olson, 1986) and rates the family along the variables of cohesion, adaptability, and communication. This family exhibited both enmeshment between the mother and her own mother and disengagement as exhibited by the oldest son's estrangement. The mother and her two youngest children were judged to be separated. They were not disengaged to the extent of the eldest son yet there was limited emotional involvement and some question as to the clarity of generational boundaries. The family's adaptability was judged to be chaotic, with mother failing to provide consistent leadership or discipline and lack of role clarity. The family exhibited relatively low levels of facilitative communication. Mother sent inconsistent messages to her daughter concerning the sexual abuse and neither child showed respect or empathy for their mother's feelings.

During the clinical interview upon which the CRS was based, the mother spoke with great pride of how accepting she was of her children's manner of dress and behavior, which was one of noncompliance with social norms. Mother also was proud of her family's ability to defy longstanding family rules as well as her children's artistic creativity. Family themes of defiance, pride, and creativity seemed to hold power for both mother and children.

Prior to presenting the metaphor, the family was told that watching them reminded the therapist of a story although she couldn't remember the ending. It was hoped that with the family's creativity they could help figure out the ending.

The metaphor was told as a story:

> There was a tribe that was small yet very proud of their tradition of defiance and of their ability to stay separate from larger more powerful tribes. While this tribe was proud, they were also tired as their size and relative power made them prone to attack. The head of this tribe was the queen whose husband had been killed many years ago, and she was proud of her ability to run the tribe without him. One day a witch belonging to an opposing tribe cast a mysterious spell over the queen that made her unable to lead her tribe. Since she was no longer able to protect the tribe from being attacked, many tribal members were hurt. The queen had become unable to hear what her tribespeople were saying to her and when she spoke, the spell caused her words to be different from her meanings. The queen became so intent on reversing this spell that all of her energy and power were focused on the opposing witch, while the tribe focused all of their attention on the queen. The tribe tried all of their creativity and magic to get the spell off the queen but nothing worked. The tribe began to succumb to despair and to lose their power.

OUTCOME

The mother was particularly affected by the metaphor. She began to cry and to talk about the effect her own mother's "spell" still had over her. The daughter, who initially appeared withdrawn and disinterested, eventually angrily asked her mother, "What happened to the princess?" This was the first time the daughter had expressed anger relevant to her mother's enmeshment with the grandmother. Hearing the metaphor and discussing different endings allowed the family to begin to talk about change in a relatively safe manner. They were able to see how the variables of cohesion, change, and communication were operationalized in their system and to look at how things might be different as they began the process of change in their therapy.

REFERENCES

Carlson, C., & Grotevant, H. (1988). A comparative review of family rating scales: Guidelines for clinicians and researchers. *Journal of Family Psychology, 1,* 23-47.

Duhl, B.S. (1983). *From the inside out.* New York: Brunner/Mazel.

Floyd, F.J., Weinand, J.W., & Cimmarusti, R.A. (1989). Clinical family assessment: Applying structured measurement procedures in treatment settings. *Journal of Marital and Family Therapy, 15,* 271-288.

Friesen, J. (1985). *Structural-strategic marriage and family therapy.* New York: Gardner Press.

Olson, D.H. (1986). Circumplex model VII: Validation studies and FACES III. *Family Process, 25,* 337-351.

Olson, D.H. (1988). *Clinical rating scale for the circumplex model of marital and family systems.* St. Paul, MN: Family Social Science, University of Minnesota.

59

Tommy and His Helpers

Glen B. Paddock

My first intervention was clearly forming as I flipped through the seemingly endless number of reports on the young 11-year-old lad who was the subject of the referral.

Although a family therapist, I was being requested to see Tommy for individual therapy. Already there were four therapists, a Child Welfare social worker, a foster family, a guardian *ad litem* and an attorney involved with Tommy and his family. I was being requested to be the fifth therapist.

FAMILIES AND MULTIPLE HELPERS

Having several "helping" professionals can lead to confusion rather than clinical clarity. At times, professional agencies with their varying service mandates and policies can work at cross purposes. The result can be demoralizing for the families who are to be the recipients of our help. Haley (1976) was one of the first to outline that professional colleagues may become part of the problem for therapy, especially when social control is an issue. In such situations the unit for therapy may not only be the client family, but the family and all those professionals involved with the family.

All too often, a network of multiple helpers has sought to reduce case complexity by bestowing blame on families. Such a posture places the helpers in a one-up, complementary position to the family, leaving the helpers blind to their own contribution to the problems being presented for treatment. Another frequent occurrence is for a helper to minimize stress between a family and themselves by triangulating in a third party, usually another professional; the salient issue of family-therapist impasse is not exposed and resolved. With more professionals becoming involved, the unspoken rule seems to become that *all* are in charge, and no one professional is above any other in a therapeutic decision-making hierarchy. While multiple helpers were recognized several years ago as a potential stumbling block to therapy, it has only been recently that guidelines for intervention with such systems have been written (Imber-Black, 1988).

THE CASE OF TOMMY'S HELPING NETWORK

Case notes revealed that Tommy had been in foster care for 8 months and he desperately wanted to be returned home. He was the youngest of four children. His sibs, 18, 20, and 21, had all established residences of their own. Tommy's parents had been divorced seven years, but had reconciled their differences such that they had been reunited for the past year. The family history was marred with allegations of sexual abuse and documentation of alcohol abuse and spousal violence. Tommy had been removed from parental care due to an incident of spousal violence. Several "helpers" were actively involved.

The request for my involvement with Tommy was coming from a therapist who had reached an impasse with Tommy's mother, Jane. Dr. Gaze had been seeing Jane for "individual issues related to the relationship violence." The impasse centered around Dr. Gaze's wanting Jane to separate from Tommy's father; something Jane would not do. Further examination revealed that Dr. Gaze had informed Jane she would *never* regain custody of Tommy unless she left Tommy's father. My initial hypothesis that I was being triangulated into a case where there was a therapeutic impasse between the therapist and the client was showing utility.

INTERVENTION

I agreed to become involved with Tommy on the condition that I first interview Tommy with his family. Following the template set out by Imber-Black (1988), I interviewed Tommy and his parents specifically about their family's relationship with "helpers." Clearly, the family members were allied in their mutual mistrust of "outsiders." They experienced professionals as people who "tore their family apart." Just as clear was the need for this family to be bonded around the mutual blame of "helpers." It seemed that the family members balanced their feelings of powerlessness with professionals with a "sense of closeness" shown in their collaborative blame of the same. My intervention with Tommy and his parents was to ask whether or not they wished to "have some say" in who worked with them. This proved to be "news of a difference." Their initial response was one of disbelief and laughter. However, I persisted with the intervention framing it as a way that they could "take some control back from the helpers." The family accepted the challenge and agreed to meet with the "helping network."

The next step was to convene and conduct the family-larger system interview. My goals were to discover how the macro-system formed by the family and the helpers had developed, what the respective roles of the helpers were, how each person saw the current problems, and to inquire about how each person saw the future (Tommy's future, the future of Tommy with his parents, and each professional's role in the future treatment of the problem).

This family-larger system interview had several important effects. First, it was an intervention among the helpers. Prior to this interview, they had never met and were not fully cognizant of each other's role. The interview highlighted differences among the helpers and how these differences impacted the interaction of Tommy's parents. It gave the helpers and Tommy's parents a new way to understand the current difficulties. Second, a theme was woven that connected the family's interactional pattern to the professional network interactional pattern, and how the two patterns impacted one another. Third, Tommy and his parents were able to have some choice regarding who would work with them and what the goals of the therapy would be.

INTERVENTION RESULTS

Information from the interview was used to formulate a treatment plan that included clear boundaries for family and helpers. Two therapists voluntarily withdrew from the case. Two others (both selected by the family) joined forces to see the family conjointly.

The idea of individual sessions for Tommy was discarded. The overarching goal of therapy was made clear, that being to have Tommy return to the care of his parents pending their evidence of no further relational violence or alcohol abuse.

Family sessions for Tommy and his parents were conducted conjointly by the two therapists for the last several weeks. There was one relational separation and reconciliation between Tommy's parents. There have been no further incidents of violence or alcohol abuse between the parents. The family-helper boundary has remained clear.

REFERENCES

Haley, J. (1976). *Problem-solving therapy*. San Francisco: Jossey-Bass.
Imber-Black, E. (1988). *Families and larger systems*. New York: Guilford.

60

A Basic Intervention in Couples Therapy

Barbara J. Lynch

Twenty years of experience as a therapist and supervisor have contributed to my belief that marital therapy is the most complex form of psychotherapy and the mode of treatment that is most susceptible to contamination by therapists' belief systems and unconscious projections. This tends to reduce the success rate of couples therapy and increase the need for effective intervention.

The definition of success that has structured my work with couples is that which states that all decisions, solutions, and resolutions affecting the couple system should be made overtly within the couple system and solely between the individuals comprising the dyad. Therefore, the objective of any intervention is to reinforce the interaction between the couple and, in the process, to deflect attempts to include others in the structure of the intimate dyadic system. Other principles that shape the formation of my strategies are the following:

1. The couple system is one which essentially is (or should be) one of peers: emotional equals without significant and unsubstantiated power and influence differences between the individuals.
2. Change in the dyadic system must occur in the context of the treatment hour. My work is present-centered, with the expectation that the continuation of learning will occur naturally when success is experienced in the here-and-now.
3. Therapist-managed anxiety, tension, and intensity comprise the impetus for change.

4. The couple is locked in an unsatisfying and dysfunctional sequence of behavior that prevents them from engaging in alternative ways of being. The homeostatic system must be unbalanced.
5. All interventions must be grounded in the reality of treatment and the couple's unique system.

I use an intervention in the first session that has several objectives. First, it establishes the ground rules for treatment and orients the couple to the therapeutic process. The intervention in progress becomes a reliable assessment, a microcosm of the interactional style. In addition, the intervention is the first restructuring maneuver of the treatment process, attending to boundaries.

The strategy occurs in the context of fee payment and should take place as a natural part of the initial session occurring early in the session as a natural part of giving policy information. The therapist, *without looking at either individual*, asks how the couple will pay the fee. Usually one individual will say "I'll give you a check each week."

Assessment possibilities: Note the use of I, individual, instead of we, couple. Who is the money manager, possibly the power holder? What is the (verbal and non-verbal) reaction of the non-speaker? Was there non-verbal checking between the individuals prior to responding?

The therapist's response should unbalance the system and heighten the intensity. A possible answer is: "I have this quirk, probably a result of my upbringing, where I tend to work for the person who hands me money. I don't want to take sides here so it would be important for me to get paid by both of you. I hope you can divide the fee in an equitable manner and reflect a joint investment in the process, so I will feel as if I'm working for both of you."

The subsequent interaction should be directed back to the couple as nonintrusively as possible. The intent is to move from a system that is likely to be overbounded between the individuals and underbounded between the couple and therapist, to one which has more clear and appropriate intra- and inter-systemic boundaries.

H | W   Thx   →   H | W   Thx   →   H | W   Thx

$$H = \text{Husband}$$
$$W = \text{Wife}$$
$$\text{Thx} = \text{Therapist}$$

THERAPEUTIC MANAGEMENT
OF COUPLE RESPONSES

H or W: "She/he earns more than I, I should pay less."

Thx: "Divide the fee so each of you pay an amount commensurate with your earnings."

H or W: "I don't have any money. I don't earn any. How can I pay you?"

Thx: "That is a problem. You two need to talk about that."

H or W: "She/he manages the money, writes the checks. I give the money to her/him and she/he pays the bills."

Thx: "This instance should be different. How can you two structure the payment so I experience being paid by both of you?"

H or W: "OK, I'll pay one week, she/he will pay the other. We'll alternate."

Thx: "That means, I guess, that you make the decisions and she/he goes along with them. And it also means you both have equal assets."

The process of arriving at a decision will continue to be fruitful ground for assessing the couple system around a "real" issue in an unexpected area. The fee payment, if it is actually forthcoming, is not as significant as the process. The following questions possibly get answered:

1. Do both individuals have a fairly equal investment in couple therapy? In decision making? In the relationship? Where is the discrepancy?

2. Who goes outside the dyad for assistance, protection, support? How is the other involved in this process?

3. Where are the potential difficulties in facilitating interaction between the partners and resisting attempts to get "caught" in the couple's process?

Since the couple is in therapy because there is a problem in their system, a functional solution may not be possible. The therapist should resist accepting an "easy answer" while still collecting a fee. This intervention orients the couple to the couple's therapy. It allows the therapist to remain in a somewhat distant position, while, at the same time, re-establishing appropriate boundaries in the dyad. It also provides the therapist with ample raw material on which to build provocative and powerful statements about the couple's process of interaction and to stay appropriately uninvolved in content.

61

Letter Writing in Family Therapy

Leon Sloman

Because the emphasis in family therapy is on the spoken rather than the written word, one finds few references pertaining to the use of letters between family members. It is noteworthy that when Bowen (1978) set out to "detriangle" himself from his parents, he initiated the process by a series of letters to other family members. Bowen's experience has been described as a major milestone in the history of family therapy and has been compared to Freud's self-analysis in that his exploration of his own feelings and relationships contributed to a conceptual leap. Although Bowen's letters were merely a vehicle whereby his theory of human change and growth was implemented, I would contend that one could pay more attention to how letters can be used. In a previous paper (Sloman & Pipitone, 1991), my co-author and I discussed how family therapists can bring about positive changes by having clients write letters to other family members, and I will expand on the topic here.

The use of letters from family therapists to families is already well known (cf. Selvini Palazzoli et al., 1978; Weeks & L'Abate, 1982; White & Epston, 1989). White and Epston argued that in order to make sense of their lives, people have to arrange their experiences in sequences across time in such a way as to arrive at a coherent account of themselves and the world around them. This account can be referred to as a story or self-narrative. For White and Epston, therapy would be a process of "storying" and/or "restory-ing" the lives and experiences of persons who present with problems. They believe that it is the meaning that members attribute to events that determines their behavior as opposed to the notion that some underlying structure or dysfunction in the family determines the behavior and interactions of family members. White and Epston's model bears some relation to "world view" schools of family therapy (Sluzki, 1983).

People differ in that whereas some can express themselves better orally, others find it easier to express themselves in writing. The thrust of this paper is to argue that writing a letter can be a creative act that enables a family member to "re-story" his/her family thus allowing him/her to initiate new kinds of interactions with other family members. One's aim is not merely to have a client write a letter; it is to provide the client with the opportunity to make productive use of his/her literary talents. At times, it also happens that a letter is the simplest means of conveying a message. White and Epston argue that literate means are of "great service in the introduction of new perspectives . . ." and "to the privileging of vital aspects of lived experience in the 'recreation' of unfolding stories, in enlisting persons in the re-authoring of their lives and relationships."

Some situations are particularly suitable for letter writing. For example, I will sometimes suggest that a parent write a letter to a child when the child is living away from home or with another parent and when the parent has difficulty in communicating with the child directly. It may be that the child is refusing to talk to the parent. I also sometimes suggest to children that they write letters to their parent(s).

I would not suggest a letter until I have a good understanding of the presenting problems and family system. When I present the idea of the letter, I try to present it as one of a number of options. It should be noted that because some people feel more comfortable than others in expressing themselves in writing, if an individual is reluctant to write a letter, I do not pressure him/her.

I may bring up the idea of letters when individuals are seeking some change in the nature of their relationships. I might ask them to define more precisely what kind of change they are trying to bring about and then discuss with them how they feel they could achieve this change. Discussing what should go into a letter provides an opportunity to explore individual motivations and conflicts: what the client might want to express as well as how s/he anticipates the recipient's reaction. Because the individual is discussing his/her motivations within a specific context, it can make these issues seem more relevant. It also means that when the individual does decide to write a letter, a lot of thought may go into what is said.

I advise clients to bring the letter to me before they mail it. This gives me an opportunity to review the letter with the client. I may draw attention to conflicting messages in the letter. With the spoken word, it is often possible for clients to deny saying something or to claim they have been misunderstood; with the written word, however, the therapist has evidence of exactly what the client has expressed.

The following is an illustration of the role of letter writing when the therapist has access to only one parent.

CASE EXAMPLE

John, aged thirteen, was the identified patient in family X. He was referred by the school because of failing grades, apathy, depression, and social withdrawal with occasional unprovoked outbursts. Mr. and Mrs. X had been separated for nine months. At the time of the separation, John chose to remain with Father; his two younger sisters went to live with their mother. At the time of assessment, Father showed an unswerving determination to obtain a reconciliation with his wife; Mother was equally determined to maintain the separation. It also emerged that John had became an instrument for Father in his quest for reconciliation. John expressed his main wish as wanting the family reunited.

Father and John refused to return after the first interview unless Mother guaranteed to return to Father, which she was not willing to do. Mother, however, was prepared to return to the therapist in order to work out the best approach to helping John. She openly admitted her feelings of sadness and hurt in reaction to John's continuing rejection of all her efforts to play a mothering role.

Faced with John's and Mr. X's refusal to attend further sessions, the therapist wondered what possible strategy could be used to detriangulate John, who had become an instrument in the parental struggle. After discussing the family system, the therapist finally suggested to Mother that she write a letter and made specific suggestions. He also suggested changes when Mother showed her first draft. When Mother wrote the final letter, the wording was entirely her own. The letter was handed to John by his mother and is reproduced here in its original form.

Dear John:

   During the past few weeks, I've spent a great deal of time thinking about you and your father and the situation we now find ourselves in.
   As I look at you and your father together, I realize how important you are to each other. I know that you, John, have made the choice to be with your dad because you know that he loves you, and that he needs you as much as you need him. In many ways you understand one another very well, you spend good times together, he allows you freedom to make certain choices on your own. I see all of this as being very good, because you are able to help and support each other. I am proud of you, because you are showing that you care very deeply about someone. Although there have been times in the past when I have not been able to understand this, I do understand now.
   However, when I look at you and me, I see how hard it is for you to be loyal to your father and be friendly to me at the same time. Right now I think it is too much to expect of you to want to see me or do things with me. This would interfere with your relationship with your father. It is not at all easy for me to have to tell you these things. Surely you must know how hard it is not to sit and talk to you about what you're doing, to watch you working or playing, to enjoy your company or just fool around with you and see you smile. However, this kind of relationship with me creates difficulties for you and I do understand the choice you've made. At no time has it ever been my wish or intention to pull you away from your father and this leads me to a very important point in my letter.
   Because it appears that I create difficulties for you in this situation, I have decided to step back from it. I have decided not to contact you as much as I have been doing — certainly not

as much as I would like to. I will call before the end of the summer and about once a month after that to find out how you're doing and what's new because it's important to me to know at least that much about you. Nothing is expected from you in return. I don't think you will want to call me; however, please feel free to do so if ever you should wish to.

From what I've noticed when I've been with you lately, you are becoming a stronger, more independent person, able to handle many things. I feel that you will understand why I choose to make this decision. I love you very much, John, and have no wish to create further problems for you.

My relationship with your father and my relationship with you are entirely separate matters. It is up to your father and me to decide whether or not we separate or get together. No one else can make either decision for us. It is much more confusing for everyone if other people get involved. From now on, I feel that your dad and I must handle our own situation and that this be kept separate from your relationship with him or with me.

Enjoy the rest of your summer, John. In time, I feel that many of our present problems will work themselves out. You may be sure that I am thinking of you often.

Love,

Mom

When she delivered the letter, John received it quietly and said he understood. The father on the other hand ridiculed the letter and said that he was not interested in their getting together unless she could give him some hope for the future, which she couldn't. Over the next few weeks, Father began to harass her with phone calls. However, Mother stated that she felt stronger and better able to fend her husband off and make decisions. Six months later, mother reported that she visited John a couple of times, and was pleasantly received by him. Although I felt that this letter had a positive impact, serious problems still remained in the family that required ongoing work for a number of years. Because there was no indication, I did not use letter writing again.

One may decide to spend a number of sessions discussing a letter before it is finally delivered. In trying to encourage the clients to be more positive, one can positively reframe negative behaviors of the other family members. For example, one might reframe an adolescent's rudeness or unwillingness to communicate as representing the adolescent's attempt to individuate and separate from his family. One might also positively reframe the parent's frustration with the child as a function of his/her parental commitment and caring. The thought or act of letter writing can be very helpful in resolving ambivalence. For example, the parent may decide she or he is too angry to write.

Letter writing can also be used as a way of strengthening the parental subsystem by asking the parents to write the letter together. In all cases, the therapeutic focus should be on the process. For example, when the parents write a joint letter, one might inquire about who was more active, how well they were able to cooperate and how they resolved any differences of opinion about what to write. Though the therapist may make suggestions, the clients must decide what they want to communicate. The therapist then gives feedback on the basis of what they write as well as their associations to what they have written. The sending of the letter and the recipient's reaction to the receipt of the letter are then viewed as providing more information about the family system.

REFERENCES

Bowen, M. (1978). *Family therapy in clinical practice*. New York: Aronson, 508-516.

Selvini Palazzoli, M.S., Boscolo, L., Cecchin, G., Prata, G. (1978). *Paradox Counterparadox*. New York: Aronson.

Sloman, L., & Pipitone, J. (1991). Parent-child letters in family therapy. *American Journal of Family Therapy, 19*, 77-82.

Sluzki, C.E. (1983). Process structure and world views: Towards an integrated view of systems models in family therapy. *Family Process, 22*, 469-476.

Weeks, G.R., & L'Abate, L. (1982) *Paradoxical psychotherapy: Theory and practice with individuals, couples, and families*. New York: Brunner/Mazel.

White, M., & Epston, D. (1989). *Literate means to therapeutic ends*. Adelaide: Dulwich Centre Publications.

62

A Change of Names

Don Brown

Strategic interventions can be used in conjunction with other theoretical approaches to couple and family therapy, provided the therapist has planned the intervention and is aware of its purpose and possible results within the system. Such interventions may be particularly useful in the early stages of couple work where the partners have capacity for growth and insight, but are and have been "stuck" in dysfunctional patterns of interaction. When I say a couple is "stuck," I am referring not only to a persistent pattern of reciprocity, but also to the words the couple uses to define their interaction (e.g., "She is not supportive of me and I have withdrawn from her to protect myself"). These descriptions often seem as though they are written in stone and usually have a "good spouse/bad spouse" bias to the definition. The strategic intervention is an assignment for an activity that is designed to alter or thwart the patterns but can also lead to a remythologizing of the definition of the relationship.

A good example of this approach would be working with substance abusing couples or couples affected by childhood traumas. Here there are often persistent patterns that are reinforced by the ways the couple defines what they are doing. A classic example may be a definition such as, "long suffering, kind, supportive wife and weak, irresponsible husband." If the strategic intervention is successful in changing a pattern or creating doubt about how the relationship is defined, then the therapist can move on to a more growth oriented model. This is increasingly possible using the resources of Twelve-Step groups.

What are some of the characteristics of strategic interventions? They are based on the presenting problem(s); they focus on present patterns or sequences of behaviors; they may involve homework assignments; and they may involve planning to set up the intervention to insure follow through.

One advantage of using this model with substance abusing couples or adult children of alcoholics is that there are good resources for further change, such as Twelve-Step groups, once an initial breakthrough has been achieved.

The following case illustrates this. Betty, a college-educated professional in her late 30's, had been married for 18 years. The couple had two children, a boy, 12, and a girl, 10. Betty sought counseling alone, seeking to work out some of her ambivalence about her marriage. This ambivalence was reflected in her opening words: "I don't know how to begin. I am unhappy — with my husband. I keep telling myself I need to accept him." She went on to describe an on/off marriage with one major separation, seven years ago, when Betty had filed and withdrawn divorce papers.

Betty came from an alcoholic family and her father, nearing 70, was still an active drinker. Betty was the oldest of four. She married young and then continued her education until she finished college and entered a profession. By contrast, her husband had held a series of jobs, even having to work for Betty's father during one lengthy period of unemployment. When Betty came in for counseling, he had been unemployed for several months. Betty was frustrated with her husband's failure to actively seek work. At the same time, she was experiencing guilt about breaking up the family.

Her ambivalence was reflected in the way she conducted herself in the sessions, being pained but also feeling good about her role in keeping the family going. She needed to continue to see her husband in a particular way. Her husband had ceased to respond to her outbursts and had turned his anger into passivity. This balance had lasted for most of the marriage.

An intervention occurred to me based on the fact that Betty never referred to her husband by his real name, Steve. In our two initial sessions she called him "Slick," a nickname that she stated she had used throughout their marriage. The continued use of the nickname suggested a relationship of "ne'er do well husband and responsible wife."

My assignment was that she would call her husband by his real name. I specified that this would take place in their personal contact, but I did not specify the time or the frequency.

When she returned for the next session she reported that she had done the assignment and when she first called him Steve he turned to her and said, "You're going to divorce me, aren't you?" Shortly after this, before her next session, she had contacted an attorney and made arrangements to borrow enough money to pay a retainer.

The changes in behavior preceded any redefining of the relationship. In the next few sessions, we continued to deal with the shift in couple patterns and later we began to redefine the relationship. This included having Betty read from adult children of alcoholics literature and visit her family to experience how she interacted with her father.

This type strategy works best with systems in which deeply engrained patterns of behavior exist, but the therapist feels that there is capacity for continued growth. The strategic intervention is focused on changing or thwarting patterns that have an addictive quality. Betty's name for her husband provided a clue to the way they interacted, and, in this case, a fitting intervention.

63

The Use of Resistant Family Members as Consultants in Therapy

Patricia Kelley

The technique described in this paper involves using resistant family members as "consultants" when only one family member comes in as the willing client. The idea of working with one individual for a family problem is not new. Brief family therapists have argued that the number of people seen is not an issue, and that work with the most motivated person in the system is useful (de Shazer & Berg, 1985; Fisch, Weakland, & Segal, 1982). The idea of using the term "consultation" rather than therapy is not new, either. Boscolo, Cecchin, Hoffman, & Penn (1987) label their work with families as consultation rather than therapy, arguing that such a term describes their work more accurately. Furthermore, this term decreases resistance and changes expectations; consultation does not offer a cure, and client choice is implied. I use the term differently, however, reserving it for family members of clients who are important as sources of information and power but who do not choose to be clients themselves. In this article, this technique is demonstrated through case examples.

In the first situation, Mr. X presented his problem to the therapist as a double bind. One: I have come to therapy for myself or my wife will leave me and I want to stay in this marriage very much. BUT, Two: Because my problems are part of a relationship conflict, I cannot change my behavior unless my wife comes to therapy with me and she has refused to do so. He claimed he learned this from his previous therapist whom his wife had forbidden him to see again because the problem had been defined as 'theirs' not his. Further discussion disclosed that he had talked about his therapy with his wife, giving his version of what transpired in sessions. Thus, I was fearful that individual therapy would be sabotaged unless the problem definition or the contract was changed.

With the client's permission, I phoned his wife inviting her in for one session as a consultant "to help me better understand" her husband's problems. I was careful not to reframe the problem as theirs. Although this approach usually works well for me, in this situation, she refused a visit. She said that the problem was his, and that he had better change or she would leave because he hit her. Even though Mrs. X did not attend a consultation, my one phone contact with her gave me important information: there was hitting. I also used the contact to extract a promise that she would not discuss her husband's therapy with him. I explained that since she was not coming in, therapy would focus on his problems, not on the relationship, and that it would dilute individual therapy if it were discussed.

After that phone contact, the contract could be set with Mr. X. It was established that since his wife would not come in, therapy could only focus on his issues and his change, not the relationship. Further, it was noted that he was not to discuss the therapy with his wife and that she had agreed to enforce that; he was given the same rationale that she had been given. Last, it was emphasized that there were no guarantees that his change would help his marriage and there was a chance that such changes might worsen the marriage. He was instructed to think carefully about it before deciding on therapy. He returned with a new resolve: to make changes himself, regardless of the risks. His renouncement of the "marriage at all costs" was a major factor in allowing change since the double bind was loosened.

Individual therapy was then begun with a new contract and the issue of stopping the "violence" (my term) was defined as the first order of business. Sessions focused on increasing self-esteem and assertiveness and reducing reactivity to others. Therapy was terminated after six months with the problem "much improved," and Mr. X reported at one-year follow-up that the improvement had been maintained. There had been no hitting since the second interview and he said such behavior was out of his repertoire. He felt more in control of himself, and labeled the marriage as better but not perfect.

In the second case, Mr. A also came in for individual therapy at his wife's insistence and threat of leaving. Mr. A said that there were major marital conflicts, but that his wife refused to come in for therapy because the problems were his. The client agreed that most of the problems were his, in that he was verbally abusive to his wife and daughter. The contract was to work on an individual basis for his personal change. After a few sessions, however, it was apparent that their 15-year-old daughter was getting caught in marital disputes, and her severe acting out behavior was causing Mr. A great concern. Since her acts were illegal and dangerous, this concern was taken seriously.

In this situation, two consultation visits were called for and held. First, Mrs. A was seen alone to get her view of the problem. From this visit it seemed clear that after years of feeling bullied and put down by her husband, Mrs. A had gained power by joining forces with her daughter against her husband. This rebalancing of power had harmful side effects on the daughter, however. Things had gotten out of hand and now Mrs. A was also concerned about the girl's behavior. A second consultation visit was called where Mr. and Mrs. A were asked to come in together with their daughter, Amy. I explained that Mr. A was my client and was "here for this session as a listener" as his wife and daughter served as consultants to me. I told Mrs. A and Amy that Mr. A was seeing me to work on his problem of temper, that he wanted to learn to express his love for them and his frustration with them in more positive ways. Information obtained from this visit showed that Amy was severely depressed; there was a sudden 15-pound weight loss and two suicide attempts. Amy indicated that she could get what she wanted when her parents were fighting because her mother disagreed with the father's rules for her. When her parents patched things up, however, Amy felt left out and lonely.

This consultation session was used to restructure family boundaries by getting Amy out of the marital disagreements. The family was told that Amy was depressed and needed strict rules clearly set and enforced by both parents working together, and that they should also give Amy more time, positive attention, and concern. I framed her acting out behavior as a call for help and said that they should work together to help her regardless of their own marital issues.

The effects of this consultation altered the family patterns radically. The parents set and enforced strict limits and Amy's behavior improved quickly. In further individual sessions, Mr. A reported that Amy was less depressed and less disruptive, that he and his wife were no longer fighting over Amy, and that he was not yelling at either of them. With Amy no longer in the middle, the marital couple now had to face their own issues. They agreed to conjoint marital counseling, a plan Mrs. A would not have agreed to two months earlier. Since I was viewed as Mr. A's therapist, it was decided that they would begin anew with a different therapist, a plan I endorsed and the case was closed.

In both of these situations, the outside contact was an important variable in the change process. Even when a consultation visit was refused, the phone contact altered the sequence that had sabotaged previous therapeutic attempts. In both situations, different alliances were formed, the view of the problem was changed, and restructuring allowed for new alternatives to be found. It is important to note that the terms were adhered to and the consulting family members were never redefined or treated as clients.

This technique was used differently in a situation in which I was a consultant to a therapist who felt stuck. The therapist's agency mandated several hours a week with the family as a whole, but the parents resisted the intervention saying the problem resided in their teenage son and he should be treated. The therapist's attempts to redefine the problem as a family problem increased the parents' anger and resentment. I recommended that the therapist go with the family's problem definition, but to ask the parents to continue to meet with her weekly for consultation regarding their son. The therapist reported a remarkable shift in parental involvement and progress ensued.

In summary, it is sometimes important to involve family members of clients in individual therapy. Using these family members as "consultants" is one way to involve them. This therapeutic technique, as others, needs to be used judiciously and based on an individualized hypothesis.

REFERENCES

Boscolo, L., Cecchin, G., Hoffman, L., & Penn, P. (1987). *Milan systemic family therapy: Conversations in theory and practice*. New York: Basic Books.
de Shazer, S., & Berg, I. (1985). A part is not apart: Working with only one of the partners present. In A. Gurman (Ed.), *Casebook of marital therapy* (pp. 97-110). New York: Guilford Press.
Fisch, R., Weakland, J., & Segal, L. (1982). *The tactics of change*. San Francisco: Jossey-Bass.

64

The Use of Fantasy
in Breaking Through Impasse

Peggy Papp

Fantasies and metaphors can be used as a powerful means of breaking through therapeutic impasse by giving clients a different perspective on their problem. One effective way to do this is for the therapist to construct a fantasy about the particular situation that he/she believes is leading to the impasse and then relate this personal fantasy to the client. The fantasy introduces a new way of thinking about the problem as it shifts the therapeutic landscape from the literal to the symbolic and metaphorical. The clients are cast into new roles in a new play that has a different meaning and, therefore, a different resolution.

Clients generally respond with a mixture of surprise, pleasure, and curiosity to the therapist's statement, "I had a fantasy about you." It makes them feel very important to know that not only are they on the therapist's mind but they have entered his/her fantasy life. The realm of fantasy, like the realm of dreams, is laden with prophetic and mythical connotation.

In the following case,* a fantasy was used to break through an impasse with a gay couple who described their relationship as being "stuck." Shirley and Maggie had been seeing each other for the past nine years, but neither felt their relationship was going anywhere in terms of a permanent commitment. Although most of the

---

*Note: This case was seen in a special project on themes in which Evan Imber-Black served as my consultant observing sessions from the other side of the one-way mirror.

dialogue in the sessions centered around this theme of commitment, it became clear that each was afraid of committing herself to the relationship and each used different ways of keeping one another at a distance. Sessions tended to get bogged down in petty arguments over who had distanced from whom, not been attentive enough, or not met a particular need at a particular time.

In gathering historical information, I was struck by the similarity of each having lost a parent at an early age. Maggie's mother died of a heart attack when she was 15. Her father died three months later and she went to live with her father's sister, her favorite aunt. She had always suspected her mother and this aunt of having a lesbian relationship because of the intensity and emotional closeness they displayed when together. It was common knowledge that her mother was unhappy and dissatisfied with her husband and that she and her aunt were constant companions. The nature of their relationship was never openly acknowledged by anyone in the family.

At fourteen, when Maggie realized she was gay, she told her mother who burst into tears and repeatedly asked, "What did I do wrong?" She tried to persuade Maggie it wasn't true and forbid her to continue to see her girlfriends. Maggie rebelled and violent fights ensued. Her mother died shortly after her revelation, leaving Maggie feeling extremely ashamed and guilty.

Shirley's father, whom she adored, died of a heart attack when she was five years old. She saw him taken from the home but was never told he was dead and was not allowed to attend the funeral. No one ever talked about him and for years she expected him to walk through the door. Shirley, although the youngest of the three daughters, became the caretaker in the family, her mother's confidant and comforter and the one who assumed responsibility for her emotional well-being. Her two sisters were now living away from home but Shirley stayed close to her mother who continued to lean on her emotionally.

Neither Maggie nor Shirley had told anyone in their families they were gay, both fearing negative reactions.

Several aspects of their situation struck me as playing a critical role in their lack of commitment and their current impasse. One was their isolation from their outside systems and the fact that their relationship had not been confirmed by their family or friends. It would be difficult for either to commit herself to a relationship so shrouded in secrecy and shame. Their entrenchment in the past and their loyalty to a dead parent also impressed me as being a stumbling block to commitment.

In light of their histories, I speculated that Maggie could not openly acknowledge her love for Shirley without feeling she was betraying her dead mother who had died disapproving of her sexual orientation. And Shirley could not acknowledge her love for Maggie without feeling she had abandoned her mother and betrayed her dead father by not taking care of her.

Because each tended to intellectualize her experiences, I decided to convey my perceptions to them through the use of fantasies. In the following session I interrupted their bickering over who was distancing from whom with, "Let me tell you about some fantasies I had about you. I think they are connected with what is happening between you now but I'm not sure. The stories you told me about your past made a profound impression on me. Maybe you can help me figure out what the fantasies mean.

"Maggie, you were an actress trying out for a play. You desperately wanted the part because you felt it was a statement about your own life and expressed your innermost thoughts and feelings. You read the part well and you got it. But on opening night you were afraid to go on stage. Your cue came up but you ran and hid in the dark wings where nobody could see you. You had seen your mother in the audience and you were afraid to play the part for fear she would disapprove of it. The message of the play was 'be true to yourself.' You were also afraid because you felt the play represented your mother's life and the things she was never able to express."

Maggie listened with rapt attention.

"I thought a lot about your dilemma and I don't know what the solution is. But I was wondering what would happen if you came out on stage and dedicated the performance to your mother — because she was never able to come out on the stage herself."

Maggie's face had gone through a multitude of emotions as she sat listening and she now started to cry saying, "That's very touching. As you were talking, you were hitting on emotions that were true. I have been hiding for so many years. Not just because I'm gay — in so many other areas of my life." This opened up a whole new vista of exploration.

I then related my fantasy about Shirley.

"Shirley, I saw you as a five-year-old child, running around the house after your father died, frightened and confused. Everything was a mystery because your family never buried him, never mourned him, so your expectation was that he would one day come through the door."

Shirley interrupted to say, "I dreamt he called the other day. He said he never really died and he was living in another state."

I said it was no wonder then that I had this fantasy and continued with, "You didn't know where to look for your father so you went into his room and there were his shoes by the bed. You stepped into his shoes and tried to make him come alive through you. The shoes were too big and very heavy but you trudged about in them trying to fulfill your father's place in the family by being this wonderful idealized image of someone who took care of everyone — all giving, loving, protective.

"In the next part of my fantasy, you were grown up. But you were still wearing his shoes, which were still heavy and burdensome and they had kept you from putting on your own shoes. In thinking about your situation, I was wondering what would happen if you stepped out of his shoes and stopped being so responsible for your family?"

Shirley replied without hesitation, "I would fall through the floor. I've never addressed what I really need and don't know what my own shoes would look and feel like."

The fantasies shifted the therapeutic ground and raised different questions concerning the presenting problem of commitment. They interrupted the squabbling over who was distancing from whom and focused attention of the central themes around commitment that ran through the lives of each. The rest of therapy was focused on the symbolic acts of Maggie coming out on the stage and Shirley stepping out of her father's shoes.

Fantasies have the power to synthesize diverse aspects of a problem and pull them together into a holistic picture. In this picture, connections can be made between different levels of functioning simultaneously: between the past and the present; between behavior and beliefs; between events and current patterns of interaction. Connecting these different threads of experience is especially important for systems therapists whose primary concern is with the interrelatedness of time, events, and relationships.

Fantasies can be used in any situation in which the therapist feels that an allegorical statement can be more effective than a direct explanation. In constructing a fantasy, I have found the following steps helpful:

1. Pull together the connecting threads that run through a person's life to form a central theme. (Maggie's theme: fear of disclosure; Shirley's theme: emotional over-responsibility.)
2. Construct a fantasy around this theme that conveys the person's dilemma in terms of the presenting problem.
3. Use the fantasy and metaphors in the ongoing therapy to continue to raise questions that point in a different direction for change.

65

Passing the Baton

Joan L. Biever
Augustus Jordan
Miguel Franco
Pamela S. Nath
Elaine F. Yee

This technique was originally developed during the live supervision of a family consisting of a mother, father, and six children. During an enactment of the family's response to Father's anger, the following pattern became clear. As the mother tried to discipline the children, Father would, in an attempt to support Mother, take over very aggressively, yelling and making demands. The children would then scatter and seek comfort from their mother because of their mutual fear of Father's behavior. This resulted in the father being more isolated and left out of the family and set up the pattern to repeat itself. Any attempts the family had made to change the pattern had not worked as all their solutions involved the father trying to take over power and ending up very angry when he was not successful.

The intervention designed was to give a "baton" (actually a rolled up piece of paper) to the parents. The instructions were that if either parent wished assistance from the other in disciplining their children, they would signal this by passing the baton. The parents also had the option of jointly holding onto the baton in order to give

---

This intervention was developed by a family therapy training team at Oaklawn Center, Elkhart, Indiana under the supervision of Joan L. Biever.

a joint message to their children. It was up to each parent as to when s/he wanted to pass the baton and each agreed to not interfere in the other's disciplining of the children until s/he was passed the baton. An agreement was made that if either parent felt like s/he was losing control, s/he would immediately pass the baton and if the other parent thought the other was losing control, s/he could ask for the baton. This intervention proved to be very helpful to the parents and they frequently used it at home, making some modifications to better fit it into their lives. Since that time the intervention has also been given to other families in similar circumstances and has proved to be beneficial in most cases.

This intervention can probably be viewed from several theoretical perspectives. The original intent was to interrupt a longstanding, repetitive, counterproductive pattern. Simply adding another step into the sequence allowed for a changing of the sequence of events. The intervention can also be viewed as a reframing technique as Father's verbal aggressiveness was framed as an attempt to join his wife in the parenting process. The passing of the baton also reframed parenting as a cooperative team event. Previously, the parents had had a subtle competition as to who had the best parenting techniques.

It is also possible to view this intervention from a structural perspective. Through the process of passing the baton, the parents formed an alliance as a parenting team, with each member relying on the other for help and support. This broke up the cross-generational protective alliance between the mother and the children. It also provided a means for the cut-off isolated father to join in the parenting process in a way that did not further alienate him. Indeed, it also allowed Father a way to ask Mother for help when he got stuck in parenting rather than simply becoming more and more angry as his parenting techniques were not successful.

This intervention is appropriate for use in two-parent families in which one of the parents is cut-off and uses verbal dominance as a means of trying to join the family. It has been useful with stepfamilies where the symbolic invitation to join in the parenting process is very powerful.

This most likely is not an intervention that should be used in families in which there is physical violence, since the implied reframing of violence as an attempt to help could be seen as minimizing the seriousness of violence in a family.

−66−

Using Bowen's Differentiation of Self Scale to Help Couples Understand and Resolve Marital Conflict

David Fenell

INTRODUCTION

When a couple enters marital therapy, each spouse has developed a stable but ineffective system for understanding his or her behavior as well as the behavior of the partner.

After establishing an effective working relationship with each spouse in conjoint treatment, I attempt to create a new system for the couple to use in understanding their difficulties. Change is more likely to occur in a relatively brief period of time if I am able to redefine marital problems and their causes in a way that fully incorporates the information the couple has presented about their situation (Fenell & Weinhold, 1989). A successful redefinition will frequently engender hope in the couple as they experience their negative behaviors in new ways.

One technique that I frequently use to help couples understand and resolve their marital conflict employs the use of Bowen's (1978) differentiation of self scale. I use the scale as a tool to help the partners experience their current situation in a new way that makes sense to them and offers solutions to their problems.

BRIEF THEORETICAL BACKGROUND

Bowen's differentiation of self scale is a theoretical scale for understanding human functioning rather than an actual instrument that measures differentiation in individuals. The scale ranges from 0 to 100. A person who is unable to separate feelings and thoughts and reacts to most situations emotionally would be located lower on the scale, somewhere between 0 and 50. A person who reacts thoughtfully to most situations and rarely allows emotions to rule rational thinking would be located higher on the scale, somewhere between 50 and 100 (Bowen, 1978).

Bowen postulated that individuals select marriage partners who are at the same level of differentiation as themselves. This selection process allows the couple to form a stable equilibrium in their marriage. Additionally, Bowen believed that individuals maintain their level of differentiation unless specific steps are taken to raise the level.

THE INTERVENTION

After developing the couple's trust and establishing credibility as someone who can help them with their problems, I attempt to find out what has been tried in an effort to resolve the marital problems that has not been successful. This serves two purposes. First, it tells me what not to try. Second, it reminds the couple that their solutions have not been successful and that seeking professional assistance makes good sense.

I then introduce the intervention to the couple by stating that I have developed an understanding of what is happening in their marriage that is leading to their present difficulties. I ask if they would like me to share this understanding with them. Invariably the couple wants to know what I have discovered and I proceed with the intervention.

I introduce the notion of differentiation of self giving Bowen full credit for the concept. Crediting Bowen adds additional expert power to the intervention. Once the couple has a clear understanding of the concept of differentiation of self, I tell them that Bowen discovered that individuals seek marriage partners with the same differentiation as themselves. To add additional credence to this statement, it is often useful to describe behaviors that each spouse has exhibited in therapy that exemplify the inability of each to separate their emotions and intellect. These behaviors are usually not difficult to identify in a troubled marriage.

When the couple has accepted that they selected each other based on their similar levels of differentiation, I draw two Differentiation of Self Scales on a chalkboard: a "Husband Scale" and a "Wife Scale." I then select a similar point on each scale to identify each partner's position before the current difficulties began. I usually select a point slightly below 50 so that the couple will not feel too dysfunctional and thus helpless but will recognize that they need to make some growth. During this phase of the intervention I disclose that increased differentiation is possible if they want it and will take specific steps to make it happen.

After the couple agrees to work toward increased differentiation, I modify one of the scales to show how one spouse has attempted to change one or more of the rules of marriage. This attempt to change a previously rigidly enforced rule is framed as an attempt to increase differentiation by one spouse. I then explain to the couple that when one spouse attempts to change a rule, it threatens the equilibrium of the relationship and the other spouse will try mightily to get the partner to return to the expected behavior. I then reveal that this normal process in marital development is causing their current problems. Thus, the new frame of reference for the couple is as follows:

"You are engaged in a *normal* process. She is attempting to change a family rule or rules which by definition will increase her differentiation of self. He is responding normally by trying to maintain the marriage at its current level. The need to grow and differentiate and the need to remain the same are not compatible. Thus, the two of you need to decide what course of action you want to take. There are several options.

1. "*You* (partner A) can return to your old behavior and stop seeking change.
2. "You as a couple can remain as you currently are and remain unhappily married or seek other solutions.

3. "As individuals you can elect to remain as you are and end the marriage.
4. "*You* (partner B) can develop additional flexibility concerning the rules being challenged and negotiate new rules."

Each of these options may be visually depicted on the two scales drawn for the couple. As the couple review these choices they generally rule out choices 1, 2, and 3. A return to the old pattern is usually not selected because it would be contrary to their previously stated goal of increased differentiation. Further, the spouse seeking change is rarely happy when giving up an attempt for personal growth. Some partners may elect this option to the marriage, however. Remaining as they currently are is not the choice usually made because this is the pattern that has brought the couple to therapy. Remaining as they currently are and leaving the marriage is also usually not selected. The couple is usually in therapy to discover ways to resolve their problems rather than leave the marriage. However, the therapist must not rule out the possibility that one or both of the spouses may want to leave the marriage.

The option most often selected is to develop additional flexibility in the marriage and renegotiate the current rules. When the couple selects this course of action I share with them that this is the first of many opportunities that they will have to increase their levels of differentiation of self. I attempt to rebalance the system by telling them that the next time growth in the marriage is needed it will most likely be the husband that initiates the growth step and that the wife will most likely initially resist. Further, as they become more familiar with the steps in the process, they will recognize it as an opportunity for growth and development rather than a threat to the stability of the marriage.

INDICATIONS AND CONTRAINDICATIONS

This intervention is particularly useful in situations which one spouse is seeking to renegotiate family rules and the other is resisting this. I have found it especially useful with couples when the wife is seeking to expand the definition of her role from homemaker to the professional person and the husband is not supportive. This technique is also useful when the husband attempts to change his role as husband, parent, or provider and the wife is not supportive of his need for change.

This technique is contraindicated for couples when severe psychopathology is present. Further, this technique identifies one spouse as the person seeking growth and the other as the person resisting growth. The therapist must be sure to rebalance the marital system so that these roles are acknowledged as temporary and the couple knows that the roles frequently alternate between partners.

CASE EXAMPLE

Mr. and Mrs. Collins entered therapy because of Mrs. Collins' symptoms of depression and her withdrawal from Mr. Collins. Through the interview process it became clear that Mr. Collins was going to quit his excellent job and start a business of his own. Mrs. Collins became concerned that they would lose their security and tried to persuade Mr. Collins to change his mind. When it became clear that Mr. Collins was determined to follow his dream, Mrs. Collins developed symptoms of depression and withdrew from him. She reported that the depression was the result of Mr. Collins' lack of love. If he loved her he would not quit his present job. Mr. Collins insisted that he did love his wife and that he was at wits end. If he did not follow his dream, he would not feel good about himself. If he did follow his dream, he would lose his wife.

The therapist used the Differentiation of Self Scale technique with this couple. Through the visualization of their situation, the couple was able to understand what was happening to them and to their marriage. This empowered them to make choices about how they wanted to proceed. Mrs. Collins gradually became willing to renegotiate the rule that Mr. Collins not take any risks concerning their financial security and began to assist him in planning for the transition to the new business. Mrs. Collins' depression lifted and the marriage reestablished itself at a higher level of differentiation of self.

A year later Mrs. Collins decided that since the kids were in high school she would return to the university for study. Mr. Collins objected to this. He told Mrs. Collins that she was threatening their marriage if she followed through with her plan. The couple returned to therapy and quickly came to realize that they were going through the same pattern with their roles reversed. The therapist reminded them that this pattern is one that most healthy marriages go through at regular intervals. Moreover, each time a marriage goes through the cycle and partners renegotiate their contract, the individuals in the marriage increase their differentiation and ability to resolve marital problems that may occur in the future without professional assistance.

REFERENCES

Bowen, M. (1978). *Family therapy in clinical practice*. New York: Jason Aronson.

Fenell, D., & Weinhold, B. (1989). *Counseling families: An introduction to marriage and family therapy*. Denver: Love Publishing Co.

67

Resurrecting the Ghost of the Master: A Split-Team Technique with One Therapist

Joseph L. Wetchler

Treatment teams have had wide popularity in the family therapy (e.g., Papp, 1980) and supervision (e.g., Liddle & Schwartz, 1983) literatures. A team of clinicians/supervisors observes the session from behind a one-way mirror and provides direction to the therapist or intervenes with the family. Team therapy appears to be clinically effective (Green & Herget, 1989a, 1989b) and is positively evaluated by treatment families (Piercy, Sprenkle, & Constantine, 1986).

Unfortunately, the use of treatment teams may not always be cost effective. The expense of installing a one-way mirror and bringing several therapists together for one case may by more than some settings can afford. While cost and availability may be a problem in the use of these techniques, they can be modified for use with one clinician.

RESURRECTING THE GHOST OF THE MASTER

A common clinical problem is the need to confront families on important issues while running the risk of their leaving treatment. Papp (1980) discusses using the team to form a therapeutic triangle to bypass this situation. The therapist allies with the family while the team takes an oppositional stance. This can be done by the team arguing against change while the therapist supports the positive aspects of change or by the team confronting the family on a certain issue while the therapist takes a confused or passive role.

The technique of "resurrecting the ghost of the master" allows therapists to create an oppositional entity while maintaining their alliance with the family. When faced with a situation in which confrontation is necessary, the therapist states what a famous therapist, either dead or living, might say to them about their problem. The therapist is free to either disagree with this statement, agree with it, or maintain a neutral stance and question the family on their thoughts about the "master's" suggestions.

RESURRECTING MILTON ERICKSON TO CONFRONT CONFLICTUAL COUPLES

Conflictual couples often blame their spouses for their marital difficulties. Each member tries to enlist the therapist as an ally against the other. Attempts to show that their marital problems are jointly shared often result in both spouses feeling betrayed by the therapist. A helpful intervention is to resurrect the ghost of Milton Erickson to confront the couple on their joint ownership of the problem. The therapist paraphrases a technique described by Haley (1973) and asks the couple how it relates to them:

> There once was a famous therapist named Milton Erickson who, many believe, was the greatest clinician that ever practiced. He had a technique for couples with problems similar to yours. First, he would listen to the husband's side of the story and then turn to the wife and say in astonishment, "He actually believes every word he says!" This would initially anger the husband while getting a chuckle from the wife. Next, he would ask the wife to state her side of the issue. After she had finished, he would proclaim to the husband with equal amazement, "She actually believes every word she says!" This time the wife would get angry while the husband would laugh. While the couple might initially be upset with him for these comments, after they had time to think about them, they would often view their problems in a new light.

I am not sure why he would do this with couples who argue.

Do you have any idea what he means and why he might say this to you?

After telling this story, the therapist can discuss it with the couple during the session or give them a homework assignment to think about it and report their thoughts the following week. Couples typically respond to this by moving from their position of "I'm right and he/she is wrong," to recognizing that they both are part of the problem.

DISCUSSION

Resurrecting a famous therapist to confront a family allows clinicians to maintain close relationships with their clients while having someone else take the role of the heavy. It should be used when an important confrontation might threaten a therapeutic relationship and not as a crutch for clinicians who are afraid of being assertive. Therapists can use other master clinicians (Carl Whitaker is an excellent source of provocative stories), famous historical figures, or present-day personalities. The use of a person in authority is helpful as it makes the intervention harder to ignore; however, therapists also can use their relatives or friends if they fit the situation.

Therapists are warned that overuse of this technique can be viewed as gimmicky by treatment families. While it may be helpful in bypassing client resistance, it is no substitute for a solid therapeutic relationship. Clinicians should have some experience with team therapy or work with a supervisor with knowledge of these techniques before attempting them alone.

REFERENCES

Green, R.J., & Herget, M. (1989a). Outcomes of systemic/strategic team consultation: I. Overview and one-month results. *Family Process, 28,* 37-58.
Green, R.J., & Herget, M. (1989b). Outcomes of systemic/strategic team consultation: II. Three-year followup and a theory of "emergent design." *Family Process, 28,* 419-437.
Haley, J. (1973). *Uncommon therapy: The psychiatric techniques of Milton H. Erickson, M.D.* New York: Norton.

Liddle, H.A., & Schwartz, R.C. (1983). Live supervision/consultation: Conceptual and pragmatic guidelines for family therapy trainer. *Family Process, 22,* 491-500.

Papp, P. (1980). The Greek chorus and other techniques of paradoxical therapy. *Family Process, 19,* 45-57.

Piercy, F.P., Sprenkle, D.H., & Constantine, J.A. (1986). Family members' perception of live observation/supervision: An exploratory study. *Contemporary Family Therapy: An International Journal, 8,* 171-187.

68

Strands of Change

Maria Flores

I adopt the view that interventions are refined human interactions that flow from the assessment of the "trouble" in the family. In my practice, I consistently find that Family-of-Origin based interventions have a character of multiple layering that continues to create strands of changes that fascinate me. My approach to this case grows out of the family-systems theory developed over the past twenty years by Murray Bowen (Kerr & Bowen, 1988). My intervention style is very different from Bowen's, but often my theoretical interpretation is based on his Family-of-Origin principles. I also often include metaphorical messages patterned after the work of Milton Erickson (Haley, 1973).

Several Family-of-Origin based interventions moved two people to a better life with creative fun. The couple's presenting problem was described as a sexual problem. The couple had been to a sex therapist who had taken them through sex exercises. However, when it was time to talk about their communication problem, the couple abruptly stopped therapy. At first they thought it was because the sex exercises, though helpful, were boring for both of them. Later, they both began to realize that the interplay between sex and communication were intricately related for them as a couple.

The subsequent interventions in their lives were based on the analysis of the family-of-origins of two very controlling people. The control theme in each family-of-origin was operating and contaminating their present family style. The husband was from a family of accountants and was the on-site accountant of a large firm. He counted everything, like his father, grandfather, and great-grandfather before him. The number of times he had sex with his wife was particularly frustrating to him: "Only twice a week," or "Four straight days without sex." He, however, would never initiate contact. If he initiated sex, she rejected him, and he was left frustrated, in pain, and waiting.

The wife was from a small town. Though her parents were prominent in the small community, her successful, debonair father and her sophisticated, stunning mother were both alcoholics. Growing up, she had been the "parent" of two charming, drunk people. Being in control was important to her. Her younger, rebellious, and angry sister went to a boarding school as a freshman in high school, then commuted to a large city for college where she became pregnant and quickly married her present husband.

When discussing the trouble in the marriage, the wife admitted she controlled their sex encounters and she agreed that she would probably reject any initiation of sex on his part. She said, "I enjoy sex when we have it." However, "My problem is that he never sets the mood for love; you know, romance." Her statement led me to believe he, the accountant, controlled the purchase mood for romance. He said, "Well, as for the flowers and diamond rings, I control the money." In further investigation, it became obvious that his control of the budget paralleled her control of sex. Every penny was accounted for with no frivolous or spontaneous spending of any kind. With all "his" wealth, there seemed to be no money for fun. For example, if she would initiate a "frivolous gift" such as buying a bouquet of flowers for $3.98, he would be grumpy and rejecting. She said, "He controls the fun, the frivolous, and rejects any spontaneous activities and this is frustrating." She told him that what was needed to set a mood for lovemaking more than twice a week was romance, yet he would not respond to any form of romance. She would wait for a flower, a pretty gift, that extra drink or cheesecake after a movie or show but none would come. Her pain was revealed when she shared that flowers cheered her up, yet she wouldn't buy them for herself for fear of his anger and rejection. He had to agree that he did not want her to initiate anything out of the ordinary. After all, she had a budget for all she needed.

This couple respected each other's area of control. As with most couples, insight alone was not sufficient to motivate change. However, with this couple, understanding what was blocking them was a valuable first step in their process. Genograms were used to clarify their insights. Once this understanding was reached, I employed basic Family-of-Origin interventions, linking their past family patterns of control to the present family patterns of control. I found that this simple interchange between them was helpful. They surrendered their outmoded behaviors of control. For example, control was admittedly useful at one time: protection for him and survival for her. Control now stifled their present relationship. He saw that he did not have to protect himself from his wife as he had from his mother. His wife did not want to dictate his behavior or for that matter possess him. She in turn learned that to survive in her family-of-origin meant she had to control relational interactions but with her husband she could relax and let down her guard since he would not exploit her. Their exchange was enough to crack and thaw the ice of the past that was still very much alive. Discussing the possibilities of how to update their attitudes toward control was fun for them. Very specifically, up until now, controlling each other seemed more important than the other person's need for the frivolous sex and frivolous romance.

In order to continue amplifying the melting of the icy control, my assignment to them was to ponder and think about whether there was space for the other person to initiate the frivolous in the other's area of control. This was planned to challenge the couple's differentiated selves. Can they share more control and maintain self? I encouraged them to draw in their minds geometric circles of how much area could be given up to the other person, thus asking them to bring a thinking process to an emotional issue. This part of the intervention was also based on Family-of-Origin information that both were introverts and enjoyed many solitary days by themselves thinking about things and images. I used old habits to create a new reality. Then I dramatically stressed that, only after very deep and thoughtful pondering, it might be possible to experiment with initiating what they wanted, ever ready to pull back if the other person was rejecting. This dramatic intervention was used to match what Bowen calls the "emotional system." I consistently attempt to match emotional systems in the couple by affect.

Two weeks passed before the next session. The couple came in saying that almost by accident something different happened the previous weekend. They went up to the university to visit their daughter for parents' weekend. They went to the football game, then had a nice dinner with their daughter and her friends. They waved goodbye and decided to stay over in a motel. Each described how the other "allowed" the other to initiate. She initiated a frivolous "stay over in a motel, an unplanned price tag item" and he initiated sex. This was the beginning of the shift to "allow" the other space in each other's realm of control. This was the first of many such encounters.

A second intervention dealt with clarifying "a small doubt" the husband brought in. He was feeling uncomfortable with the thought that there was an exchange here, money for sex, sex for gifts, etc., and he did not like it. He did not want to buy sex from her or rather, he shared embarrassingly, he wanted her to want him. She looked at him in a shocked way. She assured him that there was no exchange in her mind. She enjoyed sex with him as much as he with her. But she admitted that sex twice a week met her needs and anything beyond that was frivolous. So something more was needed for a love encounter as a special mood, an atmosphere for romance. The actual money or romance was not the issue, nor was there a sex for money or money for sex parallel operating.

What this interchange revealed was that in both families-of-origin, the lack of affection was an issue that was now spilling into their present lives. In Family-of-Origin work, I find, once the ice melts, things spilled can be dealt with effectively. She revealed that any touch from him meant sex; no affection was exchanged for the simple joy of affection, affirmation, and care. When we probed into his family-of-origin, he found there was no touching in his family-of-origin house. He shunned all touch or affection except with his wife, and his touch was meant to communicate and give the message that he wanted sex. He felt saddened that he hardly ever hugged his two daughters. He also became aware that he shunned them as he shunned his "controlling and suffocating" mother when growing up.

His wife, on the other hand, felt she had seen a lot of touching between her parents. And to her dismay, she realized that she perceived that her parents never touched unless the touch implied an anticipated sexual encounter. With this heightened awareness, both acknowledged the need for simple affection. This new information added a third dimension to their lives: the freedom to hug the teenagers was an overdue change for the family.

These Family-of-Origin based interventions created one of those culminating a-ha! moments when the husband said, "I thought I needed more sex" and the wife said, "I thought I needed more romance." And then they both acknowledged that sex and romance were not enough: They needed more, and the more was simple, unconditional affection with no demands attached.

As this interchange naturally amplified, I had two different and more exciting people at the termination of the case. Both surprisingly admitted that they felt they had greater control of their lives, even though their world seemed larger, more complicated. As she stated, "Our love life is now three dimensional: sex, romance, and affection!" to which he humorously responded, "there is so much here; no one is counting."

REFERENCES

Haley, J. (1973). *Uncommon therapy: The psychiatric techniques of Milton H. Erickson, M.D.* New York: Norton.

Kerr, M., & Bowen, M. (1988). *Family evaluation.* New York: W.W. Norton and Company.

69

"Pretend a Miracle Happened": A Brief Therapy Task

Insoo Kim Berg

RATIONALE

The task of any therapeutic intervention is to interrupt problem patterns and generate possible solutions to the problems that clients bring to therapists. Interviewing is the tool used to generate workable, feasible steps that will achieve this task.

During the interview it is more useful to focus on what the client is doing successfully already and get him/her to repeat that successful behavior than to concentrate on shortcomings and failures (de Shazer, 1985; 1988). In contrast, when the search for causal factor is emphasized, the therapeutic endeavor often appears to be one of placing blame on someone or something.

This intervention is an adaptation of the "Crystal Ball" technique (de Shazer, 1978) and is designed to help the client to project to the future when the problem is solved. Therefore, detailed attention is paid to the state of the solution: who will do what, how, when, how they will act differently, and so on.

This intervention is also an excellent tool for setting concrete goals that clients can realistically achieve since the solution is generated by the client, not the therapist. Since the image of solution is generated by the client and not the therapist, it is more congruent with the client system and, therefore, fits better.

When the client is able to describe a vivid picture of a miracle day when the problem is solved, the therapist can ask whether he/she has such days now, even once in a while. If the answer is yes, the therapist can get him/her to repeat it, thus increasing the frequency of exceptions to the problems.

TYPE OF PROBLEM/FAMILY SUITED FOR THIS INTERVENTION

This technique is suitable for all clients with a little bit of imagination, who really want to solve problems, and are willing to take some steps toward finding solutions. It is applicable to individual, couple, or family sessions. Answering these questions often generates very positive emotional responses in clients since they can see that a solution is possible, and they can imagine what can happen to the situation they think is impossible to solve.

In a family, each member may have a different "picture of the miracle," but they are usually different aspects of the same solutions and successes.

This technique is not suitable for clients who are initially "dragged in" to see the therapist and are not terribly bothered or upset by the "problem" that got them into therapy. Another unsuitable group is those clients who see no hope of their life changing; that is, clients with a view that "It is my fate" or "It is God's will" and are resigned to suffer through. These clients need other interventions before they can even imagine their problem being solved.

Therapists can often influence even those who are "dragged in" against their wishes or see no hope of changing by engendering hope and possibility for them. It is often accomplished by eliciting an "exception to the problem," such as when they were more successful, did not have to be told what to do, had more initiatives with their lives, and so on.

DESCRIPTION OF INTERVENTION

During the interview, the therapist asks the client the following question:

"Suppose you go to bed tonight and while you are sleeping a miracle happens and the problem that brought you here is solved. (Some use a magic wand.) What do you suppose will be different tomorrow morning that will tell you that something is different, that maybe a miracle has happened?''

Detailed questions about how the client will behave, feel, what others will notice different about him/her, how the client will interact with others, and so on, can be asked.

APPLICATION: CASE EXAMPLE

Tiffany, a sullen, unhappy-looking 15-year-old who frowned throughout the session, was brought by her mother. The parents had been through a bitter divorce and the mother was very concerned about Tiffany "losing out in life," saying that even though she is bright, she has had longstanding problems in school, fights, is failing in every subject, talks all the time if she shows up in classes, and skips classes even though she goes to school every day. The therapist learned Tiffany had an abortion last year. Both the school and mother were exhausted and had run out of ideas on what to do with Tiffany.

Tiffany agreed that she never, ever liked school, even though she knew she was smart because everybody told her so. She did well during the last summer school, though, because she decided that she got tired of having to go to summer school. Much attention was paid to how she managed to get Bs and Cs during summer school in contrast to the failing grades she normally gets.

Tiffany became more animated as she talked about her successes and started to talk about how she did some work at school just last week since they made an appointment. This was followed by more questions about how she managed to do so well. Through these questions about her past and current successes, Tiffany became interested in solving her problems and finally feeling good about herself.

Toward the end of the session I asked her "the miracle question," to which Tiffany had a detailed description of what she will be doing after the miracle: she will get up on time, get ready for school on her own, show up in class, pay attention, do the work, ask for extra help from teachers, and so on.

Intervention Message to Mother and Tiffany

Therapist: (To mother) "We are very impressed by the faith you have in your daughter's ability to do better even after all you went through with her. It is clear that you taught her all the things she needs to know to do better. She knows what is right and wrong; she knows how to say no to drugs. You also thought a lot about what will help Tiffany and have tried many things, such as dance and music lessons, and so on."

Mother: "I know the divorce was rough on her. To make things easier I even moved to a better neighborhood, thinking that would motivate her."

Therapist: "You really have done a lot, haven't you?" (To Tiffany) "Tiffany, we are impressed by how you know what you like and don't like, what is good for you and what is bad for you and you know what to do not to get into drugs and not to get pregnant again. That is very impressive. You have wonderful social skills and you know how to take care of yourself. Even if you have to fight, you know how to do that, too. You know exactly what you have to do, that is, get to class, stay in class, and do the homework.

"We have a suggestion for you. During the next week, we want you to pick two days of your choice and pretend that a miracle happened and do all the things you will do. Keep it a secret from your mom which days you picked. While you are doing that, we want you to guess whether your mom notices which days you picked."

To Mom: "We suggest that you do not say anything to Tiffany about what she knows and what she has to do for one week. Just get off her case for one week while you are guessing which days she picked. When you think she had a miracle day, we suggest that you do something nice for her, such as cook her favorite meal, be extra nice to her without saying anything, and see what you notice different about Tiffany."

Follow-Up

The case terminated in four sessions in three months. Tiffany made remarkable progress. She reported that even other kids and teachers commented about her being in class and one math teacher took her aside and told Tiffany how she noticed that Tiffany concentrated on doing her work and did not participate in talking to other kids.

REFERENCES

de Shazer, S. (1978). Brief hypnotherapy of two sexual dysfunctions: The crystal ball technique. *The American Journal of Clinical Hypnosis, 20*, 203-208.

de Shazer, S. (1985). *Keys to solution in brief therapy*. New York: W.W. Norton.

de Shazer, S. (1988). *Clues: Constructing solutions in brief therapy*. New York: W.W. Norton.

70

The Addict's Funeral Plans

Joyce K. Gilkey

THEORETICAL ORIENTATION: STRATEGIC

In this series of interventions, the therapist used the metaphor of "clean living" as a dangerous venture and the making of "funeral plans" to forecast caution in a cocaine addict's future. After reading the summary results of the addict's MMPI and Millon Batteries, it was determined that the coke addict's love of danger could be used to color the challenge of living drug-free after 28 days of inpatient treatment, thereby "exciting" the addict to try to live drug-free.

In the first session, funeral plans were designed with the addict's mother who was very frightened that he would be found dead eventually. She willingly and sadly planned his funeral; he attended the second half of the session and was asked to plan his funeral. At first, he balked, but then he discussed plans in the event of his death. He followed this quickly by renouncing his chances of dying and claiming his desire to live drug-free. The therapist ended the session by asking if she could light what she thought might be the addict's last cigarette. The addict scoffed but allowed her to do so. The sadness of the loss to the family was discussed a few minutes further with the addict disgustedly remarking, "I don't want to die."

The next several sessions re-emphasized the "danger" of clean living and the probability of the need for a funeral. In the second session, reports of client progress were followed by cautions and lamentations on the therapist's part. In the next two sessions, progress reports were followed by confusion on the therapist's part as to how the addict could be continuing to live drug-free. The therapist's confused remarks led to the addict's clarifying answers (attending AA and NA meetings, reading AA literature, letting go of druggie friends, playing golf, staying at home, and thinking about looking for a job). Therapy ended with the addict continuing to do all of the above, living drug-free and expressing a continual desire to live.

In this case, these interventions were used after reading the results of the MMPI and Millon Inventories. The view of self and others, the addict's love of the threat of danger, and the very real dilemma of trying to live drug-free after treatment were combined usefully with the cautionary prediction of the addict's probable demise. The danger the addict seemed to need was living "drug-free." Indications include all of the above, a slow change in attitude during treatment, the addict's early casual responses to pertinent issues in individual therapy, defiance of rules and limits in the program, and attraction towards serious risk-taking.

The addict's response to these interventions was to begin to rearrange his life drug-free. At three months, he continues to be drug-free and to be in attendance at AA/NA meetings. The mother's response was to take "one day at a time" as directed by her Al-Anon literature and remain thankful for each day of her son's life.

71

The "What-If" Technique

Leslie Ann Cotney
Christopher Hight

The purpose of this paper is to describe the use of a technique that we call "what-if." Playing the "what-if" game is nothing new to therapists. We use it frequently, but in this paper we used the technique in an innovative way. The "what-if" technique was used to address the presenting problem in a strategic framework.

THE FAMILY PROBLEM AND THE INTERVENTION

The S family presented with the oldest daughter, Mary, as the identified patient. This 21-year-old had unceremoniously left home at age 18. She was living with her boyfriend when she had an alcohol-induced psychotic episode after drinking almost a fifth of tequila. Her boyfriend called her parents when he could not control her or the damage she was doing. Mary's family placed her in a local psychiatric hospital. After a five-day stay for detoxification, she was discharged for lack of insurance and referred to the McPhaul Marriage and Family Therapy Clinic for follow-up.

Mary and her mother came to the initial therapy session. One of the first goals of therapy was to find out what the family believed the problem to be and what they believed "caused" the trouble that this daughter was experiencing. This was difficult since neither

Note: We would like to thank the University of Georgia Faculty who have made our rich experiences in the McPhaul Marriage and Family Therapy Clinic possible.

Mary nor her mother wanted to believe that it might be addiction. The attending psychiatrist had diagnosed her condition as an underlying depression and it had caused the young woman's problem. The identified patient agreed with this diagnosis, although it confused her since she related no feelings of depression. Apparently there was a difference of opinion among the referring staff since the patient was placed on a chemical dependency rather than psychiatric unit and the member of the staff contacting our clinic had requested a therapist knowledgeable in chemical dependency.

In the second session, Chris worked alone with Mary to begin exploring her preferred diagnosis since the treatments for depression and chemical dependency are very different. He took both sides of the argument to avoid working against the patient's belief system and at the same time gave a new way of looking at the problem. This offered an increased understanding of addiction and a greater likelihood of compliance with treatment.

The entire family attended the third session. The S family is comprised of Mother, Father, Mary, 18-year-old Sue, and 14-year-old Tom. In this session, the therapists used circular questioning to explore the family's feelings about Mary's drinking episode and how it had changed their estranged relationship to her. It was learned that Mary's paternal grandfather was an alcoholic who had endangered his family's lives with his drinking and acting out. Each family member gave his or her opinion about what Mary's drinking episode meant and what had caused it. The family, by and large, framed the episode as due to depression and lack of communication.

Prior to the next session, we realized that we had been organized by the family system so that we had not talked about the likelihood that Mary was suffering from addiction. We decided to promote this discussion, but not force our view on the family. Instead, we decided to talk about our "fear" that the drinking was a symptom of addiction. We again reviewed the family's theory of the cause of the drinking episode. We talked about our fears, but decided to agree with the family in the session. While voicing our hesitancy, we accepted the reframe of "depression."

In the fourth session with the family, we continued to avoid overt confrontation of the family with the severity of the symptom and the likelihood that Mary was an addict. Instead, we spent the entire hour playing "what-if": what if Mary should drink again and act out without remembering her behavior? We asked each family member what it would mean if the drinking behavior was repeated. We also asked each member what they would do if Mary's behavior recurred. We wrote a behavioral contract for the family to use in case Mary drank again. The contract would act as an emergency plan to guide the family's intervention. Chris took notes and prepared the individual contracts. In the following session we all signed each other's contracts. The family was delighted to have written agreements on what to do if the crisis recurred. Each family member agreed that should the drinking behavior recur, it was not just depression, but addiction. The prevailing opinion was that "accidents happen once, not twice." Mary has not had a relapse of the problem in three months.

The identified patient and her live-in boyfriend continued therapy for other issues relating to the arrangement. She continued to make changes in her life by getting and keeping a responsible position after having been unemployed for several months.

ANALYSIS OF THE INTERVENTION

The beauty of this intervention was that we did not directly confront the family's view of the problem. If we had tried to force the issue of reframing Mary's behavior as addiction, we would have endangered our rapport with the family. We may have lost the family because the therapists' view of the problem would have differed too greatly from the family's view. Instead, we chose to make our view just a little different from the family's while using the power of the "what-if" technique to explore an alternate view of the problem.

ADVANTAGES OF THE "WHAT-IF" TECHNIQUE

This technique made the therapists' view more acceptable to the family. This made it easier to openly discuss the possibility of Mary's return to addictive behavior since the family's rule, "don't talk about unpleasant things," enabled them to avoid the issue of chemical dependency.

The "what-if" technique allowed the family to express strong emotions in a safe way since the discussion was hypothetical. In addition, the technique helped the family believe that the therapists were supportive and would aid them again if necessary. The support was felt by our lack of direct confrontation of the family's view of the problem, our use of and participation in the contract, and availability if the problem should occur again.

The "what-if" technique was powerful because we kept the family focus of the presenting problem for so long that we were able to build the intensity and maintain it for long periods during the session. This intensity sustained the family's anxiety concerning the presenting problem. Working as co-therapists was a definite advantage in building and maintaining intensity.

The "what-if" technique also functioned as a preliminary step for the use of the family behavioral contract. It built the family's anxiety to the point that the contract was a necessary and natural step in the process of terminating therapy.

THE CONTRACT FOR THE S FAMILY

In the event that Mary begins using drugs and alcohol again.

This contract is laid down as discussed in the family therapy meeting of August 23, 1989, witnessed by the co-therapy team of Christopher Hight, MS and Leslie Cotney, MA.

The family concern, since the eldest daughter, Mary, was recently hospitalized after an extreme incident involving the overuse of the drug alcohol, is that this not occur again and that Mary refrain from any use of this or any other chemical that is intended for changes in mood. It is herein described what the family believes the consequence of any further incident will be in terms of family action.

Mary: I can't have a second accident. Something would have to drive me to do it. It would mean that the problem is more severe than I think or even understand.

If this were to happen again, I would count on my family's help and seek professional help. If I get drunk and tear up the place, then I believe that it is alcoholism. If I drink for depression or another reason, then it is alcoholism and maybe depression.

Father: It is my belief that something more than alcoholism is the cause; insecurity and low self-esteem are the problems. We can help her keep high self-esteem and she needs to control her depression. There is a chance of it happening again. She needs to reach out to us for help.

If this happens again, we need to get to her and physically force her to get help. We can stabilize the crisis situation and I can be there to help in any way I can — to get her to someone who can help her.

Mother: If this were to happen again, it could not be an accident. It would mean alcoholism. I believe it would mean we are not communicating and that there was a lack of honesty.

We would not fall apart. We would help at the moment. However, the family cannot take on the problem and we would have to draw some lines about how much we can do. We would have to treat Mary adult-to-adult and let this stay between the partners (meaning Mary and her boyfriend).

Sue: If this were to happen again, it would not be an accident. It would mean that the family has been slack and not keeping up its commitment.

I shall let my parents handle the crisis and then ask Mary what we can do. I would offer religious support.

Tom: If this happens again, it would mean that Mary has a drinking problem and that we should look at our communication patterns. If Mary starts drinking again, I think we should talk to her and offer help.

Boyfriend: If this happens again, it would be a bad sign of drinking that may become a pattern. It would be a sign that she likes to drink and it would probably mess up our relationship. If this happens again, I would call her family again and listen to no argument that was an excuse for drinking.

Therapists, Chris and Leslie: If this happens, we shall be available to the family and to Mary to aid in seeking a treatment center that Mary could afford and help in accessing the health care system for Mary and the family.

(signatures of all)

Cultural Reconnections

William L. Turner

The importance of considering cultural and ethnic influences on black families involved in therapeutic processes has been the focus of several recent investigations (Boyd-Franklin, 1989; Hines & Boyd-Franklin, 1982; McGoldrick, Pearce, & Giordano, 1982; Pinderhughes, 1982). In particular, attention has been focused on the concept of biculturality and its accompanying characteristics.

Biculturality involves an aptitude to negotiate between two distinct worlds, which for African-Americans include the American mainstream and the African-American subculture. A phenomenon associated with the African-American subculture is the victim system. Pinderhughes (1982) defines the victim system as a recursive feedback process characterized as constant, predictable, and identifiable, which maintains the subjugation of minorities through oppressive and racist behaviors and operates in a manner similar to Bowen's societal projection process. This particular system jeopardizes self-esteem and exacerbates problematic reactions in communities, families, and individuals. Psychological strain is often the product of having to cope with divergent or conflicting value systems inherent in a bicultural lifestyle (Hines & Boyd-Franklin, 1982). These conflicts are generally resolved by either maintaining a disparate relationship with the American mainstream and identifying solely with one's own subculture, identifying exclusively with the mainstream culture, or integrating the two options.

An integration of the two options would be the ideal. However, unlike other ethnic populations that have had open to them the options of becoming exclusively Americanized or of integrating the two worlds, African-Americans have all too often been denied these choices. Because of the American mainstream's continued reluctance to accept African-Americans, the remaining alternatives are either isolation from the American mainstream or identification with both cultures without being able to integrate the two fully, the latter often chosen by middle-class blacks.

Biculturality can be adaptive and some African-Americans are able to become exceptionally clear about their identities and values. Such families demonstrate comfort with biculturalism and are remarkably strong, flexible, tolerant of vagueness, comfortable with diversity, and creative with both the victim system and the mainstream majority. However, great expenditures of effort and energy are required to live in two worlds, which can result in negative consequences (Pinderhughes, 1982). For some families, efforts to adjust to these different systems can contribute to conflicts in values, roles, and power, culminating in confused identities and inflexible relationships that generate and perpetuate Powerlessness. Minorities at all socioeconomic levels are confronted by the vicissitudes of a bicultural lifestyle, although these difficulties manifest themselves in different ways (Hines & Boyd-Franklin, 1982).

For upwardly mobile African-Americans who are attempting to embrace the mainstream, a particular problem resulting from biculturality has been sociocultural isolation. Sociocultural isolation manifests itself in several forms. For black families new to the middle-class, the attainment and continuance of middle-class status might require loosening emotional ties with families of origin and other support networks (McAdoo, 1988). However, when family relationships and support systems that have served as fortifications against the victim system are disrupted, great difficulty for these middle-class families can result. For example, employment-related geographic relocations disrupt and restrict the involvement of extended family support and other supportive networks. Further isolation is experienced when adults find themselves as either the only black or the only ranking black at their places of employment. They frequently feel it necessary to work harder than others in order to prove their competence and sometimes have to endure the condescension of fellow employees who pejoratively perceive them as unqualified for their jobs and suspect them of having been hired only to fulfill an affirmative action requirement.

In keeping with their middle-class agenda, upwardly mobile African-Americans often move to predominantly white neighborhoods commensurate with their upwardly mobile incomes, only to feel unwelcome, excluded, or rejected by other residents. In order to insure a quality education, their children might attend exclusive private schools, where again there are few if any other blacks. Some of these children are rejected socially, hence social development is encumbered.

Sociocultural reconnection interventions are designed to help socially and culturally isolated families build support systems by encouraging a reconnection with their ethnic and cultural roots via social organizations. These reconnections help empower families by providing them a supportive social context wherein all family members can find the support necessary for continued development.

CULTURALLY RECONNECTING THROUGH BLACK ORGANIZATIONS AND SUPPORT GROUPS

First, family members are assigned the task of selecting and participating in a black organization. They are given the rationale that they have become socially isolated and need to reconnect in order to develop appropriately. During the session, they discuss the groups available to them and, with the therapist's direction, select an appropriate group. One goal of treatment is to enhance the ability of friends, community, and the larger social system to offer effective and appropriate support. Support networks serve as buffers and supply a necessary sense of belonging. Groups of all kinds can provide support: church, political (NAACP, Urban League), service (Big Brothers, Big Sisters, Jack & Jill), school (alumni associations), self-help, and skills-building. Church groups might prove to be particularly helpful since historically, the church has been at the center of the black social community. Some middle-class minorities have very little connection or interaction with any other minorities and consequently, experience feelings of isolation, loneliness, rejection, and disconnectedness. Black clients often express feelings of comfort when they are able to network with other blacks who have similar achievement aspirations. They frequently report feeling more accepted and less self-conscious in settings where their "blackness" can be appreciated rather than merely tolerated. Emotional and relationship needs are met through these systems such that families are energized to continue life in the mainstream or find the necessary resources to make other choices.

EXPLORING KEY FAMILY EXPERIENCES WITHIN AN HISTORICAL CONTEXT

Helping a black family see itself within an historical context can benefit the family by clarifying current functioning in the context of the past as well as forging new connections and identifications that elucidate unclear images and synthesize fragmented ones. Key experiences in their families of origin and later family experiences within the context of their minority status are the foci of exploration. Issues that need to be discussed include such topics as, "What are the problems associated with being the only black on your job, at your school, or in your neighborhood?" "How do you feel about your minority status?" "How have oppression and racism affected your work, family, life?" Often, parents have never voiced these feelings in the presence of their children. The focus should be on the strengths that have evolved. Maladaptive behaviors can be reframed as failed attempts to negotiate the greater social system and serve as a springboard for further exploration.

Cultural reconnection interventions involve efforts both within and outside of the therapy sessions and have both a present and historical orientation. These interventions are precursors to other family interventions aimed at altering internal behaviors. It may be difficult for non-African American therapists to understand the degree of isolation a black family may feel, and thus they may fail to appreciate the need to maintain and strengthen the existing supports before moving toward major shifts within the family itself (Pinderhughes, 1982). If the internal system is altered without the appropriate altering of the external system, a crisis could result. According to Minuchin et al. (1967), where fluctuations due to therapeutic intervention and the realities of extrafamilial systems are nonsynchronous, therapy will be unsuccessful. Thus, therapists' efforts to enhance internal boundaries must be concomitant with influencing the larger social system to be more supportive. Because of the existence of the racism and oppression, the goal of family treatment must be to cope constructively with those stressors and to neutralize their pervasive influence.

REFERENCES

Boyd-Franklin, N. (1989). *Black families in therapy: A multisystems approach.* New York: Guilford.

Hines, P.M., & Boyd-Franklin, N. (1982). Black families. In M. McGoldrick, J. K. Pearce, & J. Giordano (Eds.), *Ethnicity and family therapy* (pp.84-107). New York: Guilford.

McAdoo, H.P. (Ed.). (1988). *Black families.* Newbury Park, CA: Sage.

McGoldrick, M., Pearce, J., & Giordano, J. (Eds.). (1982). *Ethnicity and family therapy.* New York: Guilford.

Minuchin, S., Montalvo, B., Guerney, B. G., Jr., Rosman, B. L., & Schumer, F. (1967). *Families of the slums.* New York: Basic Books.

Pinderhughes, E. (1982). Afro-American families and the victim system. In M. McGoldrick, J.K. Pearce, & J. Giordano (Eds.), *Ethnicity and family therapy* (pp.108-122). New York: Guilford.

− 73 −

Compliments

Robert O. Morrow

Ann and John had been married for twenty-six years. Their third and last child had left home just over a year earlier and now their task was to renegotiate a relationship that did not seem to have much to build upon. They had been in therapy for three months when the therapist consulted with me. He felt stuck and asked that I function as a co-therapist with him. The couple was in agreement and I studied the case history.

The two had come to the therapist after an initial call from Ann. Her telephone conversation was very brief and to the point, stating that she and her husband wished to see the therapist at the earliest time possible. Although the intake process was usually handled by the secretary, Ann insisted that she provide the information to the therapist. Their presenting problem(s) were, from Ann, "He is not willing to consider me as a person," and from John, "She made a promise to me at the time of our marriage and I've found out that she never honored it." That promise was that she would give up certain "religious beliefs" dealing with health practices and restricting the use of medical personnel.

The fact that John was a medical researcher compounded the problem. How she could dare to commit herself to a set of ideological beliefs that discredited science was more than he was willing to take and he would prefer to be free of this heretic!

Ann, a therapist in a women's shelter, was the more reticent of the two and more reflective. Both appeared unhappy: John, in a loud, demonstrative way with body language that augmented his voice; Ann in a way that suggested a quiet strength, almost a

"Mona Lisa" quality that was something akin to a mischievous trait suggesting that she knew exactly what she was doing.

At the session before I met the couple, the therapist had given them a couple of interventions. They were to go out for dinner, perhaps dancing afterwards, and then let their hearts rule the remainder of the evening. When we met together, they were asked how things went. John reported that the evening was a waste because it did not end with sex. Ann disagreed saying that it had been fun and that she had not wanted to spoil it with sex. The therapist had asked if it would be possible to pack up all the stuff that interfered with their being closely involved and leave it outside the bedroom. "Would it be possible for you just to 'go crazy'?"

"No," John replied firmly.

John could not separate Ann's beliefs from who she was. This indicated to me a purpose for the symptom: Ann's "beliefs" kept John from having to get close.

The session continued for another thirty minutes or so with the pair's differences becoming increasingly institutionalized. Finally, I suggested a break during which time I would consult with the therapist.

THE INTERVENTION

I suggested to the therapist that we compliment them on their differences and point out that even their vocations are antithetical: John is the investigative one and deals with matters in a scientific way; Ann is a person who must treat information in a confidential, even secretive, way. It had taken John a fair number of years to arrive at his conclusion that Ann had not given up her religious practices, but he had been relentless in his search. Ann, on the other hand, had been a most cooperative partner, carefully hiding the religious pamphlets, books, and even her behaviors.

When we resumed the session with Ann and John, we did as we had discussed. I told them also that I saw no reason why this prior behavior should end; in fact, it seemed to me that it was serving a great purpose and I was going to give them some tasks to help ensure that this behavior would continue.

Ann's first task was to take place over the next two weeks. She was to hide four pieces of her religious literature and then subtly give John some clues as to where they were hidden. John's first task was to find the material and the second task, to analyze it in terms of how well it followed a scientific approach in reaching conclusions. After evaluating the material, keeping in mind his devotion to science, he was to put the material back exactly where he found it. After John had analyzed the material, Ann was to do one other thing. She was to share up to three longstanding secrets with him.

They were to have this "sharing session" a week from today at this hour. If they found this part did not work, it would be the focus at the next session we would all have together.

The couple agreed to do the tasks. At this point, the first smiles appeared on their faces. In fact, they both chuckled as if to say, "Hey, that's great. This time I'll get you!" They were both very cordial to me as the session ended. In fact, there was far more a spirit of camaraderie than I usually encourage.

Ann and John continued in therapy for another three months. During those months, the therapist reported that there was more humor and more spontaneity between them. Ann became a lady of mystery and John a sentinel of fairness. Differences were reframed and placed within a complementary relationship. In essence it did appear that religion and science could be compatible if not always harmonious.

74

The Use of Gentle Paradox
to Address Negative Loyalty

Sherry L. Rediger

> I am drawing attention to the paradox involved . . . My contribution is to ask for a paradox to be accepted and tolerated and respected, and for it not to be resolved. By flight to split-off intellectual functioning it is possible to resolve the paradox, but the price of this is the loss of the value of the paradox itself.

> $-$ D. W. Winnicott
> *Playing and Reality*

Loyalties to others can be expressed in ways that are harmful to ourselves and others. Negative loyalty is a concept developed by Boszormenyi-Nagy (1987) to describe such relational binds. Therapeutically addressing issues of trust, loyalty, and fairness in relationship often requires the contextual therapist to work in close emotional proximity to the family members and, therefore, I have not found many bottled techniques to be useful in the clinical work that I do. However, as a doctoral student in marriage and family therapy, I decided to "try on" different clinical models in an effort to integrate new approaches within my contextual philosophical grounding.

The use of paradox as a clinical intervention has been controversial in the family therapy field. Combining such an intervention within an ethical contextual framework did not seem a likely possibility to me until reading the work of Lebow (1987) who first introduced me to the possibility of a "gentle" paradox. According to Lebow, the use of gentle paradox "in the context of a close position" can be effective even though classical paradoxical technique usually results in distancing the therapist and the family members (p. 6). Although Lebow does not describe what a gentle paradox might actually be, the concept stimulated my thinking and I became open to the possibility of creating gentle paradox in my work.

I had been seeing a couple in their thirties who had come for therapy because they were ready to have a baby and had not been able to conceive. Brian and Kim had been medically evaluated, but no physical diagnosis could be found to explain their inability to conceive. Kim was from Pakistan and Brian was from a rural area in the Midwest. The couple had been quite frank about the conflicts that their different cultural backgrounds brought to the marriage and also openly discussed their sexual difficulties.

While exploring their families-of-origin, Kim told me that she had been sexually abused as a very young child by a close friend of her parents. Kim was alternately enraged that this family friend had assaulted her and quite ashamed that she might have been somehow responsible for the sexual abuse. The couple had frequently discussed the impact this abuse continued to have on Kim and on the marital relationship.

Brian had grown up in an alcoholic family and had learned to cope with pain and stress by making jokes. Kim thought that Brian's jokes were insensitive and she felt wary about trusting him to understand the past incidents of sexual abuse.

After incorporating a solution-focused framework to help the couple rework marital trust issues, the therapeutic focus shifted to the impact of the past sexual abuse on the present marital relationship. It became apparent that the clinical framework needed to address the relationships in the families-of-origin.

Kim had told her parents that she had been sexually abused by their friend about five years after the abuse had stopped. Her parents believed Kim and were greatly pained, but did not confront their friend and continued to associate with him. Kim's parents told her it would be best to put the abuse behind her and to not speak of it again.

I hypothesized that Kim's belief that she was somehow responsible for the sexual assault was an expression of her extreme loyalty to her parents and a way of caring for them. If she could in some way be responsible for the sexual assault, her parents would be justified in maintaining their relationship with their friend. This belief allowed Kim to continue her relationship with her parents without making a claim that her parents confront their friend. However, this belief was very harmful for Kim to maintain as it interfered with her daily life and happiness, with her relationship with her parents, and with her new loyalty to Brian.

I decided to begin a session by openly stating my confusion to the couple. I told Kim and Brian that I had been thinking about Kim's desire to rid herself of the thought that she was responsible for the sexual abuse. I went on to say that generally, when clients wish to be rid of something I explore how the negative is helpful so that it can be replaced by something positive that is also helpful. I wondered out loud if Kim's thought that she could have been responsible for the sexual abuse was in some way helpful. I quickly stated that I was wary of this thinking because it was obvious that Kim was not responsible for the sexual abuse and she had been very clear that her thought was extremely unhelpful; nevertheless, it was something that had come into my head. I suggested perhaps my thinking would make more sense as the session progressed, or later this week, or perhaps it would not make sense at any time.

I told Kim and Brian that I had been thinking of how this thought might be helpful to her or Brian and also perhaps helpful to her family. I spent the next part of the session exploring the reactions different family members had given her when she told them she had been sexually abused. Kim was not completely satisfied with her family members' reactions, but she went on to explain how each reaction was understandable. I talked with Kim about what she ideally would have liked her family members' responses to have been.

I offered my observation that her family was a very caring family and seemed to have different ways of showing their caring. Kim replied that her family members responded *very* differently and sometimes she didn't know the responses were caring. Kim said that her mother's response had been less of what she needed than other family members' responses. I asked Kim if she would like to hear her mother's anger and pain about the sexual abuse and Kim said that she would; however, she didn't want to "stir things up." I asked her if she did not want to burden her mother and Kim agreed that this was true.

I told Kim that it would be painful for her mother to talk about Kim's sexual abuse; however, it was appropriate for Kim to ask to talk with her mother about it because Kim is the daughter and she is the mother. Kim agreed that she needed this kind of parenting from her mother and we discussed ways she might talk to her mother about the sexual abuse without *unduly* paining her.

Kim decided she could talk with her mother by requesting her mother's help. She would tell her mother that she and Brian were unsuccessful in trying to have a baby and that intercourse was very painful for her. She would tell her mother that the memories of being sexually abused were with her daily and were interfering with her life and her marriage. Kim felt her mother could respond to this request for help in a way that Kim would feel was protective and caring.

At the end of the session I summarized the themes that had emerged from exploring the responses that Kim's family had given her when she had told them about the sexual abuse. These themes centered around "caring" and "protectiveness." I stated again that Kim's family seemed to be very caring and protective of each other and I wondered how those themes might connect with the issue of Kim trying to rid herself of the thought that she was responsible for the sexual abuse. I wondered aloud if the thought was in some way protective and caring of someone. I ended the session by saying this had just been "a thought for the day" and perhaps it would make sense at some later time, or perhaps it was just a crazy idea.

In the next session, Kim exclaimed that the previous session had been very important to her — something she would remember all her life. When asked what it was about the session that was so helpful, Kim could not be specific. She said, however, that she had called her mother over the weekend and that her mother had been more caring of her than Kim had felt in a long time. Kim was planning a trip to Pakistan and had decided she would talk with her mother about the sexual abuse and ask for her help. Kim told me that she had not previously thought of her family as a caring and protective family and now believed that it was possible that she was more important to them than their friend who had sexually abused her.

Several months later, Kim returned from her native country and told me that she had talked with her parents about the sexual abuse. She found that they were able to respond to her in a way that felt very caring and supportive of her. She felt she had been parented and nurtured for the first time in a very long time.

REFERENCES

Boszormenyi-Nagy, I. (1987). *Foundations of contextual therapy: Collected papers of Ivar Boszormenyi-Nagy, M.D.* New York: Brunner/Mazel.
Lebow, Jay. (1987). Developing a personal integration in family therapy: Principles for model construction and practice. *Journal of Marital and Family Therapy, 13*, 1-13.

75

When Words Fail

Ann Lawson

Many of the techniques used by family therapists are verbal and involve the spoken word. These techniques can be limiting since people think in images as well as words. There are some powerful exceptions to these techniques such as family sculpting and the use of art with families. I have found that adding the dimension of artistic expression to therapy is useful for those families who are not masterful with words and for those families who are skilled at verbal manipulation. Families who do not communicate well can find an alternate way to do this through artistic expression; those who are skilled at manipulating words through rationalization and intellectualization can learn more direct ways to communicate.

In my experience at the Children from Alcoholic Families Prevention and Treatment Program at the Lincoln Child Guidance Center in Lincoln, Nebraska, art techniques were particularly helpful in working with alcoholic/addict families who had strong family rules against talking about the family's problems. These family members often did not know the words to use to describe their feelings and did not conceptualize the addiction problem in family systems terms. Art therapy was useful in breaking the silence and exposing family secrets, spreading the symptom to involve all family members, and freeing family members from rigid behaviors. Sometimes

Adapted from Lawson, G., Peterson, J., & Lawson, A. (1983). *Alcoholism and the family: A guide to treatment and prevention.* Rockville, MD: Aspen Publishing.

it was easier for family members to talk about what they had drawn than what was happening within or between them.

Kwiatkowska (1978), a pioneer in art evaluation and art therapy with families, described working with a family whose presenting problem was an 18-year-old boy, diagnosed as schizophrenic. After working with the family in art therapy for several sessions, she used an evaluative technique to determine the family members' views of one another. Each family member was asked to use a symbol for family members to create an abstract family portrait. Kwiatkowska stated, "It introduced the problem of the father's drinking" (pp. 145-146). The adolescent, Donnie, had used a bottle of beer to represent his father in his picture. Kwiatkowska reported, "Donnie was bitter, contemptuous, and accusing; he spoke with disgust of his father's falling when drunk and his sleeping on the floor" (p. 146). Incidentally, this was the first time a family member was able to talk about the family secret of the father's drinking.

Art techniques can be used in the family evaluation process to assess boundaries, alliances, coalitions, peripheral family members, themes, the purpose of the symptom, and other dynamics of the family structure. They can also be used to promote communication and expression of feelings, to teach cooperation and leadership skills, to intervene in a stuck system, and to draw children into the therapy process. Children are usually comfortable using art materials like markers and drawing paper, and this allows them to feel equally important and equally as heard as their parents. The parents, on the other hand, may not be as comfortable using art materials. It is up to the family therapist to introduce these interventions in a way that makes them seem like a legitimate part of the family therapy process and to value the benefits of these techniques. Adults need to use adult art materials like markers or pastel chalks, not crayons. Therapists need to examine any fears they may have of artistic expression and self-doubts concerning their artistic ability. These techniques do not require artistic talent or training. The therapist can reduce initial resistance from the family by assuring the family that the quality of the artwork is not the focus and that only the process of family interactions will be important.

There are many versions of conjoint family drawings that can be used for evaluation or interventions. The evaluation process was developed by Kwiatkowska (1967) at the National Institute of Mental Health. The initial model of the family art interview takes two to three hours and includes six drawings. Initially, the family is asked to make a free picture – drawing anything they wish. This may be used by family members to introduce themselves or illustrate the family problem. Second, the family members are asked to each draw a picture of the family. The third drawing is an abstract composition of the family. This is the most difficult assignment, and it stirs discussion among family members about symbols used for each family member. In the fourth task, family members make scribbles on paper with their eyes closed. They must then find something in the scribble that will help them make a composition by ignoring or adding lines. The next assignment is a conjoint family scribble. Each person again makes a scribble, and the family decides which one they will use to complete as a picture. In this effort, the entire family works on one composition. The final work is, again, a free drawing that may express feelings about the process of the art evaluation. At the completion of each piece of artwork, the family members are asked to give their pictures a title and to then sign and date them. It is extremely helpful to have a cotherapist to act as an observer to the wealth of verbal and nonverbal behavior elicited by this process. Similar observations can be made in the art evaluation as in any task assignment, but in addition, symbolic art productions confront the family with expressions that cannot be denied.

The art evaluation process has been adapted, shortened, or modified by many other family and art therapists (Bing, 1970; Landgarten, 1981; Lawson, Peterson, Lawson, 1983; Rubin & Magnussen, 1974; Sherr & Hicks, 1973). Landgarten (1981) adapted the scribble technique by asking each family member to draw his or her initials on the page and then make a composition or design and give it a title. She feels it is less threatening to deal with a familiar symbol. The second assignment calls for the family to divide up into two teams to make a nonverbal, mutual drawing. Each person selects a different color so that each contribution can later be evaluated. No talking is allowed, and the family must decide what they will draw and how it will get done without words. The third task is a verbal family task-oriented art product. Each member is given a different color of plasticene clay or construction paper and must decide on an artistic product to create. Therapists can observe decision-making processes, such as who the leader is, how the artwork gets started, who initiates communication, who is ignored, and how much discussion occurs. In addition, it can be determined if the family members work in teams, individually, or at the same time. This process gives therapists three sources of data about the family structure and interactions: the art work itself, the movement and interaction of the family members during the creation, and the processing of the experience afterwards.

I used a conjoint family drawing to gain more information in a case of an eight-year-old girl who was the identified patient with a school phobia. I was interested in learning more about how the family functioned and what purpose the symptom served. When the task of the family portrait was presented to this family, they became quite anxious and resorted to their stress-coping roles. To ease the anxiety, Sally, the identified patient, jumped up and began drawing the mother (who was agoraphobic) safe in her kitchen. She then drew the withdrawn father under the car, working in the garage. After some time, the mother drew Sally in the picture, sitting at her desk in school. The mother stated that she wished Sally could go to school and be happy. This drew attention to the presenting problem and the notion of the "sick" child. The teenage girl drew herself going to the show alone, without her mother's worrying—a wish that put the focus back on the mother. Finally, the middle boy got up and drew the whole family together watching television, the ultimate wish of family unity. Sally had continued to draw members of the family all over the page, causing confusion, with each member of the family represented more than once. The father never drew anything or gave any input into the process. This exercise led to a discussion of the mother's threats to leave the family, her need to control everyone's safety, her exaggerated fear of death, and the long term marital problems.

When working with alcoholic families, I like to ask each member to draw his or her perception of the family without looking at each others' drawings. Common themes will often occur when the family views the drawings together. This was valuable in assessing a family who came to the child guidance center for work on parenting and adding a new family member.

Jean, the mother, had been a practicing alcoholic and drug addict for 20 years before going through inpatient alcohol treatment. When her first child was born, she was a member of a Hell's Angels group and did not wish to parent her daughter, Joan. Joan was given to the paternal grandparents to raise, and Jean was denied permission to see her daughter. When Jean's son was born, she kept him with her. Jean divorced her alcoholic husband, remarried, and had a third child, a son. Some years later she divorced her second husband.

At the time of the first session, Jean was living with her fiancé. Joan, 16, had left her grandparents and had come to live with her mother for the first time in her life. When the family was asked to draw family portraits, an unmistakable theme of isolation became apparent. The mother's family drawing used compartments to divide the family. She was at work while Joan was shown in a room of the house watching television. A "messy kitchen and living room" separated her from her mother. This untidy house was the source of arguments between the mother and daughter. The two boys were pictured playing ball, but they had a tree between them. Mother's fiancé was drawn in another square representing his job, which took him out of town during the week. Joan's picture showed all of the family in a neat row divided by a line separating her and her boyfriend from the rest of the family. She saw herself as the only one who was isolated. The teenage boy drew lines between each member of the family except between himself and his brother. However, he placed his brother's friend between them. The youngest boy drew family members as being busy, each doing something on their own. There was little emotional connectedness in this family.

Family art evaluation offers direct observation of family behavior, as well as graphic creations full of visual symbols that can be useful in family therapy. It further provides a record of the evaluation process that can be referred to later or can be compared with similar compositions at the completion of therapy. The therapist should use caution in interpreting the artwork and should place more value on the process of its production and the interaction patterns of the family than the pictorial content.

REFERENCES

Bing, E. (1970). The conjoint family drawing. *Family Process, 9,* 173-194.
Kwiatkowska, H.Y. (1967). Family art therapy. *Family Process, 6,* 37-55.
Kwiatkowska, H.Y. (1978). *Family therapy and evaluation through art.* Springfield, IL: Charles C Thomas.
Landgarten, H.B. (1981). *Clinical art therapy.* New York: Brunner/Mazel.
Lawson, G., Peterson, J., & Lawson, A. (1983). *Alcoholism and the family: A guide to treatment and prevention.* Rockville, MD: Aspen Publishing.
Rubin, J., & Magnussen, M. (1974). A family art evaluation. *Family Process, 13,* 185-200.
Sherr, C., & Hicks, H. (1973). Family drawings as a diagnostic and therapeutic technique. *Family Process, 12,* 439.

76

Male Mystique

Lorna Hecker

INDICATIONS FOR USE OF THE INTERVENTION

The "Male Mystique" (which can also be utilized with women as the "Female Mystique") is useful for men who are in the process of separation or divorce and are displaying "desperate" behaviors to try to recapture their spouses or ex-spouses. They are usually the "dumpees." When the more-invested spouse displays these desperate behaviors in an attempt to recapture the other's interest, it makes him even less desirable to the less-invested partner, and his solution maintains or exacerbates the problem. These clients usually come to therapy depressed and/or overwhelmed with the decision of their spouses to leave. They have difficulties mobilizing themselves and often state they would "do anything" to get their spouses back.

This intervention, of course, is not a guarantee to get a spouse back. The intervention is designed as a win-win situation. That is, if the individual follows the therapist's suggestions, he may become more desirable to the partner and may enhance the relationship. If the relationship cannot be saved, the intervention will help the individual on his way to enhanced self-esteem and self-confidence as he embarks on a new single lifestyle.

THEORETICAL FOUNDATION OF INTERVENTION

The "Male Mystique" is based on MRI theory. MRI theory holds that people persist in actions that maintain problems inadvertently and with the best intentions (Fisch, Weakland, & Segal, 1986). This intervention is used when the more-invested partner is displaying behaviors that exacerbate the problem with the less-invested partner.

DESCRIPTION OF THE INTERVENTION

This intervention is most useful for people who already have a history of engaging in desperate behaviors of trying to regain the favor of the disengaged partner. Therefore, I often give the client options for therapeutic goals in this manner:

> *Therapist:* Bob, it seems it would be helpful at this point in therapy to clarify your goals. As I see it, you have three options. However, you may have some additional ideas to add. One idea is for us to continue to find ways for you to be even more ingratiating to Sharon, to try to continue to win her back.

If you have timed this intervention carefully, the client will probably balk at this option since he has come to dislike this behavior. If he does opt for this goal, you are prescribing the symptom and could now work with the client in ways to exaggerate the symptom. This option respects the client's position, but also makes the symptom less palatable.

> *Therapist:* A second goal we could entertain is for you to accept your marriage with Sharon as over and we could work towards helping you along with your divorce.

If your client is ambivalent about the relationship and is "hanging on," this will probably not be an acceptable option for him. If he chooses this goal, it indicates therapeutic movement.

> *Therapist:* A third goal you could choose may sound a little odd. You could choose to develop your Male Mystique. What I mean by this is, we would work on strategies that would increase your feelings of self-confidence as a male. The goal here is to help you find ways to make you even more interesting and even somewhat mysterious to the opposite sex. We could work on ways that would really make your wife wonder what you're up to. My guess is, right now your wife thinks you are very predictable. She probably can guess how you will

respond in most situations: what you will wear, what you eat, what you do in your leisure time, when you are at home, and so on. Does she not? (My clients have always affirmed this observation.)

This goal is to help you get creative and increase your Male Mystique. I will help you come up with strategies to really make Sharon wonder what you are up to. It can be really simple things — like eating different foods, dressing differently, or just doing something she would never expect you to do. Can you imagine how she might react to this?

Now, there is another side to this goal. We can't control Sharon's reaction. She might not react as favorably to your Male Mystique as you might wish. The unique component of this goal is that you still win, in spite of the pain of your relationship not working out. The way that you still win is that you will increase your self-confidence in your male-ness, so that when you are ready, you will feel comfortable in your role as a single male. You will have developed some "mystique" and skills to help you maneuver in single life. I know you mentioned this was a concern of yours after having been out of the single's life so long. This is the third option of goals.

At this time, I ask the client if he has any questions or other ideas about goals for treatment. If he chooses the third goal, I brainstorm with him about it.

Therapist: Let's think about some ways you could develop your Male Mystique. What could you do that would increase your self-confidence as a male, and might just make your wife wonder what you're up to? It should be something that is out of character for you, and would really make her think you had gone off the deep end.

I then brainstorm with the client to come up with behaviors that he thinks would adequately develop his Male Mystique. This creative process is enjoyable for the client and the therapist.

Responses I have received are:

- "I wouldn't return her calls as quickly as I usually do."
- "I could clean out the car and wash it. I haven't done that since we dated. She would think I have a date."
- "I could buy some of those silky underwear. That would really make her wonder . . ."
- "I could put a sexy message on my answering machine."
- "I could go on a skiing trip by myself."
- "I could not be as accessible when she wants me to do things. I'm usually at her beck and call."

ANTICIPATING THE SPOUSE'S RESPONSE

Another step I include in this intervention is for the husband to anticipate the response of the wife and have a response ready for predictable situations. I encourage clients to be "mysterious" in their responses and to not respond in an angry manner, but very matter-of-factly. I especially encourage them to be mysterious or absurd if one has complained that the other has been overly reluctant to share information about their whereabouts, activities, the children, and so on. An example is:

> *Therapist:* What will you say to Sharon when she asks you if you have a date because you're cleaning out the car? Now remember, you must say it straight-faced, matter-of-factly.

I then help the client come up with responses if he is stumped. For example, with Bob, I said, "When she asks you about the car, you could say something absurd like, 'Well, Sharon, I have an interview as a belly dancer.'"

Bob actually did clean out his car, his ex-wife accused him of having a date, and he said, "No, Sharon, I have an interview for a job as a belly dancer." It appeared that Bob's unusually calm demeanor in answering Sharon's questions, as well as his lack of anger, threw Sharon off balance so much that she replied, "Well, Bob, you know you would never quit your regular job!"

Bob, who had been a very stuck, depressed client, later called me, laughing, and was pleased about several things as a result of this intervention.

1. He was pleased about his prediction of his wife's response.
2. He was pleased about his calm response to her and her reaction to his calmness.
3. He was brainstorming other ways to increase his "male mystique" and felt creative.
4. He said he didn't know why, but he no longer felt depressed.

SUMMARY

This intervention is effective because of the win/win nature of it's design. The Male Mystique intervention has the following therapeutic effects: (1) It helps change the client's behaviors that are exacerbating or maintaining the problem; (2) It helps the client change dysfunctional interactional sequences with a spouse or ex-spouse; (3) It empowers the client to take action at a point in his/her life when he often feels out of control; (4) It consequently decreases depression, and appears to increase self-confidence; (5) It diminishes a power inequity in the marital relationship, which either empowers the couple to reunite, or it empowers the client to proceed with getting on with single life.

REFERENCE

Fisch, R., Weakland, J., & Segal, L. (1986). *The tactics of change*. San Francisco, CA: Jossey-Bass.

77

What Are Your Children Learning?

Mary Jo Zygmond

THEORETICAL ORIENTATION

The purpose of this intervention is to produce a second order change in the parents' perception of their disciplinary techniques. This second order change is accomplished through reframing. Reframing is defined as changing the conceptual and/or emotional setting or viewpoint in relation to which a situation is experienced and placing it in another frame that fits the facts of the situation equally well or even better. As a result, the entire meaning of the situation is changed (Watzlawick, Weakland, & Fisch, 1974, p. 95). Reframing operates on the level of metareality where change in the perception of the event takes place without changing the event itself. Thus, if the reframe is successful, the event will be seen as a member of a different category or class. Because it is perceived differently, the individual can respond to the situation differently.

In order to accomplish this reframe, the therapist asks a series of reflexive questions (Tomm, 1987; 1988). The goal of reflexive questions is to trigger the release of information from the parents so that the parents can use this information to generate new patterns of cognition. If they are able to look at their method of discipline differently, they can respond to the situation differently.

DESCRIPTION OF THE INTERVENTION

The therapist asks each parent to describe the types of discipline they have used in the past. After the parents describe the types of discipline used, the therapist asks observer-perspective questions that focus on the interaction patterns that maintain the child's inappropriate behavior (Tomm, 1987). These questions help parents recognize their role in the ongoing interaction patterns. Some of the questions the therapist can use include the following: "When you use that type of punishment, how does your child react?" "When the child misbehaves how do you act?" "How does your spouse react?" When these interaction patterns are delineated, the therapist asks reflexive questions concerning the effect that these interaction patterns have on the children, particularly the behaviors and values the children are learning. Some of the questions the therapist can use are as follows: "When you do not follow through with a consequence, what are your children learning?" "When you threaten your child with a severe punishment, what are you teaching your child about you as a parent?"

Usually, the parents discover that their children are learning to be irresponsible, to lie, to manipulate, and to blame the parents. The therapist then asks each parent to describe the values and behaviors they want to teach the children. After the parents have described these values and behaviors, the therapist asks if they have been successful in teaching the children these values and behaviors. The parents usually respond that they have not been successful. At this point, the therapist introduces the idea that the parents may need to use parenting methods that will teach the children the values and behaviors the parents wish to promote.

INFORMATION NEEDED TO DETERMINE WHEN THE INTERVENTION IS INDICATED

When working with parents who verbalize that they are dissatisfied with their children's behavior, therapists often encounter parents who believe their discipline measures are fine; it is their children who need to change. Furthermore, these parents will not do homework assignments that are designed to teach more effective ways of disciplining children.

EXAMPLE

I was working with a couple who had problems with all three of their children. One child was doing poorly in school, another failed to do her household chores, and the third threw temper tantrums if she did not get her way. The parents' standard mode of discipline was to yell at the children or threaten them with severe punishments. However, when they did punish their children, they felt so guilty that they eventually recanted.

When I presented the idea that the parents had to change in order for the children to change, they agreed with my assessment. However, when we outlined the behaviors the parents needed to change and developed homework assignments that provided the parents the opportunity to change, the parents failed to follow through. If they did follow through, it was for a short period of time. When I confronted the parents about the incongruence between their verbal message that they wanted their children to behave differently and their failure to follow through on the homework assignments, they told me that they expected the children to change and that the children should change without their parents' assistance.

At this point, I decided to reframe the parents' disciplinary methods. In order to accomplish this, we examined what the parents' discipline methods had taught the children about their parents and about life in general. This discussion involved examining the patterns of interaction that maintained the inappropriate behavior. We examined these patterns from both a behavioral level and from an outcome level (i.e., What are these children learning?). The parents were amazed that they had taught their children to be irresponsible, to disobey their parents, and to be dishonest.

The couple's response to this intervention was positive; they saw the need to change their parenting methods in order to teach the children the values of honesty, responsibility, and obedience. Whenever the parents faltered in their goal to teach their children these values, I would say, "What are you teaching your children if you continue to do this?" This comment would get them back on track. At the end of therapy, the children's behavior had improved dramatically and the parents were using more effective parenting techniques.

REFERENCES

Tomm, K. (1988). Intervention interviewing: Part III. Intending to ask lineal, circular, strategic, or reflexive questions. *Family Process, 27,* 1-15.

Tomm, K. (1987). Interventive interviewing: Part II. Reflexive questioning as a means to enable self-healing. *Family Process, 26,* 167-183.

Watzlawick, P., Weakland, J., & Fisch, R. (1974). *Change: Principles of problem formation and problem resolution.* New York: Norton.

78

The Use of Meal Therapy
in the Treatment
of Families with Eating Disorders

Bill Forisha
Kay Grothaus
Ross Luscombe

THEORETICAL ORIENTATION OF THE INTERVENTION

Family mealtime is, perhaps, the single event during which systemic affect and interaction are most vivid and most available for observation, and thus, also for intervention. Students of human culture have long noted the varied ways and means by which mealtimes are carried out. According to Visser (1986), "food — how it is chosen from the possibilities available, how it is presented, how it is eaten, with whom and when, and how much time is allotted to cooking and eating it — is one of the means by which a society creates itself and acts out its aims and fantasies."

Taking his cue from the rather explicit, albeit nonverbal, dialogue that occurs in a dinner scene in the film *Tom Jones,* Forisha (1977) developed the "Sensitivity Dinner Activity" in his work with both families and groups. Characterized by prohibitions against verbal expression and the use of ordinary eating utensils, he used eating together as a way of evoking the expression of repressed

---

Note: Ross Luscombe died in May, 1989. This article is dedicated to her memory. She was largely responsible for the development of the family therapy technique described.

emotions and as a way of identifying dysfunctional communication patterns. In order to shift the focus of treatment from the anorexic patient to the familial system, Minuchin et al. (1978) reported using a "lunch session" as a means of enacting issues around eating behavior. When this shift was accomplished, usually after one session, Minuchin ceased his focus on eating issues per se in favor of other issues and curtailed or ended the use of lunch sessions.

Meal therapy was developed by the clinical staff of the Northwest Ohio Center for Eating Disorders, St. Vincent's Medical Center, Toledo, Ohio, as a continuous and primary intervention technique (Milholland, 1988). It is repeatedly utilized during the entire course of treatment for the interrelated purposes of assessment and intervention. Although often reliant on the theoretical concepts provided by structural family therapy in formulating an assessment of family functioning, treatment teams become rather experiential when utilizing meal therapy as a means of intervening in the family system.

For instance, by evoking repressed emotions and unconscious meanings ascribed to eating, the treatment team seeks to facilitate the differentiation of food intake from both familial interactional processes as well as from the intrapsychic processes of individual family members. The staging of a family meal becomes a vehicle for the exploration of the varied and interlocking meanings and patterns of behavior that family members have evolved over the years of their development as a living system. As members gain insight into the meaning and impact of their behavior on both themselves and others in the family, they are further challenged by the therapist to alter their actions in directions that are more life sustaining and enhancing.

INFORMATION NEEDED TO DETERMINE THAT THE INTERVENTION IS INDICATED

Generally speaking, meal therapy is utilized in the treatment of all clients who have been diagnosed as having an eating disorder and who consequently have been admitted to the program. It has been our observation that many eating disorder clients and their families have a history of avoiding being together at mealtime. It may be said that the use of meal therapy returns the family to the scene of the crime, that is, to the specific social context within which the presenting symptom developed.

BRIEF DESCRIPTION OF THE INTERVENTION

We ask families to eat a meal together during most therapy sessions. All members of the family who are currently sharing the same household are included in the initial sessions. Extended family members may also be included in later sessions. The therapy team is usually comprised of two co-therapists. Sometimes a nutritionist and/or physician may be invited by the therapists to participate if their expert contributions are deemed to be strategically relevant for that particular session. In fact, use of the technique is supplemented by a nutritional assessment of eating patterns, behaviors, and beliefs as they relate to the overall health status of the family.

Prior to a meal therapy session, the client is requested to order the food from the menu that is made available by the food service division of the medical center. The possible selection is deliberately varied. The food is set up in a private, comfortable dining room by the food service staff in advance of the session. The entire family and the therapists serve themselves from the buffet — the contents of which are always a surprise to everyone but the client. The session begins by asking the client to seat the family members around the table. The therapists then ask the family members to start the meal as they would do at home. Since this typically involves some kind of family ritual, a prayer being the most common, the therapists are usually provided a rather convenient opportunity — in addition to the one provided by simply the act of eating itself — for joining with the family.

The food selected by the client is noteworthy. For instance, she may try to please Mother and deliberately displease Father by her selection. Or, she may express her resistance to both parents and/or treatment itself by deliberately ordering nonpalatable combinations or simply junk food. Interestingly, as the client improves in overall health, her ordering for the meal therapy sessions becomes increasingly more socially and nutritionally appropriate. Other observations in the initial and even later sessions may involve such issues as: the seating arrangement around the dining table; the pace of eating in the family; who eats and who doesn't; who eats in a strange or even childlike manner such as pushing food around on the plate, cutting food up into smaller and smaller pieces, refusing to talk as well as to eat; how others respond to the one not eating; and who stops eating when conflictual topics are brought up.

As additional family issues emerge and as assessment increasingly gives way to intervention, patterns of interaction—such as triangulating and scapegoating—that evoke and/or support the dysfunctional eating behavior are challenged by the therapists. Specific interventions are drawn from the eclectic repertoire of the clinical staff. However, it may be said that most interventions are designed to facilitate the family's insight into dysfunctional interaction patterns and to encourage subsequent behavior change. In any case, all of this therapeutic action goes on while everyone continues to eat, or, in the case of the client, is continually reminded and encouraged to eat.

CASE EXAMPLE

This process is at least partially illustrated in the case of Donna, a 57- year-old single woman who had been both bulimic and anorexic for over thirty years. Two older sisters brought her to the center. Her age and the fact that she lives alone would seemingly disqualify Donna as being a representative case; however, the nature and course of her treatment in the out-patient program warrants her consideration.

After an initial intake session and two meal therapy sessions with Donna alone, the co-therapy team formulated an initial assessment. Donna was described as having the emotional and social demeanor of a girl in her early adolescence. At first, she pouted and whined when asked to eat her meal. However, after the establishment of some degree of therapeutic rapport, Donna developed the style of agreeing to eat followed by procrastinating in the process of actually doing so. It became clear to the therapists that it was quite important to Donna that she be liked, fussed over, and, most important, considered a "good girl."

The fact that Donna was very religious was made quite clear by her during the first session. The therapists decided to utilize and further explore her belief system while they ate together. Whenever she laid down her fork, pushed her food around on her plate, or pushed her plate away, one therapist would gently and unobtrusively put her fork back in her hand or her plate back in front of her while both therapists continued to probe the meaning of her religion in terms of basic life processes. The focus of this line of inquiry was on eating and the care and enjoyment of her body. Intermittently, she was reminded and encouraged to take another bite.

The therapists concluded during those sessions that Donna had long ago chosen for herself an impossible goal: to live a perfect life as defined by her religious beliefs. She viewed herself as undeserving of her God's forgiveness for her awful transgressions, especially her purging episodes which were "such a waste in the face of world hunger," and her periodic, but long-term feelings of jealousy and anger toward her sisters. The therapy team speculated that for Donna, the process of eating or not eating functioned as a way of managing intense feelings of guilt and shame.

The therapists further speculated that Donna's eating disorder not only relieved her guilt feelings, but had also become imbued with interpersonal power, since the threat of suicide by starvation attracted the concern of family and friends. Thus, it was decided to include her sisters in the next several meal therapy sessions. Her parents were both deceased and had been so for many years.

Particularly notable during the first two family meal sessions was Donna's response to her sisters' admonitions for her to eat. She returned to pouting, whining, and procrastinating. Her sisters addressed the therapists, each other, and Donna herself as if they were speaking about or to a very young child. It became apparent that her two sisters had for some time functioned together as co-executives in the family, alternating in their interactions with Donna between critical and nurturing behavior.

Halfway through the fourth family meal session, one of the therapists said to Donna, "When you say you are full and don't want to eat anymore, we believe that you are full with feelings — pain, hurt, **anger, and sadness — not with food.**" Her whining gave way to tears that seemed to be quite genuine. Addressing the entire family, the other therapist then shared her hunch regarding the strong likelihood that Donna had been sexually abused as a child. This hunch had begun to be formulated by the co-therapy team much earlier in the course of treatment and was reinforced during the family sessions. It was based in part on their prior experience with this population, but also on a number of current observations: Donna's apparent disdain for her body, her sexual abstinence, her discomfort with topics of a sexual nature, the continual theme of being unworthy, the apparent depth of jealousy and anger towards her sisters, and a general disinclination towards family history-taking by all three sisters.

Donna's sisters appeared to be in shock at the therapist's disclosure. They were directed to inquire for themselves; the hunch was confirmed by Donna. For the next half-hour and during the next few sessions, Donna was encouraged to more fully experience feelings and thoughts about her religion, her parents, her sisters, and herself that had gone unacknowledged for many years. Family history-taking took on a new dimension for all concerned. Of course, all were encouraged to continue to eat their meal as they worked their way through the past and back to the present.

FAMILY'S RESPONSE

As the meal sessions continued, Donna's sisters began to work on their own issues and Donna was increasingly able to respond in an effective manner to both her own needs as well as theirs. A meal therapy session held six months after the termination of therapy found these changes continuing to develop in such positive directions. Each sister had become empowered to make new decisions regarding her life in general, her health, and her relationship to each of her sisters. Structurally, the family as a system worked on the strengthening of individual and generational boundaries. Consequently, the sibling subsystem now operates in a more democratic and mutually supportive manner.

CONCLUSION

Meal therapy was developed as a means of treating families within the psycho-social context of family members eating together. Meal sessions are used in the assessment phase of treatment, as the principal component in the intervention phase, and as a means of evaluating the extent of recovery. The essence of meal therapy is to eventually provide a successful eating experience — one that is experienced apart from intrapsychic and interpersonal processes.

REFERENCES

Forisha, B. (1977, February). Family communication: A systems approach. In *The family: A spectrum of cooperative living*. Colloquium co-sponsored by the University of Illinois School of Social Work and the Association for Humanistic Psychology, Champaign-Urbana, IL.

Milholland, S.W. (1988). New frontiers with eating disorders. *Family Therapy News, 19*(6), 10.

Minuchin, S., Rosman, B., & Baker, L. (1978). *Psychosomatic families: Anorexia nervosa in context*. Cambridge, MA: Harvard University Press.

Visser, M. (1986). *Much depends on dinner*. New York: Grove Press.

79

Combining Individual
and Conjoint Sessions
in Couples Therapy

Frederick G. Humphrey

When I first started professional work with troubled couples and families almost forty years ago, the dominant theoretical orientation in the mental health field was that of orthodox psychoanalytic teaching. A cardinal rule was that therapists, in order to protect the transference relationship between themselves and their clients, never saw or spoke to spouses, parents, or children. If your identified patient was a child, the child would be in individual therapy with a psychologist or psychiatrist and, if other family members were seen, a social worker did "casework" with them. Ninety-five percent of the time, "them" was the child's mother; fathers were rarely involved in the therapy process. It was permissible for the social workers to interview the parents together on those rare instances when fathers came to the clinics because they "weren't really doing psychotherapy." After ten years of performing "casework" with parents and avoiding virtually all contacts with the "real patients," I returned to the University of Pennsylvania for doctoral studies and with hopes of learning marriage counseling. I was fortunate enough to have my advanced clinical training at the Marriage Council of Philadelphia under that esteemed pioneer, Emily Hartshorne Mudd, and her able staff. She had published her first book, *The Practice of Marriage Counseling,* in 1951 with Association Press. While she was always careful to pay homage to the medical profession, especially psychiatry, with its psychoanalytical, individualistic emphasis, Dr. Mudd has for years been advocating, teaching, and practicing intervening with couples' problems by having one therapist work with both partners in the marital system. She quoted one of her mentors, Frederick Allen, MD, an eminent Philadelphia child psychiatrist:

> The same counselor should work with both partners. By having two different counselors on a case, the focus, the dynamics, the interaction, the interweaving of the service toward a common goal, would be lost. It would be working with individuals instead of with marriage partners and complicate the problem for which help is sought. (p. 204 from a February 10, 1949 presentation by Dr. Allen)

Dr. Mudd trained her therapists not only to work with both marital partners but to interview them together or conjointly and also to see each partner alone at least once. She taught a flexible use of conjoint and individual sessions:

> If there is a joint interview, it need not cover the full hour; both individual and joint interviews can be used in the course of a single appointment. (p. 190)

As part of intake, the initial assessment process, therapists were trained to see each partner, alone and confidentially, and then to see them together for arriving at both a decision about proceeding with therapy or not and also for planning, with the couple's decision being a major factor: whether to plan future sessions as individual sessions or conjoint ones or whether to alternate between these two modalities.

I adopted this combined use of individual and conjoint sessions for my couples' therapy and have made it a regular part of both my initial and subsequent sessions. It enables me to evaluate each marital partner as an individual and as a member of a marital unit. Inasmuch as I see myself as a "psychodynamically oriented systems therapist," this combined interview method has proven to be invaluable. The individual sessions enable each person to reveal his/her own individual psyche, including family of origin and developmental issues, without the censorship ordinarily imposed by having his/her partner present to argue, question, or criticize the free flow of therapeutic revelations. It is vital for marital therapists to be reality oriented—at a very minimum in knowing and understanding what is objectively going on—and they will not achieve this if the interviewing format is primarily or exclusively done by couple or family units.

This latter statement I make in light of my research over the past 15 years into the role of extramarital relationships in marital conflict. Not only are partners often cuckolded; so, too, are therapists who fail to offer clients individual, confidential sessions. I find that extramarital affairs (EMAs) are one of the most common problems brought to therapists—constituting the majority of most couple therapy cases—and amongst the most serious ones, with about half of all couples in therapy who have EMAs separating or divorcing before therapy concludes. Individual sessions in these instances enable therapists to help clients resolve their ambivalences about continuing or ending either the EMA or the marriage. Inasmuch as many of these EMAs are unknown to the spouse, therapists who conduct only conjoint or family interviews in these instances will never even be aware of this most significant impact upon the partner and on the marital system. Even when the spouse is aware of the EMA, individual sessions work more effectively, in my experience, in resolving ambivalence.

Conjoint sessions, when EMAs are not secret, are often characterized by such hostility, probing, and threatening that the basic issue of ending the EMA or the marriage cannot be constructively addressed. However, the conjoint sessions may help the couple directly confront what needs to be done to resolve the issues in the marriage: to keep it or not, to work to improve it, adjust to the status quo, etc. Individual sessions with the spouses not in the EMAs are times for lending emotional support, for resolving their own ambivalences about their mates, and for draining off the enormous hurt, anger, and broken trust issues these clients struggle with.

When EMAs are not present, I find less value to alternating individual and conjoint sessions and ordinarily prefer to primarily offer conjoint sessions unless one or both of the partners have some intrapsychic issues that they wish to cover. Here, again, I will be guided by the wishes and needs of each couple. I wish to reiterate, however, that even with "routine" marital problems, I insist on individual sessions as part of my initial evaluation process.

I have often heard resistance to the idea of combining individual and conjoint sessions as many therapists say they worry about secrets, triangulation, and manipulation. My experience has been that if a therapist is properly trained (which ordinarily includes his/her own personal therapy) and receives adequate clinical supervision as he/she develops his/her therapeutic skills, these issues are false ghosts. All therapists have to deal with secrets of some type and all couples consciously or unconsciously try to triangulate and manipulate their therapists. It has taken the field of marital and family therapy years to "work through" the excess emphasis that the literature has placed on using the couple or the family as the exclusive unit in the treatment room. Only recently have "experts" offered the recognition that couples and families are made up of individuals with individual psyches, needs, and motivations that need to be addressed by marital and family therapists while systems' needs of these individuals are also treated. I have found that combining individual and conjoint (and/or family, if appropriate) sessions enables therapists to do this. Actually, my private conversations with therapists around the country have found that many — probably most people who call themselves family therapists — have been doing this for a long time. Unfortunately, the published literature and video presentations by prominent therapists have often led students and neophyte therapists to think otherwise. The couples and families I have worked with over the years have been virtually unanimous in accepting this treatment flexibility and purpose. The one consistent exception to doing this involves clients who suffer from paranoid ideas. They may easily interpret the therapist's individual sessions with themselves or with their partners as "proof" of someone plotting against them. In these instances, the gains of the treatment approach are often overridden by the loss of trust that ensues.

In summary, the combining of individual and conjoint sessions as a regular part of the marital treatment program, pioneered almost a half century ago by America's first marriage counselors, remains a valuable and favorite therapeutic strategy for me.

REFERENCE

Allen, F.H. (1951). Quotations from February 10, 1949 Conference. In E.H. Mudd (Ed.), *The practice of marriage counseling* (p. 204). New York: Association Press.

80

What, Where, When, How

Maxine Walton

This intervention includes moving couples from blaming each other to examining their individual responsibility for what they do and how it impacts on the marital system. In interactional terms, it is easy for couples to continue symmetrical escalations of blame. This pattern, however, does not allow individual positions to be examined or changed; each punctuation of the interaction begins with the other's distressing behavior and the speaker's "obvious" and "only" response. Interrupting the pattern by insisting on a different punctuation (beginning with self) can be powerful and beneficial.

I use a direct approach in which the continuation of treatment depends upon the couple's willingness to move from blaming to working on their issues. Strategic/structural therapy was used in the T case. The couple's eight-year-old daughter, who was extremely bright, brought them into marital therapy by refusing to eat or function in school. She was quickly released from the identified patient role during the first session.

Intervention in the marital system was blocked by each person's blaming the other and ventilation of anger. At the end of the first marital session, they decided that they were going to get a divorce and terminated.

Two months later, Mrs. T returned with her daughter, who refused to accept the IP role and was doing well. Mrs. T was still with her husband and unhappy as well as worried about his health.

For two sessions, she berated him and refused to move past her blaming position. I became visibly exasperated and refused to listen to anything except what she did, when, where, and how and asked what she wanted for herself as a separate individual. When she remained stuck, I suggested that she call for an appointment when she was ready to talk about herself. She came in three weeks later. Her affect had drastically changed. She appeared as an attractive, self-assured, smiling woman. She acknowledged her awareness of my exasperation with her and how it made her realize on the way home that she did not know how to talk about herself and who she was and what she did, which had an impact on the family. She was able to enumerate the changes in her behavioral patterns that changed the interactional patterns in the marriage and family. She had confronted her husband for an answer to her question of whether or not he loved her. She indicated her love for him, but if they were not going to work on the marriage and he didn't care, she would get a divorce and go on with her life.

Mrs. T and her husband were seen for three more sessions and terminated.

81

Letters to Families
Who Leave Therapy Prematurely

Anthony P. Jurich

"Thank you *so much* for all the help you've given us." Normally, those words ring sweetly in a family therapist's ears. They typically mean that we have done a good job and the clients recognize our efforts. However, this sentence sometimes hits us long before we expect it, when we, as therapists, feel that we are in the middle of therapy, not at the end. At that time, the same sentence takes on a whole new meaning. It now means, "We're too afraid to continue therapy and want to fire you as therapist and leave therapy before it becomes even more painful!"

This situation puts the family therapist in a terrible bind. On one hand, we obviously feel that the therapeutic work is not done and the clients should remain in therapy because, otherwise, they will not be able to achieve their own therapeutic goals. Some client families have a motto, "When the going gets tough, we get gone!" Allowing such a family to bolt therapy prematurely would only perpetuate the maladaptive family pattern. On the other hand, by both our ethics and our philosophy of systemic change, we cannot *force* a family to stay in therapy against their will. Even if we could and successful change could be accomplished, the family would view such positive change as our victory and not theirs. Therefore, we let the client family walk out of our office with the feeling in the pit of our stomachs that there is still work to be done.

When confronting such a situation, I become very "strategic" in my approach. Borrowing from the traditions of Haley (1976), Madanes (1981), and Selvini Palazzoli, Boscolo, Cecchin, and Prata

(1978) in strategic family therapy and the Rational-Emotive Therapy tradition of Ellis (1962), I attempt to use the clients' resistance to the continuance of therapy as leverage to help them see the value of continuing therapy. The client family has thanked me for helping them so much and, therefore, they are implying that they have already attained their therapeutic goals. If I confront them on their assertion, I am not only calling them incompetent at making judgments but I am also calling into question my own competence as a therapist. On a deeper level, I am also forcing them to look at their fears *at my request*, not their own. The easiest way out of this confrontational dilemma for the client family is for them to retreat from therapy. Not only does this strategy end therapy but it probably will prohibit them from reentering into a therapeutic relationship with me or any other therapist. Such an outcome is unacceptable.

Instead, I use the following procedure. I am very gracious and open to them in the last session and I try to help them, as best as I can, make the transition into "life without therapy." I always try to end the session with a statement that, if they ever have any future problems, they have an open invitation to reenter therapy with me or to contact me and ask for another therapist, in which case I will gladly make a referral. If they are still insistent on termination, I let them go. Three weeks to one month later, I write them a letter. In this letter it is important to keep the tone light, open, and friendly. If the letter drifts into sarcasm, the result will probably be anger and further cutoff. I explain in the letter that I am happy that they are doing so well. I further explain that I know this to be so because they have not needed to take me up on my invitation to come back into therapy if they needed to do so. I then recapitulate their goals for therapy and remind them that these were the goals they established at the beginning of therapy. I draw the conclusion that these goals, therefore, have been met and describe how I imagine their family life to be presently, with those problems having been solved. I add a few "warning signs," which would be early signals of impending trouble and conclude the letter with another open invitation to come back into therapy if they need to do so.

This bibliotherapy procedure has several advantages. First and foremost is that it creates cognitive dissonance between the family's reported self-sufficiency in the last therapy session and the present condition of their family relationships. It juxtaposes the family against itself, instead of against the therapist, causing the family to question the accuracy of their assessment that they had completed therapy. Secondly, it augments the differences of opinion within the family system. Each family member's viewpoint can be measured against that of the therapist. Because the therapist presents an opinion that is different from the "family party line," individual opinions are normalized and the letter often serves as a springboard for family members to express opposing views. The metamessage of the letter encourages "I think" positions, rather than a "We think" position for the whole family. Lastly, it affords the family an opportunity to reassess their family functioning vis-à-vis their original therapeutic goals. Some families may assess their progress as being very good and write me back to tell me so. In such cases, the family was stronger than I had assessed them to be and I applaud their progress.

More often, I get a call or a letter from the family confessing that they weren't as healthy as I had described in the letter and asking either to discuss that fact on the phone with me or to come back into therapy for at least a "check-up session." In either case, the door to reenter therapy has been reopened with a minimum of fear and loss of face, provided I handle that next contact with openness, caring, and empathy, while normalizing their situation as being quite typical of families in similar situations.

A CASE

I had a client family who had come to me with some relationship problems. Their 10-year-old son had been irresponsible in performing his chores. As we got into the therapeutic process, we found out that the father wanted his wife to be more demonstrative in her signs of affection (e.g., kisses) and the mother wanted her husband to focus his attention on their relationship instead of his career. Their therapeutic goals were readily recognized: (1) the son would demonstrate more responsibility; (2) the wife would demonstrate more affection; and (3) the husband would spend more time with the family. As the family started to make progress toward these goals, everyone became more uncomfortable. On some level, they all realized that their symptoms contributed to the homeostasis of the system which, in turn, masked the deeper underlying problem: both the husband and wife feared intimacy with each other and kept each other at an arm's length. As therapy began to strip away the defenses of the system, the family came into a session with that opening line, "Thank you *so much* for all the help you've given us." It was obvious that they were too uncomfortable and afraid to continue therapy. Nothing I could say or do could halt their exit.

About three weeks after they left, I wrote them the following letter:

Dear Jim, Alice, and Frank,

When we left our last session, I was really nervous that we had some unfinished work to do in therapy. I was really afraid of your sliding back into old habits. Now I see that I was mistaken and was being overly cautious. Since you left therapy with the agreement that you would call me if you had any trouble, it is obvious to me that you are doing quite well and deserve to be congratulated. In my mind's eye, I can picture Frank's now taking out the garbage with no complaints, Alice's being much more openly affectionate to Jim, and Jim's cutting back on work in order to spend more time with the family, especially Alice. Since you worked so hard in therapy, it's nice to imagine your reaping the rewards of that work. Remember, if you need me to help "tune things up," do not hesitate to call me. If Frank starts to fuss about his chores again, or Alice needs to create distance, or Jim forgets the importance of family time, those could be "warning signs" for your family. If you need me, I'm only a phone call away. Once again, let me offer you my congratulations on your less stressful life together as a family.

Sincerely,

Anthony P. Jurich, PhD

Approximately a week after I sent the letter, Alice called. She thanked me for my letter but confessed that they were having some further problems. She had tried to be more affectionate but, when she did, Jim just pushed her harder for sex. Therefore, she cut back on her little signs of affection. Jim also spent less time at work but his home time was spent more with Frank than with her. Although Frank had been doing most of his chores with a minimum of complaints, he blew up and refused to take the garbage out on the night that the family had received my letter. Consequently, Alice asked me if I could schedule a family session for them and maybe even a session for just her and Jim. They eventually came back into therapy for an additional four months and left in much better shape than they did after their original termination session.

There is no magic in this or any other therapeutic intervention. Perhaps this family would have returned to therapy regardless of my letter. However, they may not have returned to therapy as fast, if at all. If we truly believe that families must be given the responsibility to change themselves, we must not usurp their rights. However, a bibliotherapeutic letter can create the right atmosphere to help them choose a path towards greater growth.

REFERENCES

Ellis, A. (1962). *Reason and emotion in psychotherapy*. New York: Lyle Stuart.

Haley, J. (1976). *Problem-solving therapy: New strategies for effective family therapy*. San Francisco: Jossey-Bass.

Madanes, C. (1981). *Strategic family therapy*. San Francisco: Jossey-Bass.

Selvini Palazzoli, M., Boscolo, L., Cecchin, G., & Prata, G. (1978). *Paradox and counterparadox*. New York: Jason Aronson.

82

Captain's Paradise Concluded

Myra Weiss

PRACTICE MODEL

This practice model is meant to target the client's emotional, cognitive and behavioral levels. It utilizes elements from the models of Bowen (1978) and the New Hypnosis (Araoz, 1985).

STRUCTURE OF PRESENTING SYSTEM

The interventions explained in this paper deal with a triangle of husband, wife, and husband's female lover. The characteristics of these individuals, as I've experienced them, are described below. This approach has been tested with Irish, Italian, and Jewish families.

HUSBAND — married to Mom/Saint
— virtually asexual marriage
— feels guilty about wanting more out of life

WIFE — virtuous
— eternally forgiving
— repeatedly takes HUSBAND back, knowing of his involvement(s) elsewhere

LOVER — same or much younger age
— unmarried (divorced, widowed, or never-married)
— may have children of any ages
— vital, interesting, high energy
— initiates things in all areas of life
— feels guilty about "morality"

PROCESS OF THERAPY

1. Conjoint Therapy

There are two parts to the therapy. In the first part, the focus is on conjoint therapy with HUSBAND and LOVER. Usually they are self-referred or referred by an individual therapist for couple therapy.

The pattern of break-up and make-up occurs almost immediately as HUSBAND returns home to WIFE. When he resides with his wife for longer than a few weeks, I initiate a change in the contract to individual therapy for the LOVER. This must occur at the time that LOVER grasps the logical inconsistency of being "coupled" with a man who is already married. Sometimes, HUSBAND concurs with this changed treatment plan as a response to LOVER's acute pain. Other times, HUSBAND becomes angry at the therapist and is referred elsewhere for individual treatment. If the recontracting is timed properly, LOVER risks HUSBAND's displeasure and she does not leave therapy. Indeed, there are also times that LOVER's individual therapy begins only after HUSBAND and WIFE enter marital therapy with another therapist (ostensibly to prepare WIFE for divorce).

2. LOVER's Individual Therapy

This is the second part of the therapy. The goal is for LOVER to move from massive dependency needs, to experiencing herself as a person with options; that is, to raise her level of differentiation of self.

INTERVENTIONS

1. Decrease initiating/pursuing. Through coaching, client learns methods of quieting self in order to contain emotionality. This change is manifested through the client's use of distance rather than hot pursuit when she is anxious or angry.

2. Distinguish between HUSBAND's and LOVER's problems and underscore that his problems are not a personal reflection of her

(e.g., he does not return to WIFE because of LOVER's inadequacies).

3. Create a working definition of trust, which serves as a goal for client's self-growth:

> a. define behaviors that give the client examples of how she can trust herself (e.g., making her own social plans rather than sitting by the telephone waiting to respond to HUSBAND's call).
> b. learn to distinguish between HUSBAND's inconsistent words and behavior (e.g., spending time with WIFE instead of attending the birthday party of LOVER's child).

4. Work with family-of-origin material to place client's role of pursuer and her choice of involvement in an uncommitted relationship within a transgenerational context. At this stage of work, LOVER often realizes her own ambivalence about being in a coupled relationship.

Divergent paths emerge at this point between women who stay with married men and those who want a committed, monogamous relationship. Some decide that there are benefits to being the lover of a married man, such as avoidance of unresolved psychological conflicts that are evoked by a traditional intimate relationship, as well as sparing herself the mundane struggles of cohabitation. For these women, the benefits outweigh the limitations of singlehood; for example, the necessity of developing a high degree of self-sufficiency, rare socializing with couples, and feelings of loneliness during vacations and traditional holidays. The other path is for women who retain their original goal of a close, committed relationship. The awareness of their anxieties about commitment creates sadness and a mourning process begins.

During all of the above, LOVER continues to see HUSBAND, although he often remains for longer intervals with WIFE. As the mourning process occurs, LOVER takes concrete steps to leave the relationship. HUSBAND begins intense pursuit of her. She, in turn, begins to hold to her position of wanting a committed relationship.

5. Clarify future goals:

   a. use of hypnotherapy, in which client-created images are transformed to self-affirmations.
   b. focus on work life and social life, rather than sexual relationships.

6. Termination stage — With increasing frequency the client focuses on herself, with less reactivity in relationships.

OUTCOME

This work usually takes 30-45 sessions. HUSBAND divorces WIFE and makes concrete plans to marry LOVER, or LOVER is freed for a committed relationship elsewhere.

REFERENCES

Araoz, D. (1985). *The new hypnosis*. New York: Brunner/Mazel.
Bowen, M. (1978). *Family therapy in clinical practice*. New York: Jason Aronson.

83

The Divorce Ceremony:
A Healing Strategy

Florence Kaslow

This intervention is, perhaps, more in the category of "extremely useful" rather than "favorite," as it deals with sadness and loss. However, it contains a beacon of optimism in that ultimately the different parting permits "letting go" and the freeing up of bound energy to begin a new phase of one's individual and family life cycle.

Actually, this intervention as I have created and modified it over time has its rationale in elements of several theoretical schools. From the psychodynamics/object relations school comes the utilization of life cycle and stage theory concepts and the emphasis on the reassurance children need of object constancy from and with their parents. Derived from contextual/relational theory is the premise that it is detrimental to children to be placed in a position of being expected or pushed to betray their loyalty to either parent. The structuring of continuing generational boundaries and mutual responsibilities flows from both relational and structural conceptualizations. The "ceremony" as a strategic intervention reflects my own integrative, "dialectic" approach (Kaslow, 1981b).

DIVORCE CEREMONY

In the United States and in most other countries around the world, a majority of people have both civil *and* religious marriage ceremonies. Couples either choose and/or are required to be married in a church, synagogue, or mosque before the eyes of God (and their relatives and friends). For many, the religious service supersedes the civil/legal service in import; it is this ritual that consecrates the marriage and marks the specialness and sacredness of the event. Usually it signifies not only the joy and wish for fulfillment of the shared dream of the couple, but also the hopes of the new couple's respective families of origin. For all, potentially it means perpetuation of the family into the next generation.

All too often the dream of the couple to "live happily ever after" does not materialize. They are disappointed in a marriage that does not fulfill their expectations. Disillusionment and despair replace optimism and love. No matter how hard they may try, the schism of distrust and chronic discontent widens. Efforts to "communicate better," repair power imbalances, and/or restore affection and intimacy lead to naught. Ultimately, the emotional estrangement is accomplished by a physical estrangement and the couple separate. They may or may not seek assistance in marital, and later, divorce therapy. No matter whether the couple enters the adversarial system directly by contacting two separate attorneys to handle their divorce action, or whether they decide to mediate their divorce (Folberg & Milne, 1988), the process ends up in court and they receive a judicial decree that legally grants the divorce. Generally, the legal process is cold, lonely, and characterized by anger and hostility. What begins with pomp, flourish, and a mass celebration formally ends with each former partner in a dreary courtroom alone except for his or her sole attendant, the attorney—who is paid to be there and is rarely an emotionally supportive friend.

Scores of patients described to me the forlorn sense of alienation they experienced at the time of the legal ending of their marriage. Many expressed the desire to have their marital dissolution recognized and accepted by their church as their wedding had been. I encouraged patients to approach their clergy person and request that such a ceremony be developed and performed on their behalf. Some ministers assent; patients who undergo this process report a new sense of closure. A few clergy/therapist friends of mine are receptive to the idea and write ceremonies that they are willing to have me share and publicize (Kaslow, 1981a; 1984).

Eventually, it became obvious to me from much researching of the literature and discussing the topic widely that (1) only Orthodox

Judaism has traditionally recognized the need for a divorce ceremony and promulgated one through the centuries; (2) there is an enormous need for a divorce ceremony by huge numbers of couples to mark the ending of the passageway known as the divorce process; and (3) many churches are still not ready to utilize such a ceremony.

Therefore, around 1982 I created a quasi-therapeutic ceremony that is adaptable for religious purposes also. Since then, I have utilized it with dozens of my own patients and in the training of numerous other professionals in divorce therapy and divorce mediation workshops in about 20 countries. It has been refined, based on experience, and the current version, first published in 1987 (Kaslow & Schwartz, 1987), appears below. (A videotape version was made in 1988.)

THERAPEUTIC/HEALING DIVORCE CEREMONY

(Shortened Version)

The adult participants stand facing each other and the children stand facing me. We are in a square or rectangle, depending on the number of participants.

FK: Mr. Green, please thank your wife for the good years and happy times you remember.

Mr. G: (usually puzzled—pauses—chokes and responds—surprised at the positive memories this question evokes. He may say) I really had forgotten—amidst my anger—how much I once loved you. You were so lovely, talented . . .

FK: Mrs. Green, can you tell your husband about the good things you will always cherish about your marriage?

Mrs. G: (Often teary and barely audible, affirms the sharing, fun, and early realizations of her dream and how wonderful she thought he was.)

FK: (To each of the friends separately) Please tell Mr. or Mrs. Green how you are prepared to be available to them during this difficult transition time and what their friendship means to you.

Friends: You can call me at any time to talk, cry, go somewhere with you . . . . I'm here for you in any way that you need me because you're a super person and a wonderful friend.

FK: (To children) Can each of you tell your parents what the divorce means to you and what you want from your parents subsequent to the divorce?

Each child: (Something like) I am so sad that this happened but I know you tried your best. I need to know that you will each continue to love me, take care of me, let me love and care about each of you, and see you as much as possible. Please do not ask me to take sides or interfere with my relationship to Mom/Dad. (This is usually said with great sadness, wistfulness, and through tears.)

FK: (To each parent) Can you tell your children how they were conceived (or adopted) in love, born at a time when you cared very much for each other, and were delighted to be having a family? Also, let them know what your thoughts are about your future relationship to them.

Each parent: (Tells in their own words each what child has meant to them and affirms that their parental feelings and role will continue.)

FK: (to anyone else at the ceremony) Please tell Mr. and Mrs. Green what is in your hearts as you help them to feel some inner peace and some healing.

When everyone has said what they seem compelled to communicate, depending on the feeling tone being conveyed, I may ask if they all care to hug each other as a goodbye to the family in its present form.

Before utilizing such a ceremony, it is important to ascertain that the couple wishes to bring psychic closure to their marriage.

All of the families with whom I have utilized this intervention strategy have expressed appreciation for the release from the remaining unwanted emotional shackles. In acknowledging what was valuable in their relationship, they counter the feelings of failure carried for too long. In openly communicating profound feelings and memories with their children and finally listening attentively to what they have to say, a new bonding begins. Amid tears of relief, this parting occurs minus anger and the desire for further recriminations and retribution.

REFERENCES

Folberg, J., & Milne, A. (Eds.) (1988). *Divorce Mediation*. New York: Guilford Press.

Kaslow, F.W. (1981a). Divorce and divorce therapy. In A. Gurman & D. Kniskern (Eds.), *Handbook of Family Therapy* (pp. 662-696). New York: Brunner/Mazel.

Kaslow, F.W. (1981b). A "dialectic" approach to family therapy and practice: Selectivity and synthesis. *Journal of Marital and Family Therapy, 7*, 345-351.

Kaslow, F.W. (1984). Divorce: An evolutionary process of change in the family system. *Journal of Divorce, 7*, 21-39.

Kaslow, F.W., & Schwartz, L.L. (1987). *Dynamics of divorce: A life cycle perspective*. New York: Brunner/Mazel.

Videotape:

Kaslow, F.W. (1988). *Divorce consultation/divorce ceremony*. Farmington: University of Connecticut Medical School.

84

Working with Rigid Parents: Reverse Images and Reframes

Lauri Holmes

While many of the parents of families seen in outpatient family therapy clinics lack firmness and expect too little of their children, we sometimes see parents who are in fact too firm, whose expectations of their children are far beyond what is age-appropriate. Often in these families there is a "spare the rod, spoil the child" belief system, where severe physical punishment is meted out, not as with enmeshed parents who lose their tempers, but in a cold, severe way. This pattern dates back generations in the family and is almost subcultural in its roots.

In our child and family agency we have often found such rigid families in working with post-adoptive placement situations. Often it is a case of a seemingly well-functioning, middle-class, church-going couple or family who adopts an older child with a traumatic early history out of their religious concerns to help the less fortunate. When the expected (by social workers) behaviors of lying, stealing, or bedwetting occur, the parents take the traditional stance that has always "worked" in their own families and are hurt, indignant, and punitive when these traditional methods do not work.

These parents are mirror images of the uncertain, "democratic" parents typical of client families, and the usual reframes and structural moves do not work with them; often they simply make the system more rigid. Faced with such a system, the therapist quickly finds anger and frustration rising, along with the desire to say, "You're being much too hard on this kid!" We have found a rewording of this phrase to be an elegant reframe for the therapist and for the parents. It is simply, "You're being too hard on yourself!"

This phrase sets the framework for the therapy. Instead of trying to get the parents to see the kid as "more to be pitied than censured," which only sets them more firmly in their defensive posture that the kid is the one who is at fault, this frame allows the worker to "feel sorry for" the poor parents, who are working so hard. The worker can express incredulity that they really think that they have the unearthly ability to get an eight-year-old to make his bed every day or to have a teenager to willingly do chores, or a newly adopted child in the family to give up his old adaptive habits of lying, which he long ago learned in order to escape early and unjustified punishment (theirs, of course is always justified.)

Depending on the style of the family and the dramatic ability of the therapist, this theme can be elaborated on ad infinitum. Usually the more angry the therapist is at the rigid parents, the more dramatic the rendition of the sympathy, pity, and concern expressed. "Do you know many other people who have kids this age — I mean do you really talk to other parents about how hard it is?" (You hope they haven't had such conversations and usually people with this style of parenting are in fact closed and rigid in their relationships with the outside world and haven't talked much about difficult feelings with anyone — even with each other.) Strategically, this frame allows the therapist to take a one-down position, always a helpful one when faced with resistance. "I just don't know what we're going to do if you keep working so hard. My colleagues behind the mirror are really worried about you."

It must be admitted that adoptive families with this style are among the most difficult to work with. Their tradition has forged personality structures that are so at odds with the needs of a disturbed child who may never bond with even a warm, flexible set of parents that the prognosis in such a case is very guarded. But we have been able to hold together some families. Sometimes we would rather have had another choice for the child, but a move out of this rigid family would only continue an endless cycle of placement and re-placement. What this pity-the-poor parents framework has done is to give some children a less than perfect family rather than no family at all.

Biological families who show this style also are frequently long and slow cases, but they do respond to the wearing-down process that this mode of intervention effects. And, even if the parents do not really change much, there is another benefit, this one for the child. When the focus insistently is taken off the child as the villain in session after session as the therapist tends to the parents' "exhaustion" and high standards "for themselves," the child can see under the words the message that he or she (or they) are not at fault. This is a subtle version of what we call, "calling the game," where the underlying dynamics in a family are brought to light in therapy. Surfacing the family games serves to lessen somewhat the punitive impact of these parents on the child.

Biological parents who respond to this approach usually have been raised in rigid families, but it works also with parents who have been abused or neglected and are the prototypical narcissistic or borderline personality types. This "undersocialized" opposite to the rigid parents we have been describing also can respond to the "you're too hard on yourself" intervention. Their need for stroking is so great that they do not respond to reframes which attempt to help them see the child in a better light, and sometimes the sequence described above sets a more productive stance for the therapist working with such parents.

An interesting question comes to mind as we work with the "old-fashioned" families we've been looking at. One finds oneself wanting to take these parents off into a room by themselves in violation of the custom of seeing all the family members together, and talk with them about their own upbringing in a hope of softening them up in their attitude toward their child. Perhaps long-term therapy would in fact get them in touch with their own feelings of rage, hurt, and abandonment, and change their overall attitude toward their children. We usually feel that we don't have time for such long-term efforts. And so we use the more strategic methods in the whole family group.

But the impulse to take these people aside may shed some light on why in earlier decades therapists did just that. Could it be because in that time there were more of these "old-fashioned" parents who were suffering from emotionally barren childhoods themselves? Did the parent coalition-building interventions introduced by structural family therapy come into vogue because the clinical population shifted from these "old-fashioned" types of parents and moved towards a majority of more democratically-oriented parents?

In any case, these "throwbacks" make us look at our assumptions and our everyday repertoire of reframes and interventions. We may even find that the frame "you're being too hard on yourself!" is useful for therapists, who certainly find themselves working very hard with these parents, perhaps because they remind us of our own families a generation or two generations ago.

85

An Application of Programmed Writing: Arguing and Fighting

Luciano L'Abate

The pragmatic background of programmed writing can be found in the use of three different therapeutic practices. First, is the application of positive reframing in paradoxical prescriptions, based on the need to reinterpret reality in strongly positive terms for negatively oriented families (Weeks & L'Abate, 1982). Second, this type of therapy is based on principles of control and regulation that demand that families spend one hour together for every hour spent in therapy (L'Abate, 1986). Third, programmed therapy is based on the therapeutic use of writing as an additional or alternative medium of therapeutic intervention to the verbal medium. Briefly, therapeutic writing progressed from an initial stage of *open* writing, as in the use of diaries and journals, to *focused* writing, as in writing about a specific topic, like depression, to *programmed* writing, where families need to answer especially programmed lessons or workbooks on specific topics, as in the present application of arguing and/or fighting (L'Abate & Cox, 1992). Written materials of this type are considered as being *paratherapeutic*; that is, as taking place along with face-to-face contact, which is considered by definition to be therapeutic (L'Abate, in press). After a discussion of each written lesson, which is standard in each therapy session, the session may deal with other matters relevant to the family, like any other therapy session.

DESCRIPTION OF THE APPLICATION

In the case of arguing and fighting, one of the most frequent and common family symptoms, after thirty years of repeating instructions verbally, I finally wrote my instructions down according to the following progression:

Lesson 1: This form contains detailed questions concerning the *description* of arguments and/or fights according to their frequency, duration, intensity, onset, outcome, and content. Each family member, partner, parent, or teenager needs to answer each question in the lesson by themselves. Then they have to come together at a pre-established hour to exchange their lesson forms and discuss them, preferably keeping notes of their discussion for the therapist. In this way, three different feedback loops are produced: monologic, dialogic, and corrective (i.e., therapeutic).

Lesson 2: Here each respondent must answer questions concerning explanations about the various functions of arguing or fighting. This behavior is "explained" in terms of ten different positive reframings, which need to be ranked from one to ten, in order of how each explanation applies to the individual's view of what arguing and fighting does to and for the family. If respondents do not like these ten explanations, they can come up with their own.

Lesson 3: Now the arguing/fighting is prescribed in much greater detail, including time of appointment, duration (usually one hour), place, etc. This argument needs to be tape recorded. However, family members are told how they should argue (dirty!). They should use as much as possible six suicidal rules: (1) using the "You" instead of the "I" or "We" pronouns; (2) bringing up the past; (3) reading everybody's mind; (4) making excuses for self but not for others; (5) making threats and ultimatums; and (6) using emotional bribery and blackmail. The rationale and more detailed description for these three initial lessons can be found in L'Abate and Levis (1987).

Lesson 4: After the family brings the tape of the argument, they are given individual scoring sheets. Each family member has to listen to the tape, recording on the scoring sheet how often they hear themselves use each of the six suicidal patterns, or an additional seventh pattern that may be unique to them.

Lesson 5: On the basis of their scores, each family member is given a lesson dealing with the most frequent pattern. Each lesson covers the developmental origins of this pattern, its pros and cons, with a final assignment to monitor the outcome of three situations where this pattern was used and where it was not used.

Lesson 6: After a discussion of their individual and family lessons and meeting, each member is now given the lesson that covers the suicidal pattern that is second in frequency. We have not found it necessary, as yet, to go beyond the first two of these patterns, except in assigning a lesson for a pattern peculiar to the family interaction. A manual containing these and many other programmed materials has been completed (L'Abate, submitted for publication).

CASE EXAMPLE

The Bickersons consisted of the two parents and two boys. The father, 37, was in real estate, and the mother, 35, was an unemployed nurse. The boys were 12 and 10. The second son was adopted. The whole family bickered a great deal: between parents, between parents and children, and between the children. Bickering, in fact, was the major referring problem. Since the two boys were bright enough to understand the questions in each lesson, everybody in the family was given the forms for Lesson No. 1, with a specific time when they would meet to compare, contrast, and discuss their individual answers.

Typically, the mother's answers indicated an overconcern about the frequency and intensity of the bickering, while the father and the children tended to underscore and actually deny its significance. The boys' collusion with the father and the mother's loneliness in the face of this collusion were dealt with in the therapy session. While the mother was crying, it became clear that neither the husband nor the children showed any indication of empathy towards her. This is one of the many indications that often arguing and fighting may cover up unresolved or denied depression as well as make intimacy impossible (L'Abate, 1986).

A discussion of the parents' priorities produced answers dealing with "My family and my children" for the mother and "My family and my work" for the husband. The dysfunctional implications of these priorities were discussed, especially in terms of how the bridge of marriage had collapsed from pressures from below, because the parents had neglected their individual selves and the marriage, and pressures from above, allowing the children to achieve a much greater degree of importance than they deserved. ("They are visitors in your house. After they have grown and gone, what will happen to your marriage?") In leaving, they were handed forms for Lesson No. 2.

During the second session they brought back their forms with the individual rankings of the ten positive explanations of bickering. The second child had not been able to complete it. After a discussion of their rankings was completed, bickering was then discussed in terms of the parents' experiences with arguing and fighting in their families of origin. Father grew up in a family where no one ever expressed any feelings or opinions, with family members going their own ways, avoiding conflict at all costs. The mother, instead, came from a family where arguing and fighting were the norm. These two patterns were discussed in terms of their complementarity. They needed each other to give what the other did not have. In neither family of origin had either parent seen their parents cry together. Only rarely had these parents been able to comfort each other in times of need. How can one be intimate if one has not experienced what intimacy is? Toward the end of the session, a definite hour for sharing the third lesson was agreed upon by the family. Just one form for Lesson No. 3 was handed out.

OUTCOME

The family came back reporting that they had not been able to complete the assignment because the children refused adamantly to carry it out while the parents had a "very nice discussion" instead. This failure to carry out the assignment was greeted by chagrin and dire warnings from the therapist that if they did not learn to fight dirty they would not be able to fight clean! A fourth appointment was given, but the family failed to keep it, calling to cancel it because they "were not bickering anymore."

REFERENCES

L'Abate, L. (1986). *Systematic family therapy*. New York: Brunner/Mazel.

L'Abate, L. (in press). *Primary and secondary prevention with families*. Newbury Park, CA: Sage Publications.

L'Abate, L. (submitted for publication). *Manual 1: Programmed materials for individuals, couples, and families*. Atlanta, GA: Social Training, P.O. Box 450843, 30345.

L'Abate, L., & Cox, J. (1992). *Programmed writing: Self-administered approach for intervention with individuals, couples, and families*. Pacific Grove, CA: Brooks/Cole.

L'Abate, L., & Levis, M. (1987). Paradoxical therapeutic strategies: Current status and evidence. In P.A. Keller & S.R. Heyman (Eds.), *Innovations in clinical practice: A source book* (pp. 79-91). Sarasota, FL: Professional Resource Exchange.

Weeks, G.R., & L'Abate, L. (1982). *Paradoxical psychotherapy: Theory and practice with individuals, couples, and families*. New York: Brunner/Mazel.

86

Treating Information Processing Errors

Donald K. Granvold

The intervention described in this chapter is focused on the identification and modification of information processing errors that interfere with effective couple interaction. Only recently have cognitive intervention methods been specifically applied to couple interaction (Baucom & Epstein, 1990; Beck, 1988; Ellis, 1977; Epstein, 1982; Epstein & Baucom, 1989; Granvold, 1988). Cognitive distortions play an active role in the verbal, behavioral, and emotional interchanges between marital partners. In analyzing couple interaction, the behavior of one spouse is mediated by the other in terms of meaning, motivation, and etiology. What a behavior means, why a spouse behaves as s/he does, and the history of a behavior combine to form a composite appraisal of spouse A's behavior by spouse B. The interaction proceeds as spouse B completes the appraisal and responds both covertly and overtly. This appraisal may be fraught with cognitive distortions and faulty expectations. Aiding the individual or couple in the identification of cognitive errors and guiding the modification of such errors can produce constructive change in the couple's verbal and behavioral interaction and feelings toward one another.

The following are examples of cognitive distortions common to information processing (Beck, Rush, Shaw, & Emery, 1979). Due to space limitations, only a few thinking errors have been selected.

Absolutistic, dichotomous thinking – the tendency to view experiences, objects, and situations in a polarized manner: good/bad, right/wrong, strong/weak. Mary, upset with her husband, John, for forgetting to record a check in the check register says, "John, you are totally irresponsible with our finances; you don't even record our checks." In the example cited, John has acted financially responsible during the past and has failed to record a check only twice in 15 years. Mary's expectations of perfection and extreme, total conclusions are distortions requiring modification.

Selective abstraction — typically a focus on the negative in a situation, ignoring other positive (sometimes more salient) features and viewing the entire experience as negative based upon the selective view. Tom and Janet enjoyed an evening of dining and dancing during which they had a brief (10 minute), somewhat heated disagreement that resulted in a constructive resolution. The following day, Tom refers to the previous evening as a "fight night" and fails to acknowledge the pleasantness that predominated. Tom's selective, negatively focused recall represents a distortion of the evening and prompts a sense of sadness and futility in Janet.

Arbitrary inference — reaching an arbitrary negative conclusion when there is no evidence to support the conclusion or there is evidence to the contrary. Freeman (1983) describes two types of arbitrary inference as mind reading and negative prediction.

1. Mind reading — Upon his arrival home from work, Paul fails to greet Rachel with a kiss and he acts uncharacteristically quiet all evening. At evening's end Rachel says, "I know that you're upset with me, Paul. I won't stay as long at mother's in the future as I did last night." Rachel inferred that Paul's behavior was in response to her. Actually, Paul felt bad physically but failed to clearly communicate his feeling ill to Rachel. While couples become talented at reading one another correctly, unvalidated inferences may be faulty at times.

2. Negative prediction — Imagining or anticipating that something bad or unpleasant is going to happen without adequate or realistic support for the prediction. A functionally orgasmic woman has failed to reach an orgasm during the last four sexual encounters with her husband (each encounter experienced while she was very fatigued) states, "I'm never going to have an orgasm again; when you lose it (the ability), it's gone forever." She becomes disinterested in **sexual contact** with her mate, becomes cold and aloof.

Negative attribution — the view that a given behavior is produced out of negative motivation. Mahoney (1974) defines attribution as implied causality. Attributions are often simplistic statements that are perceived as accountable for a given behavior. The tendency is to attribute singular causation to complex patterns of behavior. Negative attributions can take the form of blaming—"you make me so mad"—in which the responsibility for the anger is displaced to the mate. Hurvitz (1975) presents a form of negative attributions as "terminal hypotheses" in which behavior, meanings, or feelings are interpreted such that change cannot take place. Included are such determinants of behavior as psychological classifications ("You're a manic depressive"), pseudo-scientific labels ("You're a Virgo, that's why you act the way you do"), inappropriate generalizations about innate qualities or traits that cannot be changed ("He has no willpower, was born that way; that's why he's so fat"). Epstein (1982) identifies behavior changes that are attributed to coercion or impression management. "He's doing more chores around the house because he's afraid I'll leave him if he doesn't." This form of attribution is frequently centered around therapist assigned behaviors. "You're only being nice to me because the therapist told you to be more pleasant." The implications are: (1) the *only* reason behind such behavior is the assignment, and (2) being more pleasant is actually misrepresentative of the spouse's desires.

Another form of negative attribution is malevolent intent. "You purposefully came home late to make me worry about you." "You took your secretary to lunch to make me jealous." Another negative attribution has ingredients of mind reading and inferential reasoning associated with it. "If you love me you'd know what I want from you right now." The fact that he is not doing what she "wants" is, by her inference, motivated by a lack of love—presumably considered a negative by her. To restate the attribution, "Your lack of love for me is causing you to be insensitive to what I want from you at this moment." Such a thought pattern also qualifies as an unrealistic expectation.

INTERVENTION

The intervention involves identification of client cognitive distortions evident in the couple's current interaction or those exposed through deliberate therapist questioning regarding past interchanges. These distortions may take the form of incorrect meanings, faulty expectations, or negative attributions. Couple interaction is explored by the therapist in which the meaning and motives of each partner are identified and the content of problematic interaction is explicated. The therapist continues probing until s/he has a clear understanding of the thinking that is accountable for the interactional problem or dilemma.

Once the therapist has an awareness that a thought processing error is actively contributing to the couple's dysfunctional interaction, a series of questions follow in which the erroneous thinking is exposed to the client. These questions guide the client in a process of reasoning in which clear, logical evidence is sought to support the expectations, meanings, and conclusions s/he is reaching regarding the spouse's behavior. This process serves to expose flaws in thinking. The client may learn that s/he has assigned an incorrect meaning to his/her partner's conduct or to the interactional situation. Or the client may become aware that his/her expectations are extreme, unrealistic, exaggerated, or unreasonable. Finally, the client may realize that his/her views regarding the motives behind his/her mate's behavior are faulty (negative attributions).

Once the client is aware of his/her faulty information processing, the therapist instructs the client to reconsider the interaction with his/her spouse, free of faulty thinking, which typically leads to improved communication and a concomitant improvement in feelings and interpersonal behavior. The client is encouraged to consistently seek logical evidence to support conclusions reached regarding the spouse and his/her interaction with the spouse. Homework assignments are given in which the client is to bring to the therapy session examples of occasions where s/he successfully revised his/her thinking through logical exploration. In-session review of successful information processing is conducted by the therapist to reinforce constructive changes in thought processing, to generalize common errors from situation to situation, and to pattern the application of successful modification of one type of error to other errors. Furthermore, the couple is asked to evaluate the effect the improvement in information processing is having on both their interaction and satisfaction with the marriage.

EXAMPLE

In the following case, Tom's selective abstraction regarding his night out with Janet is the focus of intervention.

Therapist: Tom, you said that the fight you had Saturday night is what captured your attention about the evening and resulted in you referring to the evening as "fight night." How do you feel when you think that?

Tom: I feel bothered, sort of disheartened . . . sad. And Janet was bothered Sunday when I referred to Saturday night as "fight night." She told me I was being negative again.

Therapist: So focusing on the fight results in some negative feelings in this case for both you and Janet. Do you think that the fight was representative of the evening?

Tom: No, not really. It was a very enjoyable evening over all.

Therapist: Then what could you think that would put the fight in proper perspective?

Tom: The evening was really a nice evening together. The argument was only a brief part of the night, we resolved it, and we didn't allow it to ruin our night.

Therapist: How do you feel as you consider Saturday night in this manner?

Tom: Much better, not nearly so bad . . . actually really good. Janet, I really did enjoy Saturday night.

USES

This cognitive intervention procedure is appropriate when the assessment exposes misunderstandings, miscommunication, emotional episodes, and interpersonal conflict resulting from a *failure* to perceive, interpret, and react to a spouse's behavior based on: (1) reasonable, realistic expectations (of self and mate); (2) positive attitudes; (3) supportable, logical conclusions; and (4) comprehensive vs. simplistic explanations. Awareness of couples' information processing errors is easily achieved in the therapy session through focused questioning regarding the thoughts, appraisals, and conclusions reached by each client in their interaction.

Couples find awareness and modification of information processing errors to greatly improve their communication and interaction patterns. While actual events may go unchanged, the meaning of those events and the way couples talk and interact in relation to events change. Couples report becoming sensitized to the positive elements in their interaction and their validation skills improve.

REFERENCES

Baucom, D.H., & Epstein, N. (1990). *Cognitive-behavioral marital therapy.* New York: Brunner/Mazel.

Beck, A.T. (1988). *Love is never enough.* New York: Harper & Row.

Beck, A.T., Rush, A.J., Shaw, B.F., & Emery, G. (1979). *Cognitive therapy of depression.* New York: Guilford.

Ellis, A. (1977). The nature of disturbed marital interactions. In A. Ellis & R. Grieger (Eds.), *Handbook of rational-emotive therapy* (pp. 170-176). New York: Springer.

Epstein, N. (1982). Cognitive therapy with couples. The American *Journal of Family Therapy, 10,* 5-16.

Epstein, N., & Baucom, D.H. (1989). Cognitive-behavioral marital therapy. In A. Freeman, K.M. Simon, L.E. Beutler, & H. Arkowitz (Eds.), *Comprehensive handbook of cognitive therapy* (pp. 491-513). New York: Plenum.

Freeman, A. (1983). Cognitive therapy: An overview. In A. Freeman (Ed.), *Cognitive therapy with couples and groups* (pp. 1-9). New York: Plenum.

Granvold, D.K. (1988). Treating marital couples in conflict and transition. In J.S. McNeil & S.E. Weinstein (Eds.), *Innovations in health care practice* (pp. 68-90). Silver Spring, MD: NASW.

Hurvitz, N. (1975). Interaction hypotheses in marriage counseling. In A.S. Gurman & D.G. Rice (Eds.), *Couples in conflict* (pp. 225-240). New York: Aronson.

Mahoney, M.J. (1974). *Cognition and behavior modification.* Cambridge, MA: Ballinger.

87

A Family Photograph

James Langford

In a special edition on the uses of humor in the *Journal of Strategic and Systematic Therapies*, Furman and Ahola (1988) write that "humor is not to be used to put people down but to help generate new points of view in order to be able to solve their problems more efficiently" (p. 5). I have experienced humor not only as a way of challenging and expanding a client's position on a problem but also as a means of tapping my own creativity and engaging abilities into the problem-solving process.

One family, in particular, brought this link between humor and positive client response to my attention. This family was a second marriage for both spouses in which a son was the mother's biological child and two daughters were the father's biological children. The older daughter (middle child in age) was being assessed for placement at the Children's Home where I was one of the family therapists. The first session was spent in a power struggle with the mother who described her relationship with the daughter as one of "trying to fit a square peg into a round hole." Initially, it appeared to the therapy team that the daughter was being admitted to the Children's Home due to this stepmother's refusal to work with such a challenging child. In a second session, with tensions building due to the stepmother's defensiveness about the placement and the therapy team admittedly identifying more with the plight of the daughter, I told the family that I needed a break from all the tension in the session. I told them that a way to defuse the tension and to facilitate my getting to know them was to do a family sculpt. I then asked them to imagine having to position themselves for a family portrait.

I would be the photographer; they were to tell me how they wanted to set up the family. Such a playful exercise not only broke the tension but it served to begin a process of building some much needed rapport with the stepmother. To the surprise of all the therapy team, she not only positioned herself close to the daughters but spoke of wishing for a much closer relationship with them. Further discussion revealed a caring, committed parent who was primarily experiencing a great deal of frustration and feelings of failure with both daughters. This creative, spontaneous exercise was not only useful in expanding our assessment of the family but, more importantly for me, confirmed again the power of humor in a tense session.

Bunny and Frederick Duhl (1981) suggest that humor is a kind of "saving grace. When one has distance, one is able to be observer to the situation that one is in" (p. 506). Humor in this situation acted to defuse the tensions between the team and the mother. It also seemed to facilitate both the therapy team's and the family's seeing the mother-daughter relationship from a very different perspective, a perspective that not only served to change the context of the presenting problem but also initiated some movement in the daughter's relationship with her stepmother.

REFERENCES

Duhl, B.S., & Duhl, F.J. (1981). Integrative family therapy. In A.S. Gurman & D.P. Kniskern (Eds.), *Handbook of family therapy* (pp. 483- 513). New York: Brunner/Mazel.

Furman, B., & Ahola, T. (1988). The uses of humor in brief therapy. *Journal of Strategic and Systematic Therapies*, 7, 3-20.

88

Silence

Sandra M. Halperin

THEORETICAL ORIENTATION

Object relations systems theory is the theoretical grounding for the intervention of SILENCE (both literal and metaphorical). The specific construct within the theory that serves as the rationale for the intervention is projective identification. This concept is defined in the Family Therapy Glossary (AAMFT, p.20) as: "a primitive defensive mechanism in individuals and an interactional style of families in which aspects or parts of an individual's personality which feel unacceptable to him are projected onto another within the family. This requires a reciprocal function whereby the other must accept the projection and act in accordance with it."

The purpose of the intervention of SILENCE (both literal and metaphorical) is to stop these powerful, intense, and enmeshing projective identification sequences and help create personal boundaries so that each person can, eventually, experience when she/he is projecting onto the other and subsequently "own" that projected, disliked part of her/himself. (Although this intervention was originally grounded within object relations systems theory, I do not feel that the intervention's use is limited to this theoretical orientation.)

DESCRIPTION OF THE INTERVENTION

The use of SILENCE as an intervention is rather deceptively simple. It is the instruction and modeling of literal silence and/or metaphorical silence by turning away, looking away, or leaving the room, in order to disengage from enmeshing projective identification interactional sequences with someone in the family. These sequences are typically very intense and the boundaries are blurred between the two individuals. What makes these interactional sequences so difficult to deal with in family therapy is that they are usually quite powerful and seemingly impermeable to change.

If an interactional sequence takes place within the session, I stop the interaction after the sequence has clearly been established and engage one of the members of the dyad by asking her/him what she/he thought was going on. I then ask them to reflect upon what just took place and ask that they describe a typical example of this sequence at home. I instruct them on the various types of SILENCE and we discuss the possible ways they can utilize SILENCE techniques to stop the pattern when it occurs at home. I encourage them to use the techniques as often as possible and bring the results back to sessions for further work.

EXAMPLE OF INFORMATION NEEDED TO DETERMINE THAT THE INTERVENTION IS INDICATED

1. At least two members in the family are reported to engage in repetitive, intense, powerful interactional sequences that they each feel compelled to become "locked into."
2. At least one of the members of this dyad must be cognitively available to "step back," observe, and analyze the sequence after it has happened.
3. At least one of the members of this dyad must be willing to try "something new" and risk feeling as if they were "giving in" to the other or losing the power struggle with the other, etc. Often there is one who feels so defeated and helpless that she/he is willing to try.
4. If/when the therapist observes that she/he has been "hooked" into participating in this projection process, the therapist has the opportunity to model for the rest of the family members and to instruct them in the "method" of SILENCE to stop this pattern.

EXAMPLE OF APPLICATION OF THE INTERVENTION

Mr. and Mrs. Anderson and their daughter Betsy, age 13, have come to family therapy because of Betsy's poor grades in school and misbehavior at home. During the first and second sessions Betsy sat passively looking out of the window and Mr. and Mrs. Anderson would alternately request, beg, demand that she look at the therapist and "pay attention." During the third session Betsy responded to the first request with rage directed towards her mother. She accused her mother of attempting to control her and make her into her "own image." When Mrs. Anderson attempted to answer, Betsy attacked her with insults. Mrs. Anderson also began to hurl recriminations back at her daughter telling her how ungrateful she was and how she didn't deserve such a horrible, arrogant daughter! But Betsy got the best of her mother, who finally broke down in tears. The therapist began to engage Betsy, asking her how she feels when she and mother attack one another. Betsy responded "How would I know? You're the one who is supposed to have all the answers, aren't you? I'd like to hear what you have to say—since we're paying you all this money!" At this point she proceeded to tear off the leaves of a plant that was located next to her. The therapist began to feel devalued and angry, and although she realized that the intensity of her anger was greater than the situation merited, she snapped at Betsy, "Get your hands off that plant! Don't you respect anything?"

At this moment, the therapist, because of her awareness of the intensity of her reaction, became aware of a projective identification process in which she had become involved. She then stopped the interaction with Betsy and looked at Mrs. Anderson. Mrs. Anderson said, "Now you know how I feel!" The therapist began engaging her, asking her if this was, indeed, the way it was at home. Mother said that it was and she felt helpless to change anything. The therapist then asked her if she had noticed what the therapist had done in the interaction with Betsy to end the interactional sequence. Mother said that she did notice that the therapist turned without a word to Betsy to speak to her. The therapist then explained to Mr. and Mrs. Anderson the technique of silence, turning away, walking away, etc. She asked Mrs. Anderson for an example that would be typical of this type of interaction between her and Betsy. The therapist asked Mrs. Anderson if she could remember just when she felt "hooked" by Betsy's invitation to "fight" and begin the interactional sequence. Mrs. Anderson was able to identify the feeling of when she felt the uncontrollable urge to react like this towards Betsy. The therapist instructed Mrs. Anderson that when she felt that feeling or when she became aware of being in this type of destructive interaction she should become silent, leave the room, turn away, speak with someone else, etc. This, the therapist encouraged, would help keep both of them from losing their personal boundaries and help Mrs. Anderson feel more in control of herself. Mrs. Anderson agreed that she would try anything. Betsy commented that they were just wasting their money. Mr. Anderson was instructed by the therapist to be supportive of his wife whenever he was present during these sequences, helping her to be SILENT, either literally or metaphorically.

FAMILY'S RESPONSE TO THE INTERVENTION

The expected outcome of this intervention is that the intense projective identification sequences will be interrupted so that the personal boundaries of those involved will be established or re-established. Once this has occurred often enough in the dyad, the members (usually the one initiating the intervention of SILENCE is the first), explore that part of themselves which they were "disowning" and projecting onto the other. They can then become aware of their own part in maintaining the intense interactional sequences. It is important to note that this intervention is not limited to parent-child interactions. It can also be quite effective with couples who are locked into the same types of destructive projective identification sequences.

REFERENCE

American Association for Marriage and Family Therapy. *Family Therapy Glossary*. Washington, DC: AAMFT.

89

The Tape Recorder as a Behavior Modification Device in Couple Therapy

James R. Fisher

Many times, couples in therapy commonly distort the statements made by each other when they are alone with each other. As Richard Bach has stated, one attribute of a successful couple is that they "fight fair." To promote this behavior, I urge couples to prepare a "laundry list" of issues they wish to discuss. Then they are asked to sit down at the kitchen table when no other parties are around and turn on a standard cassette tape recorder, preferably with a 60 or 90 minute tape in it.

Many parties are quick to say, "But she (he) will be on his (her) best behavior!" Precisely! I believe, as many of my colleagues, that behavior must change before attitude does. The tape recorder is a very reliable witness when one partner "gunny sacks" or hits below the belt. When a dispute arises as to *who* said *what* and in what tone of voice or semantic meaning, the tape recorder can be replayed for both partners to hear.

On occasion, the couple will bring a tape to a counseling session with me and we can listen together. Generally, refereeing on my part is not necessary. Most couples quickly learn to listen and analyze the tape. They get almost immediate feedback on their behavior.

I have found that *couples who use this method of communicating quickly drop many harmful habits of dirty fighting* and begin to relate in a more honest, health engendering manner.

Even when communication later occurs, and no tape recorder is around, the learned behavior tends to persist, to the benefit of the couple. Overall, I find it a quick, disciplined way of getting a couple to deal with the real issues in a way that tends to eliminate game playing. The couple can then cover more ground much faster than in conventional therapy.

George Albee, former president of the American Psychological Association, once said our duty is to "give psychology away." I believe when we teach devices clients can use on their own, we are following Dr. Albee's suggestion.

90

The Special Child:
A Multi-Use Reframe

Lauri Holmes

The term "Special Child" has replaced the terms "symptom-bearer," "scapegoat," or "identified patient" in our family therapy clinic over the last ten years of family therapy practice. We have found it a more systemic way of describing the child whose problem brings the family in for therapy. It is also a frame that implies positive intention and allows the therapist to push the parents and the child towards change. It has proved useful in two other areas as well: in training family therapists and in giving presentations to the general public.

In family therapy, the term is a reframe for the enmeshment that is so often characteristic of families seen in our clinic. The enmeshed single parent, couple, or extended parent system formed by divorce and remarriage, wants to tell the therapist how difficult the child has been, how hard they have tried with the intractable problems of the child, or how many things have happened to this poor child. Their always intense mixture of hurt, anger, and concern can break over the therapist like the rush of water into a canoe riding the rapids and threaten to swamp the therapeutic efforts.

In addition, the intensity of the parent's hurt or anger calls up intense feelings from the therapist, especially from a less experienced therapist. The simple statement, "This child has always been very special to you" can slow the pace of the session, focus the parent, give the therapist a more in-charge position, and tie up all the fragments of history that seem to be cluttering the atmosphere.

History is wrapped up in the subsequent statement, "This child is

special to you because . . . " followed by reference to those historical events, which helps the family feel they have been heard, and
which makes shorter work of the history-taking process. A future
course for the stuck parent begins to appear as the therapist weaves
the notion that, "Now, let's see if you are up to doing the things
you need to do for this child now that she/he is ____ years old."
This may come early in therapy or later as time goes on but it is the
general direction we usually take. Having such a direction is helpful
to beginning and advanced therapists alike. The specialness is also
an excellent lead-in to Evan Imber-Black's reframe that a child is
"young" (cf. Imber Coppersmith, 1983). ("He's not bad, he's not
mad, he's just young!") Special, young people can always grow
up—with help from their parents.

The "special child" reframe is equally useful for single, couple,
or extended parent systems because it speaks to the most enmeshed
person in the coalition. It certainly speaks to the single mother,
who, unless extremely narcissistic, has in fact worried a great deal
about the kids who have been left fatherless or who were fatherless
from the beginning. It can draw in the less enmeshed parent as well
by framing them as caring even though they don't show it as obviously. And it can serve to join the other less enmeshed members of
the parent system (at least some of them) by framing them as worrying about the enmeshed parent, or at least worrying about the effect
the enmeshment will have on the child.

In teaching beginning family therapists who, despite their good
intentions of being systemic, suspect that all children would be fine
if they didn't have inferior parents, the concept shows that the
symptom-bearer, rather than being a scapegoat, has often actually
been the child for whom the parents have made the most accommo-
dation and who has been the most difficult to parent despite sometimes heroic efforts.

The assignment to graduate students in family therapy to write a
paper describing a special child they know in their own family or
circle of friends produces interesting results. Children who had
been seen as scapegoats are now recognized as difficult to parent;
parents who had been seen as lacking in parenting abilities are now
seen as overloaded and exhausted. Students are given an academic-
looking outline of the Etiology of a Special Child which includes

categories from the most obvious causes, such as a physical handicap, to the least obvious, the child who never bonded (a surprising number of special children turn up in this category), and other categories such as a child born during a period of stress or a long-awaited child (born or adopted during a "positive stress" time). The students see the concept as a serious re-assessment of their reality. They are thus ready to think more systemically, to see the circular patterns of interaction that surround symptomatic behavior, and to discard their tendency to blame parents as a linear cause for children's problems because it gives them a more positive concept to replace the old ways of thinking.

Finally, the idea of a Special Child can be presented to parent groups without giving away any "trade secrets" in family therapy. Too often strategic and systemic therapists face clients who are skilled in resistance to change because they know all the psychological jargon of TA, Gestalt, Psychoanalysis, or the latest pop book. The Special Child concept does not give a parent an excuse to stay the same, but encourages overly enmeshed parents (who are the ones who usually come to parent education seminars) to back off. A workshop presenter who says, "The Special Child is the one you worry about the most," can bring tears to parents' eyes, especially the ones who feel helpless and guilty, and can open such a parent up to some direct or indirect suggestions about setting clearer boundaries in the family.

REFERENCE

Imber Coppersmith, E. (1983). From hyperactive to normal but naughty: A multi-system partnership in delabeling. *International Journal of Family Psychiatry, 3(2)*, 131-44.

Grandma, Come Help!

Judith Landau-Stanton
Pieter le Roux
Susan Horwitz
Susan McDaniel
Sybil Baldwin

The mother was heaving for breath and severely distressed. Mewling sounds emerged from the birthing room. Would mother and infant survive? The labor had been long and hard, and all present were concerned. Sounds of distress increased. The situation appeared desperate . . .

Then, Grandma arrived! She stalked regally into the room, surveyed the situation, peered into the box and leaped daintily into it. Within minutes she curled herself around her daughter, cleaned her from head to foot and purred loudly. The infant began to feed at her mother's breast; a loud purring shook the box. In the calm that followed Grandma's entrance, the kitten had begun to suckle happily, and all was well.

This actual situation exemplifies our conviction that families in general, and grandparents in specific, know best. As L. Sagan (1987) has said, ". . . the great majority of psychological problems do not require skilled or prolonged psychotherapy. Skilled and insightful grandmothers have been doing a good job of this for centuries" (pp. 192-193). No substitute exists for the love, knowledge and history that generations of family members (and surrogate family members) share. For families that do seek professional help, it is all too easy for therapists to lose sight of this; sometimes we need to be reminded by nature that our eagerness to help may obstruct the family's natural process. How do we remain sensitive to what families can do for themselves and how do we determine the best way to facilitate this process? How do we avoid getting constrained by the belief that we understand more, and can be more effective than, the natural support system? At best we are invited into the family as guests. How do we respect the family's boundaries, behave appropriately, and know when to leave?

WHY INVOLVE GRANDPARENTS?

Grandparents bring with them a wealth of knowledge about the history of the family. They enable us to share and stretch time frames, to include parts of the family history and belief systems that otherwise we would be unable to access. Grandparents' memories of their own grandparents are as fresh in their minds as their grandchildren's recollections of them. Partly because they have lived longer, are older and wiser than others in the family, and have greater life experience, they have a perspective on the family's history that no one else has about what came before and what will come after them. They also have a great investment in the perpetuity of the family. In these changing times, families need to be connected to their past: its wealth, values, and strengths, to enable them to draw on these resources to move successfully into the future (Landau, Griffiths, & Mason, 1982). Grandparents are as much a part of the future as children and are frequently a major resource to therapy as the following case illustrates:[1,2]

---

1. Names and identifying information of the cases have been altered to protect their confidentiality.

2. The therapist was Diane Greenaway, CSW, ACSW, of Buffalo Catholic Charities, who was participating as a trainee in a live supervision externship group in the Family Therapy Training Program. Her supervisor was Sybil Baldwin, MSW, ACSW.

CASE #1

Johnnie, a four-year-old boy, had been placed in foster care two years previously by Child Protective Services who were considering terminating parental rights because the parents were not maintaining contact with their son. Before terminating these rights, the Child Protective Service worker referred the parents for parent counseling in the hopes of resolving the problem. During the first session the therapy team decided to arrange a network session with the extended families and all the service providers involved. The foster family sent in a detailed letter about their wishes for Johnnie because they were unable to attend. The focus of the session was to empower the families to reach a decision about what they believed to be best for Johnnie.

During the session, it became apparent that the father's extended family was very involved with the boy, while mother's family members were relatively cut off from him. There had been a great deal of loss on both sides of the natural family, which had been dealt with very differently by the families. With the agreement of the Child Protective workers, the therapist wondered aloud whether it would be possible to give the child back to his father's family, who were invested and had already experienced so much loss. In order to do this, she elevated and empowered the grandparents by observing, "Of course you don't want to lose your youngest to a stranger. What would you like to do?" The grandparents advised their daughter-in-law to make peace with her parents and her sister so that they could be a part of this process. The paternal grandparents emphasized taking small steps rather than trying to do it all at once. Johnnie stayed with his foster parents during this period, and had frequent visits with his parents, his paternal grandparents, and other members of his extended family. The therapy team coached the family on their goals, which resulted in the grandparents' calling the mother's parents, Johnnie's other grandparents on the other side of the country, to say, "We can't do it any more without you. Please be involved and stay involved." An enactment (Minuchin, 1974) ensued in which the paternal grandparents gave their daughter-in-law back to her mother on the telephone. The other grandmother was then introduced to her son-in-law and her grandchildren, including Johnnie in foster placement whom she had never met. This grandmother, crying quietly, then proceeded to coach her daughter to reconcile with her twin sister, reconnect with her own grandmother, and to stay closely connected with her son Johnnie.

The tasks were accomplished through further therapy sessions and letters, and a visit from the distant grandmother was planned for the following spring or summer. There had been minimal contact between mother and grandmother and Johnnie's mother was really anxious. She requested that the family "See my mom for me." This was accomplished during the therapy session: both paternal grandfather and grandmother introduced their grandchildren to maternal grandmother in person for the first time. This session ended the therapy, which had consisted of six sessions extending over a period of four months.

Through the involvement and wisdom of the family elders, and by following the "small steps" that they had suggested, Johnnie's parents managed to achieve a great deal. They moved to a larger apartment with a bedroom for Johnnie, the husband had found employment and both achieved successful G.E.D. test results. Paternal grandmother taught Johnnie's mother to cook, and Johnnie successfully returned to his parents' home within six months.

Johnnie was an effective link between past, present, and future, enabling the family to reconnect and move on as an integrated whole through time. Symptomatic children are often seen as needing to be taken care of by surrogate systems, where viewing grandparents, or other extended family members as an essential resource, can be faster, more effective, and longer-lasting as well as preventing the perpetuation of problematic transgenerational family patterns.

HOW TO INVOLVE GRANDPARENTS

Johnnie's paternal grandparents were willing to come to the sessions. His maternal grandmother was involved by telephone for a portion of the therapy. The grandparents' input was invaluable, and it is dubious whether the same results would, or could, have been achieved without their assistance. There are many other ways in which the wisdom and support of grandparents can be accessed.

Unfortunately, therapists are often put off and discouraged by parents claiming that their own parents are not available. The kind of reasons given range widely: "They're too far away"; "We don't want to worry them"; "They're old and ill"; "They won't be able to handle this"; "It's not fair to them at this stage of their lives"; "They wouldn't be able to help"; "They've never been able to give useful advice"; "They don't care"; "They had to manage alone; they expect us to do the same"; "Johnnie (or Katy) wouldn't want them to know"; etc.

The manner in which one approaches this kind of statement is dependent upon the basis of the statement. In our experience, there are three common patterns, or reasons, for such statements. These are: (1) apparent cut-offs, (2) protectiveness, and (3) overt blocking (the latter often being a blend of the first two). However, a therapist can rarely go wrong if a message of invitation is given positively, for example, by saying, "I would like to invite your (grand)parents to at least one session as consultants to me."

Parents often need the reassurance that grandparents *will* want to help, *do* care, *will not* drop dead, and *will not* be blamed. As long as there is assurance of a safe context in which resources will be mobilized and supports used positively, our experience is that it is highly likely that the grandparents *will* be there.

Although some grandparents may be hard to reach, many are very available; in fact, there may be problems arising from apparent over involvement, as occurred in the following case example:[3]

CASE #2

An Italian family lived in a two-family dwelling. Elena, the 17-year-old daughter, lived with her parents in the downstairs portion of the house. The paternal grandmother, an aged Italian immigrant, lived upstairs. Elena's father was disabled, having no salivary glands and being diagnosed manic-depressive. Elena was a cantankerous young woman, who continually lied to and stole from her parents and others. The most immediate problem for the family,

---

3. The therapist on this case was Susan Horwitz, MS, and the supervisor was Judith Landau-Stanton, MB, ChB, DPM.

however, was not her lying and stealing but the fact that she argued regularly and continuously with her mother. These arguments frequently escalated to the extent that father would have to go upstairs to "console" grandmother and to "keep her company." Once there, he would immediately feel safe. When the father had left to see his mother, his wife and Elena would retreat to their respective bedrooms, and peace would ensue. Once peace was ensured, father would return downstairs.

When this pattern was described to the therapist, she prescribed the following: Elena and her mother were to have their typical heated argument every afternoon beginning at 4:00 p.m. and ending at 4:15 p.m. precisely. At 4:05 p.m., father was to go upstairs to grandmother in order to distract her attention from the noise downstairs and to protect her from the fact that his wife and daughter were not getting along. Once father went upstairs, mother and Elena were to cease fighting and separate. After the 15 minute argument, when mother and Elena were safely ensconced in their respective bedrooms, father was to return. Prior to starting this homework exercise, father was to describe the plan in detail to grandmother. The family followed the homework instructions meticulously. Mother and Elena began fighting at precisely 4:00 p.m. and at 4:05 p.m. father went upstairs to grandmother. Elena and her mother retired to their bedrooms and at 4:20 p.m., father returned downstairs.

By the end of the week, the whole picture had shifted. As Elena and her mother began to argue, father went upstairs only to find grandmother's door locked, and her yelling to him to get downstairs to take care of his own family, stop the fighting, and leave her alone. The fighting stopped dramatically.

The critical reader may now ask for an explanation of why this intervention worked. Was it the use of paradoxical symptom prescription, i.e., prescribing repeated fighting between the mother and Elena and father's continuing to protect grandmother by going upstairs, or the compression move (Stanton, 1984), i.e., sending the father home again in order to obtain support for his marriage? Whatever the explanation, the intervention could not have worked without the grandmother. When she took charge by sending her son (who had been acting as her surrogate replacement husband) back to take care of his nuclear family, she was essentially (1) giving him "permission to marry" (Stanton, 1981); (2) creating an appropriate boundary between the grandparent and parent generations that allowed her to stay connected with her son in a different way and freed him to be closer to his nuclear family; and (3) giving her son "permission to parent" (Boszormenyi-Nagy & Spark, 1973) by empowering him to take charge as husband and parent (despite his disabilities) to stop the fighting. These changes allowed the son to treat his wife like a spouse and prevent her functioning like an argumentative sibling with their daughter.

WHEN TO INVOLVE GRANDPARENTS

The best time to enlist grandparents is at the time of the initial contact (for example, during a telephone intake call). If this has not been achieved, careful family mapping should be used to determine how and when to use the grandparents' wisdom and years of experience to move the therapy most effectively. The therapist may need to move slowly and carefully if significant conflict and fusion exists between either parent and any of the grandparents. In these situations, significant therapeutic work has to be done in order to be able to elevate the grandparents and draw on them as resources.

CONCLUSION

Grandparents can be the most useful consultants available to family therapists. They bring an investment in the future generations of their family, a knowledge of long standing family patterns, and a wealth of experience that is an invaluable resource to the treatment process. Grandparents are best included in therapy during the intake procedure. If this does not occur, a request for their consultation later in therapy should be carefully framed to appeal to their strengths and experience rather than implying any blame. The most frequent reason for families excluding their elders from therapy is to protect them from harm. If blame is implied, the parents and children will close ranks in order to protect the grandparents. Psychotherapy in general has focused exclusively on the parent-child relationship. The inclusion of grandparents offers therapists a wealth of new resources and information covering a wide range of problems from marital to child-focused symptoms.

REFERENCES

Boszormenyi-Nagy, I., & Spark, G. (1973). *Invisible loyalties*. New York: Harper & Rowe.

Landau, J., Griffiths, J., & Mason, J. (1982). The extended family in transition — Clinical implications. In F. Kaslow (Ed.), *The international book of family therapy*. New York: Brunner/Mazel.

Minuchin, S. (1974). *Families and family therapy*. Cambridge, MA: Harvard University Press.

Sagan, L. (1987). *The health of nations*. New York: Basic Books.

Stanton, M.D. (1981). Marital therapy from a structural/strategic viewpoint. In G.P. Sholevar (Ed.), *The handbook of marriage and marital therapy*. Jamaica, NY: S.P. Medical and Scientific Books (Division of Spectrum Publications).

Stanton, M.D. (1984). Fusion, compression, diversion, and the workings of paradox: A theory of therapeutic/systemic. *Family Process, 23*, 135-167.

92

Engaging Men

Barbara Pressman

Power and control issues are extremely common in marital relationships and simply reflect the experience of women in the society at large. Therapists, therefore, must routinely check for these in marital assessments and family sessions by asking about jealousy, possessiveness, unwillingness for husbands to have partners visit people without them, and money decisions.

Women commonly do not recognize their right to their own voices or to speak up when what they wish is at odds with their partners' wishes. When they do, they feel great guilt at attending to their own needs.

Therapists' walking on eggshells with male clients, deferring, and applauding husbands' words to "engage," is tantamount to being inducted into an already dysfunctional system when a man is controlling and being deferred to by other family members.

CHANGE MODEL

People behave in certain ways because of their beliefs, fears, lessons in childhood, and socialized expectations. Challenge and change the basic beliefs behind the behavior, the rationale for the ineffective behavior, and they will try alternative behaviors.

ENGAGEMENT INTERVENTION

1. *Confronting husbands* (especially by female therapists) regarding controlling behavior. This enables men to experience women in a new way: as equal, knowledgeable, and as holders of information. By declaring her knowledge and perceptions, the therapist is perceived as someone to be recognized and respected, not pushed over as other women and their wives.

2. *Acknowledging another dimension of the husbands,* a dimension that is gentle, vulnerable, hurting. For example, the therapist can acknowledge that the information s/he is sharing may be difficult to hear or that the husband's ineffective means of dealing with his wife is to get his needs met. This probably leads to his feeling frustrated, distanced, and even lonely at times.

3. *Motivating him to enter therapy,* not to gain further control or to show how inadequate his wife and other family members are but because he has changes to make that will benefit not only others but also himself. Asking such questions as:

- Does what you do work?
- What is the impact on your partner, on your children?
- Do you feel good about the controlling behavior?
- What style of interacting was learned in your family of origin?
- What was the impact on you as a child as you experienced your father?
- How is this similar to the way your children experience you?
- Do you wish to learn new ways?

93

Dilemma: A Frame for Reframes

Marshall Fine

My work on dilemma as "intervention" stems initially from my interest in strategic concepts such as reframing and paradox (i.e., Selvini Palazzoli, Boscolo, Cecchin, & Prata, 1978; Watzlawick, Weakland, & Fisch, 1974). The distinction between dilemma and paradox is that paradox addresses contradictory or absurd statements, while dilemma deals with awkward situations, e.g., making a choice between unpleasant alternatives. My evolving interest has consisted of exploring ways to use reframing in the most respectful (least game-like) and effective manner possible. Over time I began to "see" or punctuate the concerns of some people as often involving personal and relationship dilemmas. For example, "If I tell my boss what I think of him/her, I might get fired; if I do not tell him or her, I might go crazy."

Some holistic brain research has recently had an influence on my thinking about dilemmas (Gazzaniga, 1985; Ornstein, 1986; Walsh, 1981). Gazzaniga (1985), for example, suggests that the brain is organized in terms of independent modules. These modules continually test beliefs preserved by our left brain's language and cognitive systems. This type of organization explains conflicts among modules (i.e., behavior versus belief), and consequently why humans may experience awkward situations or dilemmas. Schwartz (1987) uses some of these concepts when working with "our multiple selves." If valid, then presenting the client with a "fitting" dilemma as a way of explaining "problem" situations might correspond easily with mind process/experience and thereby be readily understood.

I find the dilemma "intervention" useful for a number of reasons:

1. Dilemmas are not comments on personal pathology or weakness; they are the expressions of common human experiences. For example, a husband's emotional distance may represent a personal dilemma as opposed to a negative "character" trait: "I want to be more open with my wife, but I fear that if I do, I will expose myself and appear weak." This dilemma addresses the issue while being respectful of personal "character" and worldview.

2. Dilemmas allow people to see themselves as part of the concern without being blamed for the problem. I would agree with Gazzaniga (1985) that a culture becomes more caring and humane when we all feel we are part of the solution to our problems. Dilemmas readily place people in the problem situation, but do not blame them for creating the situation. For example, when negative attention (the solution) may be part of misbehavior (the problem), a therapist might say to parents, "It must be difficult to figure out how to give your son strokes when his behavior is so disagreeable. You don't want to be good to him when he is being disagreeable and yet you must feel the positive parts of your feelings for your son rarely get the opportunity to be expressed."

3. Distinguishing a dilemma may make the covert overt, opening the area for discussion and reinterpretation. For example, "If I show my love for you, I may get hurt. If I don't show my love for you, we both may get hurt by your disappointment at not experiencing my love." The partner may now be able understand his/her partner's hesitancy about showing love in a less personal and more "workable" way.

4. Discussing personal dilemmas can be experienced as a liberation from a personal or family struggle and may help the joining process in therapy. The client may feel fully understood by the therapist and may experience relief in that others now know and understand the dilemma.

In essence, dilemma as "intervention" is a reframe and/or hypothesis to which clients can be exposed. The difference from the "traditional" reframe is that it is specifically shaped to form a dilemma (if a "dilemma" punctuation makes sense for the case). The reframe is then presented to the couple on three levels. I present a *personal* dilemma for each client and then construct a *couple* dilemma that is linked with their personal dilemmas. I would also add that the information needed for the use of dilemma-as-intervention is no more nor less than one would need for the development of a sound working hypothesis. The informational focus, however, would be specifically tailored to meaningful personal and relationship dilemmas experienced by the clients.

At this point an example is in order. A couple asked for help understanding the lack of intimacy in their relationship. One of my observations was that in 15 years of marriage they had successfully managed to avoid conflict. Further exploration resulted in a working hypothesis, which was then presented to the couple in the form of two personal and two couple dilemmas. The following is a description of the type of information that was given to the couple.

The wife had maintained an image of herself as being strong and independent. Therefore, even though she wanted more support (both in terms of intimacy and with decision making) from her husband, she could not ask for it because she thought that to ask for it would mean she would be weak. The husband had experienced himself as being powerless in his family of origin. He operated accordingly in his present relationship. If he contributed to the decision-making process he thought his opinions would be invalidated. If he didn't contribute he would often not get what he wanted.

One couple dilemma was that both personal dilemmas were contributing to the lack of intimacy they were experiencing. The wife could not ask for support; the husband could not offer his opinion — they did not share the thoughts and feelings that would have contributed to couple intimacy. However, while their personal dilemmas helped them avoid intimacy, one might ask why their desire for intimacy did not entice them to overcome their personal dilemmas. Change for the couple was therefore highlighted by a dilemma that involved conflict avoidance. The noted dilemma was then, "If I request change for the other's behavior, I may end up in couple conflict and that is to be avoided at all costs."

In this particular case, the dilemma appeared to evoke the following responses from the couple. Both acknowledged the "accuracy" of the hypothesized personal dilemmas, which helped make the covert overt in a manner the couple seemed to feel was respectful.

The presentation of the individual dilemmas also seemed to act as a "challenge," sparking both to examine their own behavior. In addition, they suddenly both had the opportunity to understand the motivation for the other's behavior in a more positive, less personally threatening way, which "allowed" them more freedom to change their personal dilemmas.

The couple dilemma seemed to have the effect of providing a good answer to the question they presented regarding the lack of intimacy in the relationship. The couple could understand "why" intimacy did not evolve. It was an acceptable answer, I think, because it fit with their personal experience, and it emphasized that both were responsible for the situation and for change, while not blaming either. The "intervention" was hopefully gender fair, in that the level and responsibility for change was in the hands of both persons.

It is my opinion that reframes, while being "interventions," are not so much meant as "cures" as much as foundations upon which to work with people.

They provide the "atmosphere" in which "change can take hold" (excuse the oxymoron).

REFERENCES

Gazzaniga, M.S. (1985). *The social brain: Discovering the networks of the mind*. New York: Basic Books.

Ornstein, R. (1986). *Multiminds: A new way to look at human behavior*. Boston: Houghton Mifflin and Co.

Schwartz, R. (1987). Our multiple selves: Applying systems thinking to the inner family. *The Family Therapy Networker, 11*, 24-31, 80-83.

Selvini Palazzoli, M., Boscolo, L., Cecchin, G., & Prata, G. (1978). *Paradox and counterparadox*. New York: Jason Aronson.

Walsh, R. (1981). *Towards an ecology of brain*. New York: SP Medical & Scientific Books.

Watzlawick, P., Weakland, J., & Fisch, R. (1974). *Change: Principles of problem formation and problem resolution*. New York: W.W. Norton & Company.

94

Supervising Client Conversation:
A Brief Note on a Contextual Structure
for Evoking Therapeutic Creativity

Bradford P. Keeney

Most so-called "live supervision" of clinical work involves a supervisor behind a one-way mirror directing the conversation of a trainee working with a client system. This supervision situation is often an enactment of a mind/body duality: the supervisor is similar to an engineer working behind a leaded mirror with his or her arms in robotic limbs to handle the radioisotopes in the laboratory. Whatever the particular supervisory structure, the goal is the same: direct the therapist-trainee to have the appropriate conduct.

An alternative method of supervision involves reversing the client-therapist relation to this supervisor. Here the supervisor says nothing to the therapist, but talks directly to the clients. A beginning rationale may be articulated to the therapist trainee as follows:

> The problem with getting therapy to work has as much to do with getting the therapist going as it does with getting the client to work. Although we often think it's the therapist who needs to say the right thing to the client, it's actually a bit more complex. The client must act upon you to get you to say what would be useful to the client.
>
> This approach assists clients in saying the sort of things that may help trigger you, the therapist, to be therapeutic. Simply

be yourself and wait for your imagination to be awakened by the client. Our job, as supervisors, is to help the client wake you up.

The supervisor now can do all the things with clients that were formerly done with therapist trainees. Phone calls to clients can take place, suggesting certain questions. Should the client become confused, he/she can step out of the room and go behind the mirror for a consultation.

Supervisors can suggest that clients ask questions such as, "I heard about another therapist who saw someone like me and suggested the opposite of what you just said. What do you think of that?" Or the client might be prompted to ask, "Do you think your colleagues behind the mirror are bored with what we're saying?" Other questions supervisors can suggest to clients include:

- "If I were to say something now to be videotaped to make you look like a master therapist, what might it be?"
- "What would I have to say for you to think I'm a hopeless case?"
- "Is my problem interesting enough to be written about in a journal?"
- "Make up three interventions you think I would never agree to do."
- "Do you think there's someone else involved in the situation that I haven't told you about, like my grandmother or grandfather?"
- "Do you think I'm capable of making one small change this week?"
- "Who in the family do you think I believe is closer to father?"
- "If I told you something really bizarre, do you think you would want to keep me in therapy any longer?"
- "Who do you think is the best therapist in the world? What do you think s/he would say to me right now?"
- "If you knew I would follow exactly what you tell me to do, what assignment would you give me for next week?"

For the supervisors, the decision to intervene is dictated solely by when the conversation is experienced as emotionally flat and boring. When the conversation is experienced as live (one can't define it, but one can recognize it), then the supervisor keeps out of the way. In this way, a contextual structure is established that enables supervisors to help clients awaken the therapist's creativity and imagination.

95

Engaging Adolescents in Family Therapy: Some Early Phase Skills

Howard A. Liddle

FAMILY THERAPY IS DIFFICULT WITH ADOLESCENTS

Several family therapy approaches are not well-suited to working with adolescents. Whereas some models have developed popular technologies for working with parents (Haley, 1981; Madanes, 1981), other schools discourage participation by family members who are not "customers" for the treatment (Watzlawick, Weakland, & Fisch, 1974), and still others advise therapists to work only with the most motivated or "well" family members (Bowen, 1966). Unfortunately, the adolescent and the development of his or her agenda are frequently ignored in such therapies. Furthermore, treatment models that emphasize themes of hierarchy, power, and control present special problems in working with adolescents in family therapy (Haley, 1981; Madanes, 1981).

One major problem with an approach that restricts its focus in this way is that such a therapy can be developmentally inappropriate. Adolescence is a time of renegotiation of parent and adolescent relations (Hill, 1980; Steinberg, in press; Youniss & Smollar, 1985), and surely one important domain of relationship change is authority and control. However, these are by no means the only or

Author Note: Acknowledgements are gratefully given to Gayle A. Dakof and Braulio Montalvo for their comments. The writing of this chapter and the research project it represents, the Adolescents and Families Project, was supported by the National Institute on Drug Abuse grant to the author (RO1 DAO3714).

even the primary variables of interest. While important, these themes are not singularly determinative of successful therapy with adolescents and their families. Too often, a constricted concentration on these areas transforms *family* therapy into *parent therapy*. While there are some exceptions to these problematic trends in the adaptation of family models to adolescent problems (see the work of Fishman, 1988 for instance), many of family therapy's major "schools" do not adequately prepare clinicians with either the knowledge base or the skills to treat teenagers from a family systems orientation.

An overemphasis on parental subsystem work can also prevent effective engagement of the adolescent in therapy. Naturally, this makes establishment of the adolescent's personal therapeutic agenda difficult, to say the least. We use a phrase, "There can be something in this for you," to literally and metaphorically represent a key aspect of the early phase engagement efforts. The present chapter illustrates one aspect of an empirically derived treatment model known as Multidimensional Family Therapy (MDFT) (Liddle, 1991; Liddle, Diamond, Dakof, Holt, Arroyo, & Watson, 1992).[1] This is a population specific approach, specializing in the treatment of adolescent problems from a family systems perspective.[2]

ENGAGING ADOLESCENTS:
RATIONALE AND CONTENT

Engagement of the adolescent and the definition of an agenda for him or her in therapy is a primary first stage goal in MDFT. It requires the therapist to work both parental and adolescent subsystems simultaneously, even though this might appear contradictory.[3] The therapist increases the probability of building a successful working alliance with the teenager by demonstrating genuine respect and interest in his/her life inside and outside of the family. This therapeutic posture is distinct from the stance that has been pejoratively labeled "child saving" (i.e., a unidimensional, partial perspective that ignores parental perceptions and needs). The therapist must honor the promise to the teenager that his or her story can be "heard" in this therapy. For adolescents to be successfully included in family therapy, therapists must believe that the teenager's viewpoint is important to elicit, and further, that it is in everyone's best interest to attend to his or her complaints and opinions.

Teenagers often feel as hopeless about family life as the parents. Drug-using teenagers do not feel personal agency or experience much control over their own lives, and relatedly, experience a profound sense of meaninglessness (e.g., Harlow, Newcomb, & Bentler, 1986; Newcomb and Harlow, 1986). Therapists who ignore or are intimidated by adolescents can do much to fuel the teenager's extant hopelessness. MDFT directly addresses these influential themes. Working with the adolescent alone for significant periods of the therapy is one way to substantively develop these content themes. Let us examine some of the requisite skills for this therapy, illustrated with transcripts from an Adolescents and Families Project case.[4]

"THERE IS SOMETHING IN THIS FOR YOU"

The therapist's first conversation with the teenager is important. We try to be upbeat but not unrealistic about the possibilities of change. Above all we are interested in the adolescent's perspective of his or her circumstances. We try to capture immediately the attention and imagination of the teenager, frequently by defining this treatment as being different from the others in which the adolescent has been involved. This process stresses the teenager's participation. Therapy is a place where the adolescent's point of view can be developed, supported, and voiced in a constructive way.

Therapy is designated as a collaborative enterprise. This collaboration is not only between the therapist and parent(s), but it *must* include the teenager as well. Family therapy involves multiple therapeutic alliances. A good alliance with the parents does not predict an equally workable alliance with the teenager. In fact, under certain conditions, an inverse relationship might exist. Therapists usually have an easier time engaging parents in family therapy. Teenagers are more of a challenge for most clinicians. Therapist attitude is fundamental to this process. We cultivate and demonstrate a keen interest in the adolescent as a developing individual and as a member of this particular family.

T: You see, I'm really interested in who you are, and I really want to know more about you. I want to know who you are in this family, and who you want to be, as your own person, Sam. But I'm going to need your help. Do you think you can help me with it?

S: I can try.

The therapist sets the foundation for engaging the adolescent, in part by defining what therapy is and what is expected. Asking for help from the adolescent gives him a new relational experience. Other family members, schools, police, and juvenile justice systems usually see these teenagers along unidimensional and incompetent lines (anti-social, addicted, disturbed). In the above sequence the therapist acknowledges Sam by recognizing that he has a point of view and further, that it needs to be expressed. Only Sam can tell his story. Furthermore, Sam must provide his own perspective on his thoughts, feelings, and reactions to life thus far. Society, parents, and other involved systems that interact with the teenager only provide partial versions of the adolescent. A plea to the teenager to tell his own story usually yields results, even with the most troubled adolescent.

WORKING THE AFFECTIVE DOMAIN

Teenagers frequently present themselves with an aura of impermeability (I'm tough, I'm hip, I don't care). Engagement can be facilitated by accessing different aspects of the teenager than are commonly explored. Vulnerability, sadness, and tenderness, for example, are usually assumed to be therapeutically inaccessible with teenagers. However, we have found that with skill and an appreciation of how to explore certain themes in therapy, therapists can facilitate engagement *and* develop substantive content by working these underappreciated and avoided domains of a teenager's existence. Respect, compassion, perseverance, and sensitivity represent core therapist behaviors in this regard. Consider this statement from one of our therapists to a teenager who is unsure about what his participation in the therapy should be.

T: You told me last week when the big fight happened with your father, that you don't like dealing with your anger that way.

S: I don't, man, but that doesn't mean any of you are gonna make me change . . . Maybe I'm wrong, I'm not saying I'm not.

T: Would you be interested in learning how to deal with things better?

S: (Pauses) Yeah. I am.

T: That's something we could do here. (Pause) You know, you didn't look so happy when you were hitting your dad. (Sam kicked his father in the family assessment the previous week.) And you told me you hate when you get mad at him. I didn't think you looked too happy. Tonight I felt like there were times when you weren't happy. You didn't like what they were saying, maybe you don't feel like they understood you enough. Maybe you feel like you get in between them. You know, it's a hard situation, your parents being split up. They're still working out their things. It's going to influence you. I know that's rough. So, I want to help you work through some of that in a way that would work out well for you. But I'm gonna need your help.

MDFT operates in the multiple spheres of people's lives. In this sequence, we define work in the affective realm both as inherently useful, and as a potentiating process. Work in this realm is a holon, in the sense that Minuchin and Fishman (1981) have used it — something that is both a whole and a part. Acknowledging this teenager's unhappiness about how he handles his anger is singularly helpful, since it touches an aspect of this teenager's functioning that others ignore or try to control. Additionally, focusing on emotion also serves to potentiate work in other domains, such as in the cognitive realm.

Emotional communication is hardly simple catharsis, as contemporary, systems-oriented theoretical and empirical work on emotion demonstrates (Campos, Campos, & Barrett, 1989). Dealing with, in this case, the adolescent's emotional reactions creates a process that reveals other aspects of functioning, frequently in the realm of attributes about how his parents "really are." That is, as emotion becomes the focus of our work with teenagers or parents, the core beliefs concomitant with these emotions become apparent. In this example, the teenager's feeling of disconnection from his father, hopelessness about change, and his belief that the father does not care about him were stimulated by first working the affective realm. Thus, a prime early target of our work is the teenager's emotional world. This concentration aids the adolescent's engagement by establishing his personal agenda in the therapy, and installs the therapist as a person who can understand, confirm,[5] and, sometimes at least, take their side.

DEFINING THE TERRITORY

The environment of therapy is a strange and foreign place for many teenagers. The therapist must succinctly yet deftly sketch in this landscape, always stressing core themes of collaboration and compassion, experimentation, communication style, and responsibility.

> Therapist: There's times I'm gonna ask you to talk to your folks and be straight with them. There's times I'm gonna ask you to do things in here or at home and try out new things. There's times where we're gonna meet alone and I'll want you to be straight with me and say what's on your mind, so that you can really get some of your own needs met. Because I feel like you're not getting what you want right now. What does that all sound like? Do you want to give it a try?

Articulation of the teenager's concerns is paramount in the early stages of therapy. This expression is framed accordingly: The previous ways of communicating one's disagreements and self-definition have not been received kindly by the teenager's parents or most adults. Thus, a new, more effective form of expression on the teenager's part is declared necessary. This therapeutic construction is critical and, to accomplish it, one must frequently use the crisis that often presents itself at the outset of adolescent therapy. On other occasions, using events from the teenager's past can help. The adolescent's new communication ability, or as we refer to it with the teenagers, the new "language," is defined as crucial to his or her very survival. The therapist offers himself or herself as one who can assist the teenager in this regard. S/he designs therapy as an arena that will push for some experiments toward change. In short, action and attempts at change are included in the agenda with the teenager.

Although we are careful not to be become over-organized and pessimistic by disinclined teenagers, we do accommodate to this adolescent's position. He or she can be given psychological space to work out a way to participate. Nonetheless, the therapist needs to make a strong and confident statement that she would like to work with the teenager and give some indication of what this work might be like. The therapist is careful to pace her/his definitional process and requests for commitment. The following comes at the end of the first session with the teenager alone:

> It's something (our work together) that might evolve over time. It's not something that you just say yes to. But, I do want you to go home and think about it. I want you to think, "Am I willing to be honest with myself in this therapy, and if I can do that, am I then willing to be honest with them? With my folks and with Guy (the therapist)? Am I willing to really take stock of who I am, what I want, what's the best way to get it, what's not working, what do I want to change, and whether I'm willing to give it a try?" And I'm only asking for your best shot. I'm not asking for perfection, and I don't expect you to come in with big plans. It'll be a process. It's something to just start working on. But, if you're willing to say, "Okay, I'll put my foot in the door," then we can give it a try. So, I don't need a big answer or a commitment. It's purely something to ponder over, to think about over the week. Next week we'll meet again and see what you think . . . Are you willing to be honest with yourself?

CONCLUSIONS

There are several crises ahead for family therapy (Liddle, Gurman, Pinsof, & Roberto, 1990). One is whether training models can evolve in the needed direction. The schools of thought themselves, as well as the "schools approach" to training, inadequately prepare trainees for the real world of clinical practice (Liddle, 1991). Ours is not a world of training tape cases or of Masters interviews. Treating teenagers is an example of what is, for many therapists, a population and set of problems for which they are clearly unprepared. Given their training, and the challenges posed by this age range, it is easy for therapists to avoid and trivialize adolescents. Taking our cue from society and the popular culture, we pathologize adolescence (Offer, Ostrov, & Howard, 1981), making erroneous, and therapeutically unhelpful assumptions about teenagers. A leading family therapy text, for example, falsely proclaimed adolescence as "a time of normal psychosis" (Pittman, 1988). We need to progress on this front. To do so we must build treatment manuals and models with an accurate knowledge base that is clearly tied to empirical work in the clinical and basic realms.

NOTES

1. Funded by the National Institute on Drug Abuse, the Adolescents and Families Project is a randomized clinical trial of family therapy's effectiveness with substance abusing and conduct disorder adolescents. The research began in 1985 at the University of California, San Francisco, and moved in 1990 to Temple University with the relocation of the Principal Investigator, Howard Liddle. Over 250 families entered this research project with randomized cases into one of three conditions: multidimensional family therapy, group therapy for the adolescents alone, and multi-family treatment.

2. To achieve this we rely on an in-depth understanding of the contemporary adolescent development literature (see reviews by Peterson, 1989; and Powers, Hauser, & Kilner, 1989). A guiding value of the Adolescents and Families Project and MDFT has been the translation and incorporation of research findings from this area of developmental psychology into the clinical realm. We have discussed elsewhere the major molar level constructs that have informed the clinical model building (Liddle, Schmidt, & Ettinger, in press).

3. This chapter emphasizes some early phase skills of doing a multidimensional, multisystemic therapy through the adolescent subsystem. This is not meant to imply that skills needed to work for adolescent, parent, and family change

through the parental subsystem are somehow less vital. The modules for working with such subsystems as the parental and extrafamilial subsystems will be developed in other publications. Important themes in the parental subsystem, for example, have included the establishment or rekindling of parental hopes, dreams, and aspirations for their adolescent. This revitalization of a parent's commitment, which could be said to address the "parental imperative," can be accomplished by working themes that promote forgiveness, perspective taking, and a stance of negotiation on the parent's part. As one can see, these foci serve as a necessary complement to the control-and-authority oriented interventions commonly thought of in work with the parents of teenagers.

4. The therapist in this case was Guy Diamond; the supervisor was Howard Liddle.

5. Understand and confirm perhaps do not carry enough of the connotation of how these realities are both understood/confirmed and shaped, sometimes simultaneously. At this earliest stage of the therapy and the developing therapeutic alliance between therapist and teenager, however, it is more accurate to say that the therapist aims for a more pure understanding and confirmation of the adolescent's life as he or she experiences it.

REFERENCES

Bowen, M. (1966). The use of family theory in clinical practice. *Comprehensive Psychiatry, 7*, 345-374.

Campos, J.J., Campos, R.G., & Barrett, K.C. (1989). Emergent themes in the study of emotional development and emotion regulation. *Developmental Psychology, 25*, 3, 394-402.

Fishman, H.C. (1988). *Treating troubled adolescents: A family therapy approach.* New York: Basic.

Haley, J. (1981). *Leaving Home.* New York: McGraw-Hill.

Harlow, L.L., Newcomb, M.D., & Bentler, P.M. (1986). Depression, self-derogation, substance use, and suicide ideation: Lack of purpose in life as a mediational factor. *Journal of Clinical Psychology, 42*, 1, 5-21.

Hill, J.P. (1980). The family. In M. Johnson & K.J. Rehage, (Eds.), *Toward adolescence: The middle school years. Part I.* University of Chicago Press.

Liddle, H.A. (1992). The adolescents and families project: Multidimensional Family Therapy in action. In *ADAMHA Monograph from the First National Conference on the Treatment of Adolescent Drug, Alcohol and Mental Health Problems.* Washington, DC: United States Public Health Service, Government Printing Office.

Liddle, H.A. (1991). Family therapy training and supervision: A critical review and analysis. In A.S. Gurman & D. Kniskern (Eds.), *Handbook of family therapy* (Volume II). New York: Brunner/Mazel.

Liddle, H.A., Diamond, G., Dakof, G.A., Holt, M., Arroyo, J., & Watson, M. (1992). Multidimensional family therapy with adolescent substance abuse. In

E. Kaufman & P. Kaufman (Eds.), *Family therapy of drug and alcohol abuse, 2nd ed.* Boston: Allyn & Bacon.

Liddle, H.A., Gurman, A.S., Pinsof, W., & Roberto, L.G. (1990). What's wrong with family therapy? Papers presented at the 48th Annual Conference of the American Association for Marriage and Family Therapy, October 5, 1990. Washington, DC.

Liddle, H.A., Schmidt, S. & Ettinger, D. Unpublished manuscript.

Madanes, C. (1981). *Strategic family therapy.* San Francisco: Jossey-Bass.

Minuchin, S., & Fishman, H.C. (1981). *Family therapy techniques.* Cambridge, MA: Harvard.

Newcomb, M.D., & Harlow, L.L. (1986). Life events and substance use among adolescents: Mediating effects of perceived loss of control and meaninglessness in life. *Journal of Personality and Social Psychology, 51,* 564-577.

Offer, D., Ostrov, E., & Howard, K.I. (1981). The mental health professional's concept of the normal adolescent. *Archives of General Psychiatry, 38,* 149-152.

Peterson, A.C. (1989). Adolescent development. *Annual Review of Psychology, 39,* 583-607.

Pittman, F. (1988). *Turning points.* New York: Norton.

Powers, S.I., Hauser, S.T., Kilner, L.A. (1989). Adolescent mental health. *American Psychologist, 44,* 2, 200-208.

Steinberg, L. (in press). Interdependency in the family: Autonomy, conflict, and harmony in the parent-adolescent relationship. In S.S. Feldman (Ed.), *Normal adolescent development.* Washington, DC: Carnegie Council on Adolescent Development.

Watzlawick, P., Weakland, J., & Fisch, R. (1974). *Change: Principles of problem formation and problem resolution.* New York: Norton.

Youniss, J., & Smollar, J. (1985). *Adolescent relations with mothers, fathers, and friends.* Chicago: University of Chicago Press.

96

The Blanket

John Madonna
George Roix

THE INTERVENTION

This intervention is a form of multiple sensory impacting (MSI). It consists not only of an insight-oriented discussion of transactional marital issues, but a visual and, in this case-example, a tactile/thermal experience of the issue. In the example, a blanket was used as a physical metaphor for emotional suffocation and was used to envelop an abusive husband during a marital session. In other cases, appropriate metaphors can strategically rebalance power structures in marriages.

INFORMATION NEEDED TO PLAN THE INTERVENTION

The intervention is useful when (1) excessive dependency and emotional smothering is a transactional issue in a marriage or family; (2) clients are predominately action oriented, have a limited proficiency in communicating verbally, are easily swept away by their emotions, and are unable to maintain focus on the issue(s); (3) there is a trusting relationship between the clients and therapist; and (4) the client can sufficiently tolerate the intervention. It is important for the client not to feel ridiculed.

CASE EXAMPLE

The husband was highly dependent upon his wife, impulsive, and abusive toward her. He was not very bright and had not talked very much in therapy. The wife felt smothered in the marriage, unable to tolerate her husband's dependence or abuse any longer. Direct attempts to change this relationship were unsuccessful. The therapist placed a heavy wool blanket over the husband during the session. While the client was covered with the blanket, the therapist talked with the wife about her experience of suffocation.

OUTCOME

The husband began to understand his wife's experience as he experienced the sensation of not being able to breathe. He also was very hot under the blanket. He began to understand that his dependency was pushing her away from him and was as unbearable for her as sitting under the blanket was for him. He began to allow her greater freedom and negotiated more balanced distance between them.

97

Frank and Jimmy

Cynthia R. Zeldin
Thorana S. Nelson

THEORETICAL APPROACH

Transgenerational theories often explain how people interact in patterned ways through multiple generations. Framo (1982), using ideas from object relations theory, discusses how children develop distorted perceptions of their parents and then act toward significant others in later life based on those perceptions. They see their spouses and children through the lens of this distorted perception, and miss the unique characteristics of important others. Framo suggests that bringing parents and adult children together in therapy helps people share perceptions and understand each other as real people rather than distorted images. This often helps free clients to improve relations with both parents and current significant others.

The first author, using her own modification of Framo's basic ideas, employs the conjoint parent/adult child interview to help people illuminate their distorted perceptions of each other and open the way for healing and new ways of relating.

PREPARATION

The therapist helps the client prepare for the session by discussing agenda items. The purpose of the session is to assist the client in letting go of the past so that relationships in the present can be more significant and satisfying. The therapist makes it very clear that the purpose of the session is not to obtain an apology from the parent(s), but to allow the client to express him/herself and to gain a better understanding of the parent(s)' views of the time and situations under discussion. The therapist informs the client that rapport must be built with the parent(s) in order for them to feel comfortable, taking time while the client waits for the business to begin.

After the client understands the purpose and agrees to the conjoint interview, the client invites the parents to attend the session. The therapist coaches the client about ways to make this invitation nonthreatening and appealing. When parent(s) live out of town, the therapist plans sessions for Friday and Saturday to allow sufficient time for joining, conversation, and processing. The family may discuss the items introduced on Friday after the session, allowing the Saturday session to be used for closure.

THE INTERVIEW

After joining with the parent(s), the therapist guides the discussion by asking them what kind of child the client was—what s/he was like growing up and what life was like from the parent(s)' perspective. The therapist supports and encourages the parent(s) in their perceptions of their child's life. The therapist frequently states that parent(s) are not being blamed, that they did the best they could, and that the therapist is requesting this information for consultation so that the client can better understand the parent(s) and the past. The tone is continually nonjudgmental and matter-of-fact. The therapist encourages moderate but not excessive affect.

The first part of the interview often takes about one hour after which a break is taken. These breaks usually occur naturally, but the therapist may initiate them if necessary. The client and parent(s) continue talking if they wish while the therapist excuses him/herself. This conveys a message of trust to the client and parent(s): they don't need the therapist and can begin the process of communicating in new ways on their own.

The next part of the interview involves helping the client tell each parent the client's perception of important events and relationships as well as his/her feelings about those events. The therapist helps the parent(s) listen to the client without feeling guilty, clarifying interactions. The therapist insists on I-statements and self-responsibility. At no time are the parent(s) asked to apologize. The purpose of the session is not to establish blame or seek forgiveness, but to bring different perceptions into the open so that the client and parent(s) can understand each other differently with less distortion. If the parent(s) are feeling excessively hurt or express guilt, the therapist may see them alone at another time. Unresolved feelings may require extra sessions.

After the client and his/her parent(s) have discussed the past, the therapist guides them to the present, establishing new levels of trust and encouraging them to move on in new directions in their relationships. The therapist continues to work with the client after the conjoint session, helping to establish new ways of relating to other important people as well as to the parent(s). Healed relationships with parent(s) is one of the rewards of this mode of therapy.

CASE EXAMPLE

Jimmy's father, Frank, left Jimmy with his mother when he was 9 months old for service in World War II. Jimmy and his mother lived with her father until Frank returned. A second son was born one year later. Frank is a successful businessman and Jimmy works with him in the family business. They have a good professional relationship, but Jimmy feels distant from Frank as a son. Jimmy's mother drank excessively while he was growing up and was often depressed and withdrawn. Frank worked very hard during this time, leaving Jimmy and his brother in the care of a housekeeper. Jimmy remembers preferring to be at his friends' homes to his own. Frank and his wife later divorced and she subsequently committed suicide.

Frank described Jimmy as a good kid, easy to discipline and never in trouble. He explained how he worked hard to keep things going at home, trying to raise the boys and protect the family from his wife's alcoholism. He obtained treatment for her once, but it was not successful. He was sad and confused about her problem and his feelings of inadequacy toward her and his children. He felt competent only at work and so worked a great deal. Much of this information was a surprise to Jimmy since his father had always seemed distant and cold to him, but competent and confident. He hadn't known what his father thought about him, his mother, or her drinking problem. He told his father he had been afraid of his mother and her anger. Frank was surprised to learn that Jimmy was afraid since Jimmy had always been so helpful, caring, confident, and competent.

Frank and Jimmy were able to understand each other much better after each learned of the other's pain, confusion, and sadness. Like his father, Jimmy had learned to withdraw from problems to avoid conflict, a pattern that was influencing his marriage negatively. Hearing his father explain how he had made decisions helped Jimmy understand that his father had not withdrawn out of fear of conflict so much as to protect his children and family and provide some peace in the house. The therapist encouraged both men to express their anger and sadness with each other and to join each other in expressing these emotions in addition to their love for their wife and mother. Jimmy was able to tell his father that he wanted to be closer to him emotionally. The therapist helped them discuss ways they could make this happen, keeping in mind that old patterns cannot (nor should they) completely change.

After the conjoint session, Frank and Jimmy began to spend more personal time together. Jimmy talked with his father about his relationship with Frank's second wife and was able to improve his interactions with her. He also was able to reexamine his relationship with his wife, talking with her instead of withdrawing during arguments.

DISCUSSION

This intervention is useful when adults are unable to break destructive interactive patterns with their spouses or important others that are connected to unresolved family of origin issues. It also is useful when the client wishes to openly discuss unresolved issues with his/her parent(s) and is willing to do this in a conjoint session without expecting apologies or requesting forgiveness.

This intervention helps the child within to heal so that the adult can grow. Childhood hurts are painful, but there are many ways of perceiving those events. The conjoint family of origin session can help bridge a gap between different perceptions, freeing the client and his/her parent(s) to choose new ways of relating to each other and to others.

REFERENCE

Framo, J.L. (1982). *Explorations in marital and family therapy.* New York: Springer.

REFLECTIONS ON INTERVENTION

Questions as Metaphor

Arthur Mandelbaum

Dear Dr. Thorana Nelson,

As I enter my senior years of practice and supervision of family therapy, I no longer think of intervention as one of the primary ways of changing behavior. Indeed, I no longer push for change, but leave that up to my clients. When I speak to my clients, I do it in the form of raising questions. I think of such questions as metaphors, as language which presents images. What lies below visible behavior is always imagery, pictures, the imaginative. One might think of this as a kind of poetry.

One example of this is the family member who spoke of his father as a mighty oak. This metaphor was explored through questions, such as asking the father, "What experiences in your life have led you to become a mighty oak?" Using this as a metaphor not only about the father but about family experiences led to the disclosure of a tragic loss the father had experienced in early adolescence. As the father wept, his wife and children joined him in his grief by weeping with him. I thought of the lines in Macbeth:

> What, man! Ne'er pull your hat upon your brows.
> Give sorrow words. The grief that does not speak
> Whispers the o'erfraught heart and bids it break.

From then on in the treatment process, the metaphor of the mighty oak, led into where the father had frozen, had become stuck in his development at the time of his great loss, impacting that severely on his marriage and on his children. This theme was developed in a variety of ways, stimulated by the imagery and inventiveness of family members and a variety of strategic and structural techniques by the therapist that fitted the temperament and value system of the family. This resulted in the father halting the projection onto his youngest son of his rage and bitterness rooted in the father's early loss and the son ended his delinquent behavior at school.

What has been helpful to me has been the contribution of Daniel Stern, who wrote that experienced clinicians

> search with the patient through his or her remembered history to find the potent life-experience that provides the key therapeutic metaphor for understanding and changing the patient's life. This experience can be called the narrative point of origin of the pathology, regardless of when it occurred in actual developmental time. Once the metaphor has been found, the therapy proceeds forward and backward in time from that point of origin.

The psychoanalyst, Elvin Semrad wrote:

> If you think about where the patient is stuck in his life and what issues he's failed to work out and integrate so that he could continue his development you'll have a much greater chance of therapeutic success than if you try to put a label on him or call him a diagnostic name.

A system can get stuck also and slowly grind down and each member is affected by its key metaphors, gets locked into them, and becomes part of a patterned choreography.

In this period of integration of family therapy theory, each therapist is inevitably influenced by what is experienced, read, seen in the work of his colleagues, and what is learned from practice. Many interventions are tried and in time those that work for a particular therapist become his or her possession. I owe much to the gifted leaders and teachers we have had in our work as well as students and families.

Sincerely,

Arthur Mandelbaum

REFERENCES

Rako, S., & Mazer, H. (Eds.). (1980). *Semrad: The heart of a therapist.* New York: Jason Aronson.

Shakespeare, W., "Macbeth." In G.B. Harrison (Ed.), *Shakespeare: The complete works* (pp. 1184-1218). NY: Harcourt, Brace, & World. Original work published 1791.

Stern, D.N. (1985). *The interpersonal world of the infant: A view from psychoanalysis and developmental psychology.* NY: Basic Books.

99

Intervention in Context

William C. Nichols

Dear Dr. Nelson:

This is in response to your communication concerning a book on family therapy interventions. Thank you for asking me to make a submission to the book.

I appreciate being included on your list of potential authors, but must decline. What you are asking is something that is out of character for my approach to clinical work with couples, families, and individuals. I simply cannot teach interventions except in context. As my students have heard over the years, "I don't teach interventions as such – in the classroom or in the abstract, although I may teach a thousand of them in supervision," including the "Pollyanna" approach, the "Columbo" approach, and a number of others of varying sizes and uses.

Hence, if I were to respond it would be with something kind of dull such as:

> My favorite intervention is whatever kind of approach can be tailored to a particular couple, family, or situation either primarily by the therapist or by the therapist in explicit collaboration with the client/client system to meet the particular needs and exigencies of the time and phase of treatment, life, and development in an effective manner. Interventions for me don't have an independent life of their own, although there are permissive conditions for the use of some and contraindications for the use of most of them. Hence, I don't know specifically what interventions are going to be used until we reach a

particular phase or situation in therapy and both the initial and ongoing assessment work indicate that it is appropriate to make such an intervention. The outcome may or may not be readily evident — sometimes you have to wait for years to know how effective something was. The more satisfying interventions are those in which the client/client system is able to take an increasing amount of control over her/his/their own behavior and life and to work the therapist out of a job either temporarily or permanently.

That may sound pretty stuffy and may lead to a response of, "Sorry I asked." It certainly is not the kind of thing out of which one can construct a book on interventions.

Again, best wishes with your endeavor.

Sincerely,

Bill Nichols

100

Beyond Intervention

Eric E. McCollum

The invitation to submit a piece for this book came just before I went into a session. The family I saw was having a lot of trouble with their son Ted, seventeen. He was just expelled from school for skipping and had been drinking on weekends with his friends even though he is diabetic. He quit his job a week ago. Since then he has been sleeping in his car out behind a friend's house because "everyone gets on my case at home."

In the session, Ted sat slumped in his chair, curly hair hanging down in his face, wearing a dirty fatigue jacket. His mother was sitting on the edge of her seat, ready to let me know how much worse Ted had been this week. Ted's father sat over in a corner, leaning back, eyes closed, present only because his wife "made him" attend. It was a scene I'd encountered weekly for the past few months. I asked what had been going on.

"Nothing," Ted said. "Everything's boring."

"That's not what the police said when they brought you home the other night," Ted's mother chimed in.

Ted leaned back in his chair, much like his father, and closed his eyes, too.

"Whatever," he said, with the hint of a grin. As Ted withdrew, his mother got more intense. She turned to me.

"What are we going to do?" she asked. I thought I saw Ted's father scoot his chair back a little as his wife focused on me. "The police said they found him outside a store that had been robbed. They think Ted was involved but they can't prove anything. It can't go on like this. What are we going to do?"

I could feel my energy drain out of me as she spoke. My head was getting fuzzy and I didn't know what to say. I looked over at the clock on the bookshelf, hoping a miracle had moved it to the end of the hour, but there were 45 minutes left.

"Oh, boy," I said to myself. "I'd better do something. If I ever needed an intervention, now's the time."

My meeting with Ted's family got me thinking about interventions. For me, "intervention" has a specific connotation, differing, perhaps, from how others think of it. To me, an intervention is a well-defined, circumscribed action I can take in a session that has a consistent, definable result.

Although the action may be based in theory, it doesn't require much thought at the time to carry it out. There's a cookbook aspect to it. Adolescent suicide threat? Use recipe A. Extramarital affair? Try recipe B. It's what participants are asking for in workshops, I think, when they say, "Enough talk about theory. Tell us what to do!"

I was pretty interested in gathering together a "bag of tricks" when I was a younger therapist. "Intervening" is what therapists do, after all. The masters were cooperative models. I moved more furniture than North American Van Lines after I saw Minuchin in the early days. When Haley came to town, I began to prescribe ordeals left and right. Then I read Selvini Palazzoli and my clients got more mail from me than from Publisher's Clearinghouse. Other things followed. Genograms the size of Rhode Island after I learned about Bowen. Sex therapy. Biofeedback referrals. Cognitive therapy. Medication. Hospitalization.

While all these actions have value, my interventions never proved completely satisfying. Sometimes they worked, but often they didn't. I finally decided that what went wrong was that my interventions were usually aimed at the wrong party in the therapy room. I made cookbook interventions hoping to get the family to change when the real problem was what I was feeling.

"Head 'em up, move 'em out" interventions came when I got anxious. They were designed to inject missing motivation into the family. It was what I felt with Ted and his parents. I had to get them to do something different. Why wasn't this boy worried about his health? How could I get his father more involved and his mother calmed down a little? The problem I was trying to solve with these interventions was: "How come I'm more worried about your life than you are?"

"You can't get away with that!" interventions came when I got mad. Mute adolescents like Ted are one sure trigger for me. If I'd been supervising behind the mirror, I'd have a little smile on my face as the therapist struggled with Ted's refusal to participate and his parents' inability to get him to.

"I'll put a paradox on that rascal," I'd be thinking to myself. "He can't get away with that." The real problem, of course, was that Ted and his family weren't helping me be a competent, successful therapist. And it made me mad.

Interventions—at least the cookbook variety I'm talking about here—don't solve the problems with me. What does make a difference is stopping to pay attention to myself when I feel an urgent need to intervene. It's kind of a therapist-focused intervention, I guess. How is it helpful? There are several ways.

First, I stop doing things based simply on my own anger or anxiety. Those interventions rarely work well because they don't come from a clear, thoughtful plan. Now, when I feel like making a cookbook intervention, I first try to pull back and look the situation over. If some focused intervention makes sense, it will still work after the little time it takes to consider it.

The second advantage to a therapist-focused intervention is that my own feelings are often a clue to understanding the family. If I act too quickly, I lose that information. With Ted, for example, I felt angry, stymied in every effort to be successful, yet stubbornly not wanting to give up. That's a lot of what a boy who has a chronic illness must feel. Nothing he does will cure it. It sets him apart from his friends and the only way to have some control is to resist, whether it's parents, school principal, or therapist. His parents must experience similar feelings—sadness about the situation but anger at their son's refusal to help himself. Recognizing these feelings in myself led me to be more patient with Ted and his parents, and to realize what Ted would lose by giving up his oppositional stance.

Finally, a therapist-focused intervention helps me stay clear about what's possible in therapy and who's responsible for it. For me, the impulse to "intervene" often comes when I've lost track of the limits of therapy and of my responsibility. If I get more worried than my clients about their troubles, I may push them toward solutions that are premature or frightening to them or go beyond the goals they have for themselves. Other times, I have to accept that therapy can't always provide happy endings. Some problems go unsolved. The more I can remember these things and not get hooked on finding the perfect intervention, the more satisfaction I seem to have in my work. It's the best prevention for burnout I've found.

My struggle with the idea of intervention results from a fundamental shift in my practice over the years. Whereas I used to concentrate on "what to do" as a therapist, I now find myself much more interested in "how to be" with a family. My first job is to calm myself before I consider what to do about the other person. If I can slow myself down, instead of jumping for a cookbook formula, I am much less likely to become part of a dysfunctional therapy system. Then what I do will come from an empathic understanding of the family, based on my own experience of them. That's the most basic intervention of all, it seems to me. Of course, if anyone does know a good way to get a resistant, withdrawn adolescent to talk, let me know immediately. I rescheduled Ted and his family for next week and I'm already starting to worry about what to do about that kid.

Comfortable Interventions

Tom Andersen

Intervention seems to be the core word of this book. I want to share my definition of it as a part of my relating to the concept itself and the activity it reflects.

In terms of the semantic aspect of the word, Webster's Dictionary tells me that its first component (inter) means *between* and the second (vention) may have two slightly different meanings with roots from old English and old German *to come* and with roots from Latin and Greek *to walk* or *to go*. Concerning the pragmatics, Webster mentions various possibilities: to occur or lie between two things; to enter or occur or fall between two points of time or two events; to come between by way of hindrance or modification (which, according to Webster, is close to *interfere*: use of force or threat).

When I am uncertain of a meaning, I ask my intuition for advice. In this case it tells me that, according to the semantic part, *to come* is a very active word *and* it is static: "I have *come* and I *am here*." *To walk* contains a lot of varieties as the walker proceeds (as part of a process). *To go* is similar to walk, but also different. To walk contains the walk and all that follows in terms of impressions the walker receives as s/he walks: sounds, smells, touches, colors, shapes, etc. To go is more "effective": "I go from somewhere to somewhere."

The three meanings of the pragmatic aspects have an increasing tendency of influencing — from the slight *to occur* to the more heavy *to force* or even *to threaten*. McNamee (1988), among others, has recently advocated the idea that every search for something new is an intervention.

What is the request or what are the requests various consultees bring us when they come to "therapy"? I often hear them say, "I don't know what to do!" I think at this point in time that implicit in this statement are more statements: "What I do in my present difficulties does not help me." Or more implicit: "The way I understand my difficulties has not helped me." Or even more implicit: "The way I describe my difficulties has not helped me." Or: "The language I use in order to describe and understand, and through that find a way to act on my difficulties, has not helped me."

I see, at this point in time, that my professional contribution to those who consult me is to participate in conversations in order to search for new actings, new descriptions, new understandings and/or new nuances in the language they use or even new bits to their language.

The crucial word above is *to participate* and the question raised in that context is: how can I best participate in these searches?

At this point in time I find it crucial that I participate in such a way that I feel comfortable, or at least not uncomfortable. Part of not being uncomfortable is to talk with the consultees in such a way that *they* feel comfortable, at least not uncomfortable.

If one accepts Sheila McNamee's position above, the question can also be formed: "What kind of intervention do I prefer to provide?"

I like to walk and let that walk occur between the two (or more) aspects of the dilemma(s) that a difficult situation comprises. Where and how that walk shall be I intend at this point in time to let my intuition tell me. The intuition is my body telling me from second to second which of my own contributions to a conversation I feel uncomfortable with. I become more and more alert to the uncomfortable instances. The comfortable and successful instances do not need attention, they take care of themselves. These ideas have been very much inspired by an expression of Harry Goolishian, Galveston Family Institute, Texas: "If you know what to do, it limits you pretty much. If you know more *what not to do*, then there is an infinity of things that might be done."

My experiences so far have told me that consultees are extremely sensitive about being told that they should be other than they are. Humberto Maturana, a Chilean, has, from a biological point of view, pointed out that the body is extremely sensitive to the pertur-bations it is challenged by. Some are welcomed and become a stim-ulus to change, some are too alien and will disintegrate the body or parts of it if they are included. Norwegian physiotherapist Aadel Bulow-Hansen has noticed that much of what stimulates us from outside influences our breathing such that inhalation increases fol-lowing exhalation. She also understood that tension in the body was released through that exhalation. As air goes, she says, tension goes. If the stimulations from outside are inappropriate, the person inhales, but stops breathing and keeps the air inside. Keeping the air inside keeps the tension inside as well.

This has become more than a metaphor for my working. The breathing of all of us who participate must flow freely, as the flow of the conversation itself must be free.

Meanings, tasks, advice, and interventions aimed to change "from outside" will easily be understood by those who receive them as: "They want to give me this because they think what I have myself from beforehand is not good enough. I am not good enough." It is hard to think of such, and I believe most people feel uncomfor-table in such moments.

My interventions are questions that my intuition tells me are not too unusual for the receiver. Such questions are often directed to-wards the language that is used. The interventions also contain loose ideas about which descriptions and understandings might ex-ist *in addition* to those that are already there. There is more of this in Andersen (1990a and 1990b). A main idea is that a person cannot be changed or learned. But the person can change and learn.

REFERENCES

McNamee, S. (1988). Accepting research as social intervention: Implications of a systemic epistemology. *Communication Quarterly, 36,* 50-68.

Andersen, T. (1990a). *The reflecting team: Dialogues and dialogues about vari-ous dialogues.* Kent, UK: Borgmann Publ.

Andersen, T. (1990b). Search and re-search for being with. In S. McNamee & K.J. Gergen (Eds.). *Social construction and therapeutic process.* CA: Sage.

About the Contributors

Jerome Adams, PhD, is Assistant Professor of Family Therapy, University of Rhode Island, Kingston, RI.

Eleanor Adaskin, RN, PhD, is in private practice; is Assistant Professor of Nursing and Medicine, University of Manitoba; and is Director of Nursing Research, St. Boniface General Hospital, Winnipeg, Canada.

Scot Allgood, PhD, is Assistant Professor of Marriage and Family Therapy, Utah State University, Logan, UT.

Tom Andersen, MD, is Professor of Social Psychiatry, Institute for Community Medicine, University of Tromso, Tromso, Norway.

Michele Baldwin, ACSW, PhD, is Assistant Professor of Psychiatry and Behavioral Sciences, Northwestern University Medical School, and is on the faculty of the Family Institute of Chicago, Chicago, IL.

Sybil Baldwin, CSW, ACSW, is a former faculty member in the University of Rochester Family Therapy Training Program, Division of Family Programs, Department of Psychiatry, Rochester, NY.

D. Ray Bardill, PhD, is Dean and Professor, School of Social Work, Florida State University, Tallahassee, FL.

Charles P. Barnard, EdD, is affiliated with the University of Wisconsin-Stout, Menomonee, WI.

Marilyn Belleghem, MEd, is in private practice in Oakville, Ontario, Canada.

Amith BenDavid, PhD, is in private practice in Haifa, Israel.

Insoo Kim Berg, MSW, is affiliated with the Brief Family Therapy Center, Milwaukee, WI.

Joan L. Biever, PhD, is affiliated with Our Lady of the Lake University, San Antonio, TX.

James R. Bitter, EdD, is Chair, Department of Counseling, California State University-Fullerton, Fullerton, CA.

Diane B. Brashear, PhD, is Assistant Professor, Department of Obstetrics and Gynecology, University Hospital, Indiana University, Indianapolis, IN.

Gregory Brock, PhD, is affiliated with the University of Kentucky, Lexington, KY.

Glenn I. Bronley, PhD, is Coordinator, Family Psychology Internship, Harlem Valley Psychiatric Center, Wingdale, NY.

Don Brown, STD, is Director of the Substance Abuse Program, Cheaha Mental Health Center, Sylacauga, AL.

Edmund Cava, MD, is a clinical faculty member, Department of Psychiatry, University of Miami, Miami, FL.

Norman H. Cobb, PhD, is Assistant Professor, Graduate School of Social Work, University of Texas at Arlington, Arlington, TX.

Leslie Ann Cotney, MA, is affiliated with the McPhaul Marriage and Family Therapy Clinic, University of Georgia, Athens, GA.

Au-Deane Cowley, PhD, is Associate Professor, Graduate School of Social Work, University of Utah, and is in private practice in Salt Lake City, UT.

Don Dinkmeyer, Jr., PhD, is Associate Professor, Western Kentucky University, Bowling Green, KY.

Don Dinkmeyer, Sr., PhD, is President, Communication and Motivation Training Institute, Coral Springs, FL.

Sandra Diskin, PhD, is Clinical Supervisor, Family Services, Inc., Lafayette, IN.

Matthew Eastwood, PhD, is Supervisor of Social Work, Bellefaire/Jewish Children's Bureau, Cleveland, OH.

David Fenell, PhD, is Associate Professor and Chair, Counseling and Human Services Program, University of Colorado Springs, and Director, Rampart Family Institute, Colorado Springs, CO.

Marshall Fine, EdD, is Associate Professor, University of Guelph, Guelph, Ontario, Canada.

James R. Fisher, EdD, is a licensed psychologist in Eustis, FL.

Maria Flores, PhD, is Co-director, Marriage and Family Therapy Institute of San Antonio, San Antonio, TX.

Bill Forisha, PhD, is affiliated with the Department of Applied Human Ecology and the Department of Human Development and Family Studies, Bowling Green State University, Bowling Green, OH.

Bruce D. Forman, PhD, is Associate Professor, Department of Psychiatry and Department of Family and Community Medicine, University of Miami, Miami, FL.

Miguel Franco, PhD, is affiliated with the University of Notre Dame, South Bend, IN.

Amy D. Frankel, MA, is a private practitioner affiliated with the Akron Family Institute, Akron, OH.

Jane Gerber, MSW, ACSW, LCSW, is a private practitioner and training psychotherapist in Evanston, IL; a senior faculty member, Satir Avanta International Training Network; Co-founder, Oasis-Midwest Training Center; and a Founding Fellow, Chicago Gestalt Institute, Chicago, IL.

Joyce K. Gilkey, PhD, is Assistant Professor of Marriage and Family Therapy, Fairfield University, Fairfield, CT.

Maria Gomori, MSW, is an international family therapy teacher of Satir-based interventions and theory, and is Associate Professor, Faculty of Medicine, University of Manitoba, Winnipeg, Manitoba, Canada.

Donald K. Granvold, PhD, is Professor, Graduate School of Social Work, University of Texas at Arlington, Arlington, TX.

Richard L. Graves, PhD, is in private practice in Houston, TX.

Kay Grothaus, RN, MSN, was formerly Assistant Vice President, St. Vincent's Medical Center, Toledo, OH, and is now in private practice.

Julia Halevy, Dott Ped, is Chairperson, Department of Applied Psychology, and Director, Marriage and Family Therapy Program, Antioch University, Keene, NH.

Sandra M. Halperin, PhD, is a private practitioner of marital and family therapy in Auburn, AL.

James L. Hawkins, PhD, is in private practice in St. Paul, MN.

Lorna Hecker, PhD, is Assistant Professor of Family Therapy, University of Nebraska, Lincoln, NE.

Christopher Hight, MS, is affiliated with the McPhaul Marriage and Family Therapy Clinic, University of Georgia, Athens, GA.

Lauri Holmes, MSW, is Director of Family Services, Family and Children Services of the Kalamazoo Area, Kalamazoo, MI.

Susan Horwitz, MS, is a faculty member in the University of Rochester Family Therapy Training Program, Division of Family Programs, Department of Psychiatry, Rochester, NY.

Frederick G. Humphrey, EdD, is Professor of Family Studies, University of Connecticut, Storrs, CT.

Jannah J. Hurn, PhD, is affiliated with the School of Social Work, Florida State University, Tallahassee, FL.

Mary L. Ideran, RN, MA, is Clinical Director, The Changing Woman Counseling and Educational Center, Calumet City, IL.

Evan Imber-Black, PhD, is affiliated with the Department of Psychiatry, Albert Einstein College of Medicine, Bronx, NY.

Augustus Jordan, MA, is affiliated with the University of Notre Dame, South Bend, IN.

Catheleen Jordan, PhD, is Assistant Professor, Graduate School of Social Work, University of Texas at Arlington, Arlington, TX.

Anthony P. Jurich, PhD, is affiliated with the Marriage and Family Therapy Unit, Department of Human Development and Family Studies, Kansas State University, Manhattan, KS.

Florence Kaslow, PhD, is Director of Post Doctoral Residency in Family Psychology, Florida Institute of Technology, West Palm Beach, FL, and is Director, Florida Couples and Family Institute.

Bradford P. Keeney, PhD, is Professor and Director of Scholarly Studies, Department of Professional Psychology, University of St. Thomas, St. Paul, MN.

Patricia Kelley, PhD, is Associate Professor, School of Social Work, University of Iowa, Iowa City, IA.

Pat Kessler, MSW, ACSW, is a caseworker in San Antonio, TX.

Luciano L'Abate, PhD, is in private practice in Atlanta, GA.

Judith Landau-Stanton, MB, ChB, DPM, is a faculty member in the University of Rochester Family Therapy Training Program, Division of Family Programs, Department of Psychiatry, Rochester, NY.

James Langford, MSW, is practicing family therapist in Fort Worth, TX.

Ann Lawson, PhD, is Director, Marriage and Family Therapy Training, U. S. International University, San Diego, CA.

David Lawson, PhD, is affiliated with the Department of Counseling/Special Education, Stephen F. Austin State University, Nacagdoches, TX.

Pieter le Roux, DLitt et Phil, is a faculty member in the University of Rochester Family Therapy Training Program, Division of Family Programs, Department of Psychiatry, Rochester, NY.

Howard A. Liddle, EdD, is Professor of Counseling Psychology and Director of the Adolescents and Families Project, Temple University, Philadelphia, PA.

Ross Luscombe, MSW, was Program Director, Northwest Ohio Center for Eating Disorders, St. Vincent's Medical Center, Toledo, OH, before her death in 1989.

Barbara J. Lynch, MS, is Chair, Marriage and Family Therapy, Southern Connecticut State University, New Haven, CT.

John Madonna, EdD, is in private practice in Worcester, MA.

Arthur Mandelbaum, MSW, is in private practice in Topeka, KS.

Martha Gonzalez Marquez, MSEd, is a doctoral candidate in the Marriage and Family Therapy Program, Purdue University, West Lafayette, IN.

Eric E. McCollum, PhD, is Assistant Professor, Marriage and Family Therapy Program, Purdue University, West Lafayette, IN.

Susan McDaniel, PhD, is a faculty member in the University of Rochester Family Therapy Training Program, Division of Family Programs, Department of Psychiatry, Rochester, NY.

M. Ellen Mitchell, PhD, is Assistant Professor of Clinical Psychology, Illinois Institute of Psychology, Chicago, IL.

Tammy Mitten, MA, is a doctoral candidate in the Marriage and Family Therapy Program, Purdue University, West Lafayette, IN.

Robert O. Morrow, PhD, is Professor of Psychology and Counseling, University of Central Arkansas, Conway, AR.

Pamela S. Nath, PhD, is affiliated with Bel-El Children's Center, Belle Fontaine, OH.

Thorana S. Nelson, PhD, is Director of the Marriage and Family Therapy Program and Associate Professor, Department of Family and Human Development, Utah State University, Logan, UT.

William C. Nichols, EdD, is an organizational consultant and a marital and family therapist in Tallahassee, FL.

Glen B. Paddock, PhD, is Assistant Professor of Marriage and Family Therapy, Seattle Pacific University, Seattle, WA.

Peggy Papp, MSW, is affiliated with The Ackerman Institute for Family Therapy, New York, NY.

Fred P. Piercy, PhD, is Professor of Family Therapy, Family Therapy Doctoral Program, Department of Child Development and Family Studies, Purdue University, West Lafayette, IN.

Barbara Pressman, MEd, is in private practice as a feminist family therapist, and is an adjunct faculty member in the Social Work

Department, Wilfrid Laurier University, Waterloo, Ontario, Canada.

Judith Rae, MS, MA, is in private practice in Indianapolis, IN.

Sherry L. Rediger, MFT, is a doctoral candidate in the Marriage and Family Therapy Program, Purdue University, West Lafayette, IN.

Yolanda Reyna, MS, is a counselor with Project SER (Service Employment Redevelopment), and is in private practice in San Antonio, TX.

Janine Roberts, EdD, is Associate Professor, University of Massachusetts, Amherst, MA.

Thomas W. Roberts, PhD, is Assistant Professor, Western Kentucky University, Bowling Green, KY.

George Roix, MA, is affiliated with the Human Resource Center, Athol, MA.

Don D. Rosenberg, MS, is affiliated with Family Service of Milwaukee, Milwaukee, WI.

Connie J. Salts, PhD, is Associate Professor and Director, Marriage and Family Therapy Program, Department of Family and Child Development, Auburn University, Auburn, AL.

Lynne Shook, PhD, is Family Systems Specialist, Department of Pediatrics, Harbor-UCLA Medical Center, UCLA School of Medicine, Los Angeles, CA.

Leon Sloman, FRCP(C), is Associate Professor, Department of Psychiatry, University of Toronto, and Coordinator of Family Therapy, Clarke Institute of Psychiatry, Toronto, Ontario, Canada.

Vincent Taylor, PhD, is in private practice in San Antonio, TX.

Susan Toler, MS, resides in Pittsburgh, PA.

William L. Turner, PhD, is Assistant Professor, Department of Family Studies and Department of Family Psychiatry, University of Kentucky, Lexington, KY.

Robert A. Urlacher, MS, is a doctoral candidate in the Marriage and Family Therapy Program, Department of Child Development and Family Studies, Purdue University, West Lafayette, IN.

Emily B. Visher, PhD, and **John S. Visher, MD,** are Stepfamily Specialists in Lafayette, CA.

Maxine Walton, MSW, CSW, is a certified marriage counselor in Detroit, MI.

Myra Weiss, DSW, is in private practice in Rockville Center and New York, NY.

Joseph L. Wetchler, PhD, is Assistant Professor and Director, Marriage and Family Therapy Program, Department of Behavioral Sciences, Purdue University-Calumet, Hammond, IN.

S. Allen Wilcoxon, EdD, is Associate Professor of Counselor Education, University of Alabama, Tuscaloosa, AL.

Elaine F. Yee, MA, is affiliated with the University of Notre Dame, South Bend, IN.

Cynthia R. Zeldin, MS, is in private practice in Indianapolis, IN.

Mary Jo Zygmond, PhD, is Assistant Professor of Education, University of Akron, Akron, OH.